THE

CHURCH MEMBER'S MANUAL,

OF

ECCLESIASTICAL PRINCIPLES, DOCTRINE, AND DISCIPLINE: PRESENTING A SYSTEMATIC VIEW OF THE STRUCTURE, POLITY, DOCTRINES, AND PRACTICES OF CHRISTIAN CHURCHES, AS TAUGHT IN THE SCRIPTURES.

BY
WILLIAM CROWELL,
AUTHOR OF "THE CHURCH MEMBER'S HAND BOOK."

"For one is your Master, even Christ; and all ye are brethren;—And are built upon the foundation of the Apostles and Prophets, Jesus Christ himself being the chief corner-stone."

WITH AN INTRODUCTORY ESSAY
BY HENRY J. RIPLEY, D.D.,
PROFESSOR OF SACRED RHETORIC AND PASTORAL DUTIES IN THE NEWTON THEOLOGICAL INSTITUTION.

NEW REVISED EDITION.

BOSTON:
GOULD AND LINCOLN.
NEW YORK: SHELDON, BLAKEMAN & CO.
CINCINNATI: GEO. S. BLANCHARD.
1857.

T. B. SMITH, STEREOTYPER,
216 WILLIAM STREET, N. Y.

PREFACE.

AMONG the recollections most sweet and mournful to the writer, are the little incidents of his last meeting with the lamented Knowles. It was the closing day of our last Winter Term at the Newton Theological Institution. A six weeks' vacation, to be followed by a brief Summer Term, was all that remained to us, before our final separation for the toils of the Christian Ministry. The exercises of the hour ended, we lingered a moment around our beloved teacher. He had spoken to us of a particular branch of Pastoral Duty. Conversation having turned on the topic of the lecture, he who now writes, remarked, that a treatise on our church order and discipline, for the use of young ministers and church-members, was much needed. Other members of the class confirmed the opinion, inquiring where such a guide could be found; when he modestly said,—as we hoped he would,—that he had such a work in preparation, which might be expected in a few months. Gratified with this intelligence we separated, with his warmest wishes for our welfare till we should meet again. But alas!——We did meet, when early summer had decked that hallowed spot with beauty, a sad and stricken class, to pour our tears on his freshly covered grave.

His manuscript was placed in the hands of judicious brethren,—the intimate friends of its author,—who after careful perusal decided that to publish it would be an injustice to his memory. It was a first hasty draught, and lacked the finishing touches of his graceful pen.

When, by the providence of God, it fell to my lot to be the conductor of a public religious journal, the want of such a book became still more manifest. A few articles, hastily prepared for the CHRISTIAN WATCHMAN and other periodicals, having met with unexpected favor, I resolved to study thoroughly the principles of church polity for my own benefit. The task was so pleasant, and the materials for a book so abundant, that a few hints from my brethren, added to what seemed an inward conviction of duty, were sufficient to convince me that at some distant day the results might be given to the public. At my request, Mrs. Knowles readily placed the manuscript of her late husband in my hands, with liberty to make such use of it as I judged proper. His plan was found to be very different from mine; but his sound judgment and correct taste, his catholic spirit and practical wisdom as a pastor, qualified him in an eminent degree to give good counsel for the government of churches; and his judicious remarks have rendered me valuable assistance in preparing the Third Part of this work.

That the result will be as satisfactory to others as the labor has been pleasant and useful to myself, is too much to expect. My post of duty made me an involuntary spectator of the assaults on our church principles with which the organs of various ecclesiastical bodies were teeming; while the evils arising from the misapplication of those principles were equally manifest. The partisans of prelacy, apostolic succession, and territorial churchism, represented us, like forsaken Israel of old, as "without a king, and without a prince, without a sacrifice and without a pillar, without an ephod and without teraphim."

In the prosecution of these inquiries, my only desire was to follow truth, wherever it might lead. For the ties of sect I care little; for names, still less. If the Baptist churches were not true churches, I would leave them. My first inquiry after the true principles of church constitution, therefore, was, What and where, is the church? And what oracle must I consult? The church? Must I ask the church to tell me what and where is the church? I might as well go to Delphi, or Dodona, or the shrine of Jupiter Ammon, to inquire who is the god, and where is his temple. Yet this gross begging of the question, helped out by a little circle reasoning, where the more conclusive arguments of the dungeon and the rack are not available, is all the answer that bigoted churchism has to offer. Do we appeal to tradition? The responses are like the echoes of Babel. They have led some to believe that their Jerusalem is the only place where men ought to worship; others to contend as strenuously for "this mountain," or for their Themis, their Delos, or their Bura, according to the responses which they fancied were divine. But we demand an independent, unimpeachable witness: we therefore reject them all, and turn to the inspired oracles of the living God.

To the Bible—the Bible only—this primary question is referred:—What is the church? This is the real point of divergence from the divinely modelled culture of Christ's visible spiritual kingdom, into the cheerless mazes of Abrahamic covenants, faith by proxy, ordinances without faith, territorial churches, prelacy and popery. This is the great question of the age. The Rationalist is laboring to solve it — in his sense of the term—by the help of unassisted reason, if that can be called reason which runs riot from its Maker; the Papist by abjuring reason in his blind submission to what he calls "the church;" the Baptist by exalting reason to be the interpreter and reverent pupil of God's word. The first would set up human reason to judge the Bible and the church; the second allows "the church" to judge the Bible and to impose on reason the most abject silence; the third maintains that the Bible, interpreted by reason, is to rule the church. The first deifies, the second debases, the third exalts, reason to her true place. The Bible is the church's supreme law, reason is her court. The Bible is the compass; reason, lighted by the spirit of God, is the binnacle lamp. If all Christians would go to the Bible for an answer to this first question, if they would accept none but that which the Bible gives, if they would abide by that—that only—union would soon take the place of discord. But error on this point is fruitful of other errors. And here the grand error of Christendom arose — that ancient error, whose pestiferous seeds have filled the world with tares. Old as it is, it must be rooted up, for our Heavenly Father hath not planted it.

Hitherto, Baptists have paid but little attention to the subject of Church Polity. As the bold advocates of spiritual Christianity in its primitive form, as faithful martyrs of religious freedom, as laborious missionaries to the heathen, they have contributed to every other department of theological literature; but the organic principles of church constitution have received little of their attention. So far as I know, this is the first attempt to exhibit the Baptist Church Polity in systematic order. Some portions of the work will, of course, occupy a field which I have attempted to explore without a guide. In those portions which have long been common ground, it is quite probable that I have fallen into some trains of thought similar to those whose works I have read. As the design of the book is to prove what is true, rather than to expose what is false, it contains no controversy. It was undertaken for the special benefit of all Baptists, as members of Christ's visible family, not to settle disputes on minor points, but to exhibit, in their native strength, beauty, and harmony, those great principles on which they all, or nearly all, unite; in the belief that it will thus be more extensively useful. It claims no authority over the judgment of any church, or individual. It must stand or fall by its own merits. But the principles which it advocates will stand forever, and be honored as the bulwarks of all true liberty, of sound doctrine, and of active piety.

It is proper to acknowledge my indebtedness for valuable suggestions, to the Reverend Professors Ripley and Sears, of Newton Theological Institution, to whom the manuscript was submitted, and to the Rev. Dr. Sharp of this city, who examined portions of the work. To the Rev. Baron Stow, D.D., who in addition to an examination of the manuscript, has read all the proof sheets as the work was going through the press, I return thankful acknowledgdments.

Go, then, child of many prayers, on thy unpretending mission of light and love; promote in some small degree, the intelligence, the harmony, the spirituality, the beauty, the stability, the usefulness, of the household of God, and the author will be amply rewarded for all his toil. For while thus employed among the outworks of Zion, telling her towers, marking her bulwarks, considering her palaces, it has been delightful to contemplate the surpassing glories of that inner temple, where the Church of the Redeemed behold the King in his beauty, and all are filled with his love. May that love animate all his churches below, that Zion may be the joy of the whole earth, that her righteousness may go forth as brightness, and her salvation as a lamp that burneth.

W. C.

Boston, March, 1847.

PREFACE TO THE SECOND EDITION.

THE public voice having invited this "Manual" to a place among the permanent religious literature of our country, it has been revised, line by line, to prepare it for that honorable position. Its plan, principles, and doctrines, remain unchanged; yet corrections have been made on almost every page. The author's highest aim has been to make it a true exponent of that simple, yet beautiful, because divinely taught, church order which is the strength and the glory of Baptists. As such, it has received the sanction of the wisest and best among us: may it henceforth share as richly the Master's favor.

W. C.

St. Louis, Mo., January, 1852.

CONTENTS.

PART I.

PRIMITIVE CHURCH CONSTITUTION.

CHAPTER I.

PRINCIPLES FUNDAMENTAL TO THE EXISTENCE OF A CHURCH.

1*

CHAPTER II.

PRINCIPLES INVOLVED IN THE FUNCTIONS OF A CHURCH.

CHAPTER III.

PRINCIPLES OF ORGANIZATION.

PART II.

DOCTRINES.

CHAPTER I.

OF GOD, AND DIVINE REVELATION.

CHAPTER II.

CHARACTER AND STATE OF MAN.

CHAPTER III.

THE WAY OF SALVATION.

CHAPTER IV.

THE FUTURE WORLD.

CHAPTER V.

POSITIVE INSTITUTIONS.

PART III.

CHURCH GOVERNMENT.

CHAPTER I.

CHURCH MEMBERS.

CHAPTER II.

CHURCH OFFICERS.

CHAPTER III.

CHURCH MEETINGS.

CHAPTER IV.

CHURCH DISCIPLINE.

CHAPTER V.

VARIOUS USAGES.

INTRODUCTORY ESSAY.

THE following work aims to unfold the principles which regulate the constitution and government of Christian churches, and their modes of action, considered both individually as separate bodies, and relatively to one another. It does not profess to discuss questions which directly affect personal Christian character, or which relate immediately to the soul's future destiny. Its utility must not, therefore, be estimated by bringing it into comparison with books which design to nourish the soul viewed in its internal spiritual relations. But while advancement in true piety must ever occupy the highest place in point of importance, neither truth nor a regard to the welfare of the cause of Christ would justify an indifference to the external form and arrangements of a church. The soul of man is of prime importance; but his body is not, therefore, to be neglected. The mutual relations and influences of the soul and the body are worthy of deep consideration, and must be duly regarded in order to secure man's vital interests both for time and for eternity.

Design of the Work.

Since from the very nature of men and their circumstances in this world, there must be some external organization of churches, it is important, all will admit, that the organization be adapted to the purposes contemplated in the existence of churches. Of the great diversity of forms in which church-organization exists, it must be obvious to every one that some are more, and some are less, adapted to promote individual Christian character, and the prosperity and extension of the Christian cause regarded as a great universal interest. That some are better adapted than others to prevent a wide-spread defection from inspired truth, or to effect a return to the old paths in case of a departure, can hardly be doubted even by a superficial reader of ecclesiastical history, or a superficial observer of religious affairs.

Importance of the inquiries here pursued.

There is, then, room for choice in regard to actually existing, or to conceivable, forms and arrangements; and we might be guilty of a culpable indifference, if, even viewing this matter as wholly committed to human wisdom, we should allow ourselves to be borne along, without any principles, on the current of prevalent opinion, or should fail, through a supreme regard to present convenience, to make a judicious selection. If, however, while human wisdom, or policy, has to a very great extent treated this subject as though it were submitted to man's control, and as though man were competent to a matter which may touch the religious interests of multitudes, in communities greatly diversified, and not only in one age, but in all subsequent ages, if, I say, we have reason to believe that certain guiding principles have been fixed by Him whose authority is law, whether personally exercised or through the agency of appointed representatives, then the subject assumes a higher importance, and we are not to inquire into the best comparative methods, in order to make a selection. If this shall be found to be the case, we can have no doubt that He, who knew what was in man, has made provision for arrangements which, should they be fully carried out, would most happily contribute to the great design of the gospel for man viewed individually, for men viewed in their social relations, for men of any one age and country, for men of all ages and all countries. Not only would arrangements, conformed to the principles which He has established, ultimately prove themselves thus worthy of their origin; they would, also, be found, if not entirely free from imperfection as applied to imperfect men by imperfect men, yet far less encumbered with hindrances and involving far less difficulty and liability to abuse, and far more adapted to the progressive state, as well as to the forming period, of Christian communities, than arrangements which have been extensively modified by men. If there be such principles, traceable to ultimate authority, it is immensely desirable to ascertain them; for we may be sure, they are just the principles which the case requires.

The following work, then, if it truly exhibit the scriptural principles of church-organization and government, has a claim to public attention on the score of utility. It will, however, be more particularly interesting to members of Baptist churches; because they profess a special desire to ascertain scriptural principles, and nor should diverse preferences produce such diverse parties as cannot, in all *matters of obligation*, flow together.

The principle, just stated, seems strictly to accord with the spirit of Paul, in his endeavors to unite in harmony dissentient brethren; and as an appendix to it, his own words may also be adduced,—Nevertheless, whereto we have already attained, let us walk by the same rule, let us mind the same thing. (Phil. 3 : 16.)

Union on such a principle is feasible among the true-hearted and self-denying disciples of Christ: to other men, called Christians or not, the union which is valuable in the sight of Christ does not pertain. Such a union, we say, is feasible. But it would require a sacrifice in various quarters; and it would, after all, be more a union of heart, such as now exists, really, and, to a considerable extent, visibly, among the followers of Christ, than of outward forms and worship. On the one hand, let the simple principles of the New Testament which regulate church-membership, the government of the church, the nature, duties, and powers of the ministry, be universally adopted, and let nothing be *enjoined* that is not enjoined by scriptural authority; on the other, let an enlightened, enlarged, yet scriptural, liberality be cherished in regard to matters not regulated by scriptural precept, or example; then the obstacles to union would be removed, even in respect to the outward mutual relations of Christians. Since the union which is often sighed for is an outward union, and must of course depend very considerably on external matters, an attention to these externals assumes no little importance; and inattention to them on the part of individual Christians, and especially of ministers, really tends to perpetuate and propagate division. If those externals in religion, concerning which Scripture furnishes precepts and precedents, are, notwithstanding, held to be submitted to human wisdom, or to convenience, the evil of division is of course allowed to extend itself; and any who may seek, in their outward obedience, to be entirely guided by scriptural views, though they may thus follow the only true standard, a regard to which would produce all desirable uniformity, must yet often bear the reproach of disuniting the followers of Christ, or of putting asunder what God has joined together. It is not they, clearly, that create disunion; the cause of disunion will rather be found at the door of those, if such there be, who do not seek and obey the Lord's will in reference to the outward organization and to other externals, as well as to the soul.

No reproach is intended in this language. It will, probably, apply in various directions, and perhaps, where it is least suspected. It is intended to awaken thought on this subject; a subject, which is too easily thrust aside, but which has too much importance to be neglected.

Source of information.

If it be asked, now, from what source we are to seek information, the reply is easy. The New Testament gives us authoritative instruction. Here is recorded the practice of inspired Apostles and of the first churches under their guidance; we have here, too, instructions to churches and individuals from Apostles, which contain principles touching this subject; we have, also, the instructions of Christ, which contain the seeds of that order of things which grew into shape during the Apostles' ministry. The ministry of the Apostles extended over so many regions, and through so long a period, and was exercised amid so much diversity of character and circumstances, that we have reason to believe there is no deficiency in regard to the development of principles which regulate the whole subject of church-membership and government. Not that a minute system of external arrangements is exhibited in the New Testament; but the essential principles are easily discernible. These, as might be presumed from the nature of Christianity, are presented as occasion required, sometimes incidentally; they are few and simple, and give rise to certain necessary inferences, thus embracing the whole subject.

Reverence for antiquity.

A strong tendency prevails in some quarters to overlook the instructions of the inspired records on this class of subjects, and yet to set up a plea for certain forms and practices on the ground of antiquity. The antiquity which is thus contended for, labors under the misfortune of not being sufficiently ancient; for it did not enjoy the presence of inspired men. If it be said, that the third and fourth centuries furnish the best results of the apostolic beginnings, and that in those times we find specimens of character and outward arrangement which we should feel ourselves required to imitate, it must not be forgotten that those same centuries present developments, not very honorable to the Christian name, which some men have thought might be naturally traced to an inspired source. But it is very unsafe for our reason thus to mark out a path, or to subject itself to the reason, perhaps to the whims, quite likely to the perversions of those ancient times. Let us, as the men of those centuries ought to have done, go at once to a more ancient time, to that of inspired men. By walking in the footsteps of inspired men, imbibing their spirit, and regulating ourselves by developments which they sanctioned, we may have assured confidence that we are in the path on which the light of heaven has shone. Reverence for antiquity is exceedingly prone to misguide on subjects which require a different standard; and particularly on subjects of Christian faith and duty, antiquity, aside from the inspired records, has no authority, and may be dispensed with in our inquiries, except indeed as adding confirmation to opinions drawn directly from the word of God, or as showing at how early a period, and to how great an extent, the simplicity of Christian truth became corrupted. The great question should be, What says the New Testament? An observance that is venerable by a hoary antiquity, has no claim to our religious respect, unless it is evidently sanctioned by that book.* A church that came into existence yesterday, in strict conformity to the New Testament principles of membership, far away from any long-existing church, or company of churches, and therefore unable to trace an outward lineal descent, is a true church of Christ;—for Christianity is not a religion of circumstances, but of principles;—

* The remarks in this paragraph are particularly applicable to those writers, who seem to consider the ecclesiastical arrangements which were in vogue in the third and fourth centuries, as a sort of perfected model of Christianity. The spirit of them is also applicable to the manner in which Neander, the distinguished Lutheran of Germany, thinks infant-baptism may be vindicated as agreeing with Paul's sentiments. For while he distinctly acknowledges that infant-baptism was not instituted by Christ; that it did not originate from the primitive church in Palestine, nor from the Apostles who preceded Paul; that it was not introduced among the Gentile Christians by Paul—inasmuch as such a substitute for circumcision would "agree least of all with the peculiar Christian characteristics of this Apostle;" that it cannot be infered "from the instance of the baptism of whole families;" that faith and baptism were originally connected with one another; that no trace of infant-baptism appears till the time of Irenæus [who suffered martyrdom in the year 202]; and that it first became recognized as an apostolic tradition in the course of the third century, and that this circumstance "is evidence rather *against*, than *for*, the admission of its apostolic origin;" while he makes all these distinct acknowledgments, he yet thinks that the practice was "*necessarily developed*," in an age subsequent to that of the Apostles, from some of Paul's views of the influence of Christianity.—See. *Neander's History of the Planting and Training of the Christian Church by the Apostles*, pp. 101–103.

while a church, so called, not standing on the apostolic principles of faith and practice, and yet able to look back through a long line up to time immemorial, may have never belonged to that body of which Christ is the head.

Proper use of this book.

A word or two, in regard to the proper use of such a book as this. It is not to be read through hastily, and then laid aside. As it is a book of principles relating to church matters, designed also to show their practical operation on the various occasions which arise in a church and in the religious community, it ought to be read in short portions and at intervals. It may be considered as a reference-book, to be examined on the particular topics which will claim attention in the transactions of a church, and on the questions which will arise in the religious community concerning the order and discipline of a church, and the connections of churches with one another. Whatever may be thought of the correctness of the opinions which it presents on particular points, it cannot fail to be profitable to one who should thus employ it. And without presuming to endorse every opinion and statement which it contains, I take this occasion to recommend it, particularly to the members of Baptist churches, as a book which they would all do well to read with much care. May I also suggest, that pastors would find it serviceable in their endeavors to form in the more youthful professors of religion just and enlarged views of the relations and duties of church-members? Pastors know, too well, that this whole range of subjects, unless indeed the primary topics be excepted, is too little understood. And yet circumstances may at any moment arise, which would prove it important for members of a church to understand their church-relations, as well as the doctrine of repentance towards God and faith in our Lord Jesus Christ.

H. J. R.

CHURCH MEMBER'S MANUAL.

PART I.

PRIMITIVE CHURCH CONSTITUTION.

A Christian church, viewed as an organized society, is a peculiar institution. The character of its members and the principles of their union, its powers and the mode of their exercise, its organization and purposes, are all peculiar to itself, as a church of Christ. As it is the visible representative of an invisible kingdom,—a kingdom not of this world,—the principles of its constitution are necessarily different from those of all societies of human origin for temporal purposes.

Every associated body of men involves certain elementary, constituting principles, on which its existence depends, by the operation of which it became a society. Civil government is founded on principles peculiar to its nature and its purposes; and it is by conforming to these principles that individual human beings become a civil society, or state. A voluntary society, formed for the mutual improvement of its members, in science, literature, or the arts, in manners or in morals, is constituted on different principles; a benevolent, or philanthropic society on principles still different; and a church is constituted on principles different from them all. The first point of inquiry into the constitution of a church, is, in relation to the elementary principles of its corporate existence.

When a society of any kind is formed, it necessarily comes

to possess certain powers, which its members, as individuals, did not possess. The powers of a church, and the principles on which they are exercised, are very different from those of civil government, or of a common voluntary society. The source, nature, and extent of those powers, and the manner in which they should be exercised, must next be inquired into. A church, too, like every affiliated body, must be organized, and have officers or public servants, appointed to the discharge of certain duties. The principles of its organization, therefore, form the last topic of inquiry into the *constitution* of a church. Within this three-fold division, all that relates to the structure of churches may be contemplated.

But by what means are the principles on which the existence, the powers, and the organization of churches depend, to be ascertained? It is evident that they cannot be discovered from the light of nature alone, for Christianity is a revealed religion. Its doctrines, duties, and ordinances, are matters of record. This record claims to be divinely inspired, infallible, and perfect. And the purpose for which it was given to men, "by inspiration of God," is, "that the man of God may be *perfect*, thoroughly furnished unto *all* good works." The simple question now before us is, Do they reveal all the *principles* which are essential to the constitution of a church; Are the Scriptures *alone* sufficient for this purpose, or do they need the addition of some other writings, of oral tradition, or of human legislative wisdom? This question must first be settled.

We proceed, then, to state as a first great principle, that THE SCRIPTURES FURNISH SUFFICIENT, AND THE ONLY RULES AND LAWS FOR THE FORMATION, ORDER, AND GOVERNMENT OF CHRISTIAN CHURCHES. We unanimously appeal to the Bible, the whole Bible, and to nothing but the Bible. The instructions of our Saviour and his Apostles, illustrated by the practices of the apostolic churches as recorded in the New Testament, comprise the standing law, the rule, and the authoritative examples to Christians, ministers, and churches through all succeeding time. The churches formed under the ministry of the Apostles are the models after which all others should be formed.

For, if the Scriptures are the infallible, the sufficient, and the only rule of faith and practice to individual Christians, they must also be to churches. Do they contain precepts, and examples, to regulate the belief and the conduct of individual Christians? They do also of churches. Many portions are addressed directly to churches, giving specific directions to meet particular cases, or laying down general principles of action. Is there any reason to believe that the commands, the warnings, the threatenings, and the promises to churches, in relation to their order and discipline, are defective, or stand more in need of uninspired additions, than those addressed to individual Christians? If tradition, or human inventions are necessary to the one, they are equally so to the other. Whoever, therefore, presumes to maintain that the Inspired Volume does not contain all needful instructions for the formation and government of churches, must remember that he is assaulting the integrity, and destroying the authority, of that Divine Word which opens the only way of salvation to the human soul.

It is certain that the Scriptures often make mention of bodies called "churches," and they inculcate important duties on believers in relation to them. In other words they enjoin duties which could not be performed unless churches were in existence. How, for instance, could the Saviour's directions, Matt. 18: respecting an offending brother, or those of Paul, 1 Cor. 5: and 2 Cor. 2: in regard to the exclusion of an offending church-member, and his restoration on repentance, be obeyed, unless churches, such as Christ and Apostles approved, were in existence? The same classes of duties are obligatory on Believers still, and from the nature of the case must continue to be so, to the end of time. But no one could know how to obey the Saviour's directions, nor even understand the meaning of those

directions which relate to a church, unless he was also told what kind of an institution is entitled to that name. The reception of the idea of a church involves necessarily the knowledge of what constitutes a church, and if the Scriptures do not furnish this knowledge, they contain commands which can neither be understood nor obeyed. How can a man be required to unite with, or to perform any duty towards, an institution which is not described to him, and which he has never seen? If the Scriptures do not describe a church, nor furnish the means of knowing what a church is, how can they enjoin on us duties towards such a body? Aye, if the Scriptures do not furnish this knowledge, how can we know that such an institution exists, or ever did exist, in the world? We must, therefore, take the New Testament description of a church, or have none at all. And we must discharge our duties towards such bodies as are there described by the name of churches, or experience the consequences of disobedience to a large portion of the commands of God.

It is certain, however, that collective bodies of believers in Christ came into being through the labors of the Apostles, which they called "churches," all constituted, so far as the record informs us, on precisely the same principles. If, then, we would know what kind of societies the Apostles then called, or would now call *churches*, we must examine the description of those bodies to which they applied the term. As the Scriptures give us no reason to suppose that the principle on which those churches were formed are ever to be changed, it is the duty of all Christians to study them diligently, and to connect themselves with churches formed on the same principles as those described in the Word of God.

The object of this FIRST PART of the present work is, to unfold the scriptural account of *the structure, the powers, and the officers of those churches which were formed under the ministry of the Apostles, as authoritative in the formation of churches for all future time.* Receiving the record as inspired, and consequently perfect, the examples and precepts will be treated as of equal authority. It is true there are many actions and customs mentioned in the Scriptures, which, growing out of the state of society, the habits of the times, or some peculiarity of circumstances, are of no authority to us. But *principles*, expressed by precept or illustrated by example, in the Scriptures, are still in full force, and should receive the unqualified assent and obedience of men. The rights and duties of Christians, of ministers, and of churches, are the same in every age, however customs and forms may change.

To accomplish this object, it is proposed to find out, and set in order, in as brief space as the nature of the subject will admit, the principles of the SCRIPTURAL CHURCH POLITY; and, as far as it is possible, to pursue this investigation without regard to the views or the practices of any existing sect. The discussion will be purely Scriptural. At the same time we have no doubt that the principles here brought to view prevailed substantially in the churches through the two centuries which succeeded the age of the Apostles. To illustrate this and other collateral points, a few brief testimonies from early Christian writers, and ecclesiastical historians of undisputed scholarship and candor, will be presented in notes. The lessons of history are of great value in tracing corruptions to their origin, and pointing out the sources of danger to the churches, whenever they can be clearly ascertained and correctly understood. Yet it must be remembered that we do not rely on ecclesiastical history, even to furnish a basis for interpreting and applying the principles revealed in the Scriptures. We rely on the Bible alone, interpreted according to the known laws of language. The early Christian writers are often quoted in such a manner as to deceive, and thus to serve a bad cause, for the criticism of ancient writers is a distinct science, and even the learned are liable to be deceived by the extensive forgeries of those early days, and the *pious frauds* which were perpetrated by monks and other papal writers to support the errors of papacy.

In conducting this investigation, the *presumptive argument* is sometimes introduced. By this is meant the reasons for *presuming* a proposition to be true, irrespective of any positive arguments adduced in support of it. This presumptive argument must in all cases be refuted, or shown to be groundless, before any other arguments can avail to prove the proposition untrue. For instance, men have a natural right to choose their civil rulers; and the presumptive argument is, that they have also the right to choose their spiritual rulers, until it is proved that the Scriptures teach the opposite doctrine. They have a natural right to choose their scientific teachers; the presumptive argument is valid and good that they also have the right to choose their religious teachers, until it is proved that the Scriptures have forbidden it. All societies have a natural right to admit and exclude members, by a vote of the body, according to their established customs, rules, or laws; the presumptive argument is that churches have the same right. The opposite cannot be proved by showing that the Scriptures do not expressly give this right, it must be shown that they expressly take it away. And so, generally, where the teaching of nature is clear, and the Scriptures teach nothing to the contrary, the presumptive argument is good.

CHAPTER I.

PRINCIPLES FUNDAMENTAL TO THE EXISTENCE OF A CHURCH.

SAYS the learned Richard Hooker, "The mixture of those things by speech which by nature are divided, is the mother of all error. To take away, therefore, that error which confusion breedeth, distinction is requisite."

There are two forms of extended visible unions among men which are of Divine appointment; civil governments, and Christian churches. The first grow up out of the social nature, the physical weakness, and general selfishness of mankind. However small their number, or extensive their domain, human beings naturally desire to form themselves into compact communities; their dependent condition and varying capacities render mutual protection, assistance, and division of labor, needful; while their selfish propensities, and defective moral perceptions, absolutely require government and laws, sustained by sufficient sanctions, to preserve them from each other's rapacity, and political society from anarchy.

Christian churches would, on the contrary, as naturally spring from the purified social nature, the spiritual weakness, the brotherly love, and the holy benevolence of renewed men. Their social feelings, transformed by the Spirit of God, and elevated by the love of Christ far above the promptings of natural affection, attract them powerfully towards each other, and repel the companionship of worldly men; conscious of great imperfection, of exposure to the dangers of error and sin, they seek each other's watchcare, admonition, and counsel; while the new, heaven-born passion which animates their hearts, of love to their Saviour, and for his sake, to the souls whom he died to save, leads them to combine their wisdom and strength to honor their Master by doing good to their fellow-men. Mutual protection against other men, and mutual temporal assistance in any form, do not belong to the nature or the design of a church. Its origin and its objects are purely spiritual, self-sacrificing, and benevolent.

The principles, therefore, on which the existence of churches depend, necessarily differ widely from those of civil government. The origin, nature, objects, materials, and structure of one of these institutions are all diverse from those of the other. One is temporal, the other spiritual; one is territorial, the other local; one is to protect the rights of persons and property, the other to train souls for heaven. Citizenship in the one depends on the place and circumstances of natural birth, membership in the other is for those only who are born of the Spirit. One is adapted to the wants of all men in the world, the other only to "men chosen out of the world." One must enforce submission to laws by pains and penalties, the other has no need nor right to use them. A church is a voluntary society in *one sense*, that all its members became so from choice; civil government is not voluntary in this sense. Men are born, not into a church, but into the world; and usually into some civil society or state; a circumstance which depends on boundary lines, but no national, diocesan, nor parish boundaries nor laws, can make them members of a Christian church. This relation depends not on the circumstances of birth, such as country, parentage, or pedigree, but on specific elements of character, and free, intelligent choice. Had these important and very obvious distinctions between civil governments and Christian churches always been kept in view, many profound and eloquent fallacies which have been written on the "Laws of Ecclesiastical Polity" might have been spared. In order rightly to understand those laws and their application, we must first consider who are the true and proper *subjects* of them. The brute forces of nature, or the animal tribes, are scarcely less adapted to be the subjects of municipal law, than are unconverted men to be the subjects of those laws under which Christ has placed his churches. The laws of Christianity are for men actuated by Christian principle. When a church undertakes to extend its laws over others it must adopt force, and make use of pains and penalties—the sanctions of civil government—to secure obedience, and then it ceases to be a church, and becomes an odious, and usually a very oppressive, worldly institution.

Let us now, with deep humility and prayerfulness, open the Inspired Volume to ascertain the true elementary principles which are essential to the *being* of a Christian church. In doing which, we must, first, settle the Scriptural meaning and application of that term; second, ascertain what sort of persons are proper members; third, consider the working of the divine energy in preparing and uniting these materials; and fourth, the constituting act by which they become a church. And may the Spirit of all grace be our guide, that we may understand the truth clearly, and receive it in meekness and in love.

SECT. 1. *Origin and Meaning of the word* CHURCH.

The English word *church** was probably derived from a Greek work which signifies *belonging to the Lord.*† It is not used in the English version of the Old Testament, but often in the New, as a translation of the Greek word *ecclesia*; the primary meaning of which is, an *assembly*, or a *congregation*, called together for any purpose. This word occurs three times in Acts 19: where it is used to designate the tumultuous gathering at Ephesus, and is translated *assembly*. In Acts 7 : 38, it is translated by the word *church*, where it clearly refers to the whole body of the Israelites. "This is he that was with the church, [ecclesia, *congregation*,] in the wilderness." But with these exceptions and a very few others, *ecclesia* is uniformly translated *church*, in the New Testament.‡

* Greek, κυριακὸν; Saxon, *circe;* German, *kirche;* Scottish, *kirk.* Its Greek origin is inferred from the fact that it is found in all the German dialects, as well as in the Swedish, Danish, Polish, Russian, and Bohemian.

† With the article prefixed thus, τὸ κυριακὸν, it was used by the early Christian writers to signify a *temple or house of the Lord*, i. e. the Lord Christ. In Rev. 1 : 10, this adjective in the feminine form, in connection with the Greek word *day*, κυριακη ημερα, is translated *Lord's Day*, i. e. Christ's day, in distinction from the Jewish Sabbath. Some derive κυρι -όν from κύριος and οικὸς, signifying the household or family of the Lord.

‡ The word ἐκκλησία, from which comes the English word *ecclesiastical*, occurs a few times in the Septuagint, the Greek version of the Old Testament, as a translation of the Hebrew עדה, though that word and קהל, which often occur, and in the English version are rendered *congregation, assembly*, are usually translated in the Septuagint by the Greek word *synagogue*, i. e. a *coming together*.

2*

The prevailing use of the word is to denote a company of Christians. "At that time there was a great persecution against the church which was at Jerusalem." "Now there were in the church that was at Antioch certain prophets and teachers." "Unto the church of God which was at Corinth." "If the whole church be come together into one place." "Great Priscilla and Aquilla, * * likewise the church that is in their house." "Nymphas, and the church which is in his house." "The churches throughout all Judea, and Galilee, and Samaria." "As I teach everywhere in every church." These are but specimens of the ordinary use of the word. Its primary meaning is indicated by its formation from two words signifying *to call out of*; as a public meeting of *qualified* citizens is called to transact important public business; but the New Testament usage has made this general meaning specific, by applying it to a society of the disciples of Christ, called out, chosen, and separated from the world.

In a few instances it is used to include all believers. "And he [Christ,] is the head of the body, the church." "Christ loved the church and gave himself for it." "Gave him to be head over all things to the church, which is his body." If these passages are carefully examined in their connection, it will be seen that they may be applied to any particular church; for Christ is head over all things to each, and as he stands in the same relation to one as to another, the remark includes them all. Thus we say, God is the rightful ruler of man; by which we mean all men,—the human race,—yet we do not mean by this expression that the human race is one individual. If we follow the Apostle's reasoning through, Eph. 2: we find, v. 22, that it was not a universal, but a particular church which he had in mind, even in these passages; for having spoken of the union of Jews and Gentiles "in one body," as "fellow-citizens with the saints," then as "the household of God," to illustrate the great truth that in "Jesus Christ, the chief corner-stone, all the building fitly framed together groweth to an holy temple in the Lord," he immediately adds, as if to prevent the error that there is but one visible church for the Lord's earthly temple, "In whom YE [the church in Ephesus,] also are built together, [formed into a church,] for AN habitation of God through the Spirit." If the Ephesian church were one habitation of God, then every other church is so.

In one instance the word includes all saints and angels: "To the general assembly and church of the first-born." Heb. 12: 23. But these uses are rare. It is never applied in the New Testament to a national, provincial, or geographical church, of any description. The idea of such a body was developed in a later age. A church, in the language of the inspired writers, is a society of believers, who meet in one place for the worship of God, and for the united observance of the ordinances of the Gospel.*

* In this sense the word occurs in the singular number upwards of fifty times, and the word *churches* upwards of thirty times, in the New Testament. It is used with other significations in about sixteen or eighteen instances.

According to Chancellor King, an Episcopal writer, this was the prevailing use of the word during the first three centuries. In his learned and impartial "Inquiry into the Constitution, Discipline, Unity, and Worship of the Primitive Church that flourished within the first Three Hundred Years after CHRIST," he says, "The usual and common acceptation of the word is, that of a particular church, that is, a society of Christians meeting together in one place under their proper pastors, for the performance of religious worship and the exercising of Christian Discipline."

This is evidently the prevailing use of the word by the early Christian writers. Dionysius Alexandrinus, when banished to Cephro in Lybia, writes Πόλλη συνεπεδήμησεν ἡμῖν ἐκκλησία, *a large church collected with us*, &c. Eusebius, lib. 7. 11. So Irenæus, *Ea quæ est in quoque loco ecclesia*, that church which is in any place, &c. Op. lib. 2. c. 56. So Cyprian, Ignatius, and Origen speak of "the church in Smyrna," "the church in Antioch," "the church in Athens," "the church in Alexandria." So Dionysius Alexandrinus speaks of the *churches* throughout the east, the churches of Cilicia, &c. Eusebius, lib. 7. c. 5. Tertullian says, *Ubi tres, ecclesia est, licet laici*, i. e., three are sufficient to form a church,

Had the Saviour designed to set up a kingdom for worldly purposes, a visible ecclesiastical unity would have been necessary; as his kingdom was not of this world, it is both unnecessary and undesirable. The phrases, kingdom of heaven, and kingdom of God, were employed by him to include all churches, and all Christians, and indicate that they are *one* only in their relation to himself. The first church was that formed at Jerusalem, under the ministry of the Apostles. To speak of a church founded on the covenant with Adam, or with Abraham, or with Moses, is but wresting words from their proper meaning. The Jewish commonwealth was, in all its leading features, unlike a Christian church. It is evident, therefore,

That the primary meaning of *ecclesia*, church, a select assembly, or congregation, being in its nature limited to a local company, is, in the New Testament, the distinguishing term applied to a company of believers in Christ.

Should one church extend its authority over many other churches or congregations of Christians, so as to control all their actions, it could never make them a part of itself, nor fuse them into one church.

To apply the name *church* to an extensive heirarchy, or national religious establishment; as the church of Rome, the church of England, the Episcopal church, or the Methodist Episcopal church, is an unscriptural and improper use of the word. They are not churches, and God has given us no leave to call them so.

SECT. 2. *Many distinct Churches were formed.*

The question to be considered is, Did the Saviour or the Apostles establish, or intend to establish, one visible organized

although they are laymen. The learned Dr. Owen fully maintains, that in no approved writer, for two hundred years after Christ, is mention made of any organized, visibly professing church, except a local congregation of Christians.

body, to be called THE CHURCH, of which all the local societies of believers should be constituent, subordinate parts or branches; or had each body of Christians an equal right to the distinctive name church, according to the proper Scriptural meaning of that word? Was the church at Antioch, for instance, a church in the same sense as the church at Jerusalem, or was it a part of that church? When a company of believers was gathered in any place, did they by any means become a church, for all the purposes of such visible union, or were they merged in the whole fraternity of Christians, as possessing, collectively, the exclusive right to that title?*

* This inquiry, it will be seen, is a fundamental and most important one. The true issue between the advocates of spiritual Christianity and religious freedom on the one hand, and papists and prelatists on the other, arises here. Ecclesiastical history bears unequivocal testimony to the fact, that the idea of a catholic or universal church, in ecclesiastical organization, first corrupted Christianity by destroying the supremacy of the Word of God, crushing the right of private judgment, breaking down the independence of churches and the equality of ministers, exalting bishops, patriarchs, cardinals, and finally popes, to lord it over God's heritage.

Dr. Merle D'Aubigné, of Geneva, author of the excellent History of the Reformation, in his late work entitled 'Puseyism Examined,' pp. 30, 31, says:—"At the epoch of the Reformation, if I may so speak, three distinct eras had occurred in the history of the church.

"1. That of Evangelical Christianity, which, having its focus in the times of the Apostles, extended its rays throughout the first and second centuries of the church.

"2. That of Ecclesiastical Catholicism, which, commencing its existence in the third century, reigned till the seventh.

"3. That of the Papacy, which reigned from the seventh to the fifteenth century.

"Such were the three grand eras in the then past history of the church; let us see what characterized each of them.

"In the first period, the supreme authority was attributed to the revealed Word of God.

"In the second, it was, according to some, ascribed to the church as represented by its bishops.

The presumptive argument is in favor of many churches. We should expect, from analogy, that God intended there should be distinct churches, equal in powers and rights, no one subject to another, nor to any earthly head. For no necessity exists in the nature of the case for a universal or catholic church, any more than for a universal monarchy. God has seen fit to place nations under distinct, separate civil governments, and though many evils come from this arrangement, yet it obviously prevents much greater evils. It is neither possible nor desirable to subject the whole human race to one ruler, or unite them in one form of government; nor would the least good be effected by bringing all Christians under one hierarchy, order of ministers, or form of church canons and discipline, were it lawful in itself, and practicable. This argument in favor of many distinct churches is alone sufficient and irrefragable, unless the Scriptures expressly establish one church only.

But the Scriptures do not even intimate that all Christians are to be members of one united visible church. On the contrary, the inspired use of the word, as we have seen, applies in five instances out of six, to a local company of believers. Can anything be plainer than that we are bound to abide by that meaning of the word which the Holy Spirit has so fully sanctioned?

Nor is this all. The word *churches*, as every reader of the New Testament knows, is often applied to local bodies of

"In the third to the Pope.

"We acknowledge cheerfully that the second of these systems is much superior to the third, but it is inferior to the first.

"In fact in the first of these systems it is God who rules.

"In the second it is Man.

"In the third it is, to speak after the Apostle, THAT WORKING OF SATAN, with all power, and signs, and lying wonders. 2 Thess. 2 : 9."

The system of the third period is Popery, of the second Episcopacy, of the first that form of Evangelical Christianity which is explained and advocated in these pages.

Christians living in the same province, and very near each other. As, "The churches throughout all Judea." Paul "went through Syria and Cilicia confirming the churches." "So were the churches established in the faith and increased in number daily." We read of the churches of Galatia, the churches in Asia, Macedonia, &c. Paul speaks of the church in Corinth, and of the church in Cenchrea, a port or harbor of Corinth, a few miles distant. He says to the Corinthian church, "I robbed *other churches*, taking wages of them to do *you* service." The force of the appeal rests wholly on the churches in question being regarded as separate, distinct bodies; otherwise he should have said, 'I robbed other *branches*, or dioceses, or parishes of *the church*, to supply *this branch*.' John writes, not to the Asiatic church, but "to the seven churches in Asia," and then addresses each as a church separately. There are general Apostolic epistles addressed to all Christians, and epistles directed to particular churches in cities, and to several churches in a province; but no instance of any one to *the* holy catholic or universal church, nor to a provincial or diocesan church. The plain inference from which is, that the Apostles did not form nor recognize any such body, and if they did not, no other Christian ought to do so.*

* Archbishop Whately in his Essays on "The Kingdom of Christ," says: "The Church is undoubtedly *one*, and so is the Human Race *one;* but not as a *Society*. It was from the first composed of distinct societies; whieh were called one, because formed on common principles. It is One Society, only when considered as to its *future* existence. The circumstance of its having one common Head, (Christ,) one Spirit, one Father, are points of unity which no more make the Church One Society on earth, than the circumstance of all men having the same Creator, and being derived from the same Adam, renders the Human Race one Family." And again: "The Church is *one*, then, not as consisting of One Society, but because the various societies, or churches, were then modelled, and ought still to be so, on the same principles; and because they enjoy common privileges,—one Lord, one Spirit, one baptism. Accordingly, the Holy Ghost, through his agents and Apostles, has not

Had the Apostles intended that there should be but one church, or that there should be national or diocesan churches, they would have plainly told us so. They would not have left so important a doctrine to depend on the plainest inference; for it is the manner of Inspiration to teach all great truths positively and fully. Yet not only are we left to infer exactly the opposite, as from reason and the nature of the case we should do, the language of inspired Apostles, repeated in many forms and connections, illustrated and confirmed by their recorded actions, furnishes positive proofs, clear and indisputable, that churches were constituted as separate, distinct, local bodies of believers. These Apostles had just been instructed by the Lord Jesus personally in things pertaining to the kingdom of God, and they certainly must have received directions on this point. Being Jews, their prepossessions and habits of thinking and speaking were altogether in favor of a national religion and priesthood, an idea which when incorporated into Christianity, which they knew to be a universal religion, would have led them to form one universal or catholic church. How shall we account for the fact that their language and proceedings were so entirely opposite to this, but by supposing that they received particular instructions from the Saviour's lips to establish separate local churches as they did?

And, finally, the circumstances show the impossibility of any such extended or combined church. For, if there were such an organization, the seat of its authority must have been somewhere. The earliest church—that at Jerusalem—was gathered

left any detailed account of the formation of any Christian society; but He has very distinctly marked the great principles on which all were to be founded, whatever distinctions may exist amongst them. In short, the foundation of the church by the Apostles was not analogous to the work of Romulus, or Solon; it was not properly, the foundation of Christian societies which occupied them, but the establishment of the principles on which Christians in all ages might form societies for themselves."

under the preaching of inspired Apostles. But could it for these reasons, or did it as a fact, claim authority over other churches? Apostles also preached at Antioch, at Corinth, at Ephesus, and at Rome; and churches sprung up in those places as the consequence. Neither could claim precedence on account of Apostolic origin, and no one can suppose that priority of existence could give any claim to it. Other churches sprung up under the labors of men who were not Apostles, yet they were no less the fruit of Christian doctrine, and some of them afterwards enjoyed the privilege of Apostolic instruction and oversight. Could these churches possibly owe allegiance to the church at Jerusalem, or to any other, or to the ministry of any other church? Certainly not.*

The conclusion is irresistible, that there were many churches constituted under the ministry of the Apostles, each one entitled, in the fullest sense, to the name, the immunities, and the authority of a *church* of the living God.† We therefore infer,

1. That all claims to universal, national, provincial, or

* To the correctness of this view the best ecclesiastical historians of the early churches bear ample testimony. Gieseler says, vol. i. s. 29, "The new churches everywhere *formed themselves* on the model of the mother church at Jerusalem. At the head of each were the Elders, all officially of equal rank," &c.

† Archbishop Whately fully sustains this view. He says: "It appears plainly from the sacred narrative, that though the many churches which the Apostles founded were branches of one *spiritual* brotherhood, of which the Lord Jesus Christ is the heavenly Head,—though there was 'one Lord, one Faith, one Baptism,' for all of them, yet they were each a distinct, independent community *on earth*, united by the common principles on which they were founded, and by their mutual agreement, affection, and respect; but not having one recognized Head on earth, or acknowledging any sovereignty of one of these societies over others. Generally speaking, the Apostles appear to have clearly established a distinct church in each considerable city; so that there were several even in a single province; as for instance, in Macedonia, those of Philippi, Thessalonica, Beræa, Amphipolis, &c.: and the like in the province of Achaia, and elsewhere."

diocesan church power, are of human origin, are contrary to Apostolic practice, and should be discarded and resisted as usurpations.

2. That the plurality of distinct, visible churches is no more a proof nor a cause of schism, than a plurality of cities or villages, of literary or benevolent societies, or families, states or nations.

3. That the real authors of schism are those who press the claims of one church to extensive or universal authority.

4. That a plurality of churches, all similar in their structure, polity, and doctrines, all taking the Bible for their guide and obeying it, form, indeed, but one church, of which Christ is the Head—one kingdom of heaven on earth, of which he is the King.

Sect. 3. *Of whom true Churches are composed.*

Professed believers in Christ, and no others, were admitted as members in the Apostolic churches. This might have been expected from the nature and object of our Saviour's mission, to set up the kingdom of God in this world, the subjects of which "must be born again." "My sheep," says he—speaking to the Jews, who supposed themselves God's covenant people in virtue of their pedigree—"hear my voice, and I know them, and they follow me." "He that believeth on me hath everlasting life." "He that believeth not, is condemned already." The only people on earth who retained any of the elements of true religion were sunk in mere ceremonial worship, trusting to external righteousness; he, therefore, required a change of heart, and faith in himself as the Saviour, in all the subjects of this new spiritual kingdom.

As might be expected, therefore, the primitive churches were formed of believers only.* The three thousand persons who

* Mosheim says, vol. i. p. 82, that, in the first century, "whoever professed to regard Jesus Christ as the Saviour of the world, and to

on the day of Pentecost gladly received the word, became disciples of Christ, "continued steadfastly in the Apostles' doctrine and fellowship, and in breaking of bread and in prayers," "and all that *believed* were together." We are next told, "the Lord added to the church daily such as should be saved," or such as had been just described; all of whom had been baptized as a solemn renunciation of their Jewish prejudices, their former hopes, and their sinful practices, and a joyful profession of their faith in Christ. When a fierce persecution was kindled against the church at Jerusalem, "they were all scattered abroad and went everywhere preaching the word." None but true believers would have done this. When "the churches had rest" they "were edified, and walking in the fear of the Lord and the comfort of the Holy Ghost, were multiplied." The church at Ephesus is called a "flock," of which the Holy Ghost was the patron, to appoint its overseers, and as "the church of God which he hath purchased with his own blood."

The churches are always addressed by the Apostles as composed of saints only. "Paul, unto the church of God which is at Corinth, to them that are sanctified in Christ Jesus, called to be saints." "To all the saints in Christ Jesus which are at Philippi, with the bishops and deacons." "Paul and Sylvanus, and Timothy, unto the church of the Thessalonians which is in God the Father, and in the Lord Jesus Christ: grace be unto you and peace from God our Father and the Lord Jesus Christ. We give thanks to God always for you all, making mention of you in our prayers, remembering without ceasing, your work of faith and labor of love, and patience of hope in our Lord Jesus Christ in the sight of God our Father; knowing, brethren beloved, your election of God."

To the church in Corinth these decisive Apostolic instructions were given: "Be ye not unequally yoked together, [connected

depend on him alone for salvation, was immediately baptized and admitted into the church." "The congregation of the elect," says Clement of Alexandria, "I call the church."

or mingled,] with unbelievers: for what fellowship hath righteousness with unrighteousness? and what communion hath light with darkness? and what concord hath Christ with Belial? or what part hath he that believeth with an infidel? [that is, an unbeliever.] And what agreement hath the temple [the spiritual temple, the church,] of God with idols? for ye are the temple of the living God, as God hath said, I will dwell in them and walk in them, and I will be their God, and they shall be my people. Wherefore *come out* from them and be ye *separate*, saith the Lord, and touch not the unclean thing, and I will receive you, and will be a Father to you, and ye shall be my sons and daughters, saith the Lord Almighty." This passage plainly teaches that a church should consist of believers only, that they should publicly profess their faith in Christ, and separate themselves from an unbelieving world.

Our Saviour has also warned his ministers and his people not to receive into church-membership nor to the privileges and ordinances of His house, unsanctified persons, who live devoted to worldly appetites. "Give not that which is holy to the dogs, neither cast ye your pearls before swine; lest they trample them under their feet, and turn again and rend you." The history of the papacy and of every ecclesiastical body which has violated this rule, affords melancholy proof that such warnings are needed. Baptized unbelievers, aptly compared to dogs and swine, have not only trampled church privileges under their feet, but have rent the children of God more than all the unbaptized infidels and pagans together.*

Believers were also baptized, as a pledge of their faith in Christ, as a symbol of their spiritual change previous to their becoming members of the churches. The Apostolic commission was, Go and *disciple* all nations, or bring them to become believers, then *baptize* them, in token of their union to God, and to his visible church, next, *teach* them all the com-

* See *Biblical Repository,* Second Series, vol. 12, No. 23.

mandments of Christ. Baptism is joined with faith. "He that believeth and is baptized shall be saved." These instructions the Apostles obeyed, both in spirit and to the letter. "Then they that gladly received his word were baptized." "When they believed Philip, preaching the things concerning the kingdom of God, and the name of Jesus Christ, they were baptized, both men and women." Ananias came to Saul, put his hands upon him, "and he received sight, arose and was baptized." Writing to the church at Rome, Paul reasons from their baptism their obligation to be holy. "Know ye not, that so many of us as were baptized into Jesus Christ, were baptized into his death? Therefore we are buried with him by baptism into death; that, like as Christ was raised up from the dead by the glory of the Father, even so we should walk in newness of life." This passage not only takes for granted the baptism of the members of that church, but assumes as a universal fact, that all the members of Christian churches are baptized persons. The same thing is inferred of the members of the church at Colosse: "Ye are circumcised with the circumcision made without hands, in putting off the body of the sins of the flesh, by the circumcision of Christ; buried with him in baptism, wherein also ye are risen with him through the faith of the operation of God, who hath raised him from the dead." It was the uniform practice of the Apostles to administer baptism immediately to believers, after which they became members of the churches.

It is evident, therefore, that the only proper members of a church are baptized believers in Christ. The Scriptures make no exceptions on account of age or sex, or nation, or civil rank: "Ye are all the children of God by faith in Christ Jesus. For as many of you as have been baptized into Christ have put on Christ. There is neither Jew nor Greek, there is neither bond nor free, there is neither male nor female: for ye are all one in Christ Jesus." "Believers were the more added to the Lord, multitudes both of men and women." "Let your women keep silence in the churches." These passages settle the question of female membership. Those who do not or cannot exercise faith in Christ, have no right to baptism, nor to church-membership. If, in the Galatian churches, filled as they were with Jewish prejudices and wedded to Jewish customs, especially that of circumcision, "as many as had been baptized into Christ had put on Christ," by a public profession, it is plain that there were no baptized infants among them. The Gospel being designed for moral agents, capable of spiritual exercises, presents its claims, and proffers its instructions to such only as are able to receive it. Nothing is said or intimated in the New Testament respecting infant members of churches, nor are the children of believing parents described as sustaining any relation to the churches different from that of other children, or as any more entitled to the ordinances or subject to the discipline of the churches.

As Christian churches, then, should always be composed of baptized believers only, and as the nature of a church requires that all its members become so by their own free, intelligent act, the initiatory rite must be performed on the same principle. It matters not what has been done to the believer by parents, or guardians, or sponsors, in his unconscious infancy; the knowledge of which may have come down to him by tradition, by testimony, or by parish records, nor with what sincerity, nor in what form it was done; since it was not *his own act.* *No owning of the covenant* can make the act his own. His duty is to believe and be baptized for himself, without which, he cannot be a proper member of a Christian church.

SECT. 4. *Churches the fruit of Christian Doctrine.*

"And I, if I be lifted up from the earth, will draw all men unto me," said the Divine Redeemer, in speaking of his cross, the grand spiritual magnet of the world—the central sun in the system of revealed truth. Christ crucified, the great, and often the exclusive theme of Apostolic preaching, the standing memorial of the sinner's guilt, ingratitude, and ruin; and of God's awful justice, compassion, and love, the admiration of angels, the terror of demons, possesses the strongest spiritual attractions. The soul that has felt its power exclaims, "I am crucified with Christ, yet I live by the faith of the Son of God, who loved me, and gave himself for me." "God forbid that I should glory save in the cross of our Lord Jesus Christ." "If we are beside ourselves it is to God, if we are sober it is for your sakes: for the love of Christ constraineth us." The Gospel commences its work by transforming the individual character, and here is the first element of a Christian church.

The influence which transformed his character is social, benevolent, diffusive. He becomes a spring of holy influence to relatives, to near friends, to countrymen, then to those afar off. "Andrew . . . first findeth his own brother Simon, and saith unto him, We have found the Messiah." "Come see a man who told me all things that ever I did: is not this the Christ?" The converted persecutor exclaims, "I am not ashamed of the Gospel of Christ; for it is the power of God unto salvation to every one that believeth." Thus "the kingdom of heaven is like unto leaven, which a woman took and hid in three measures of meal, till the whole was leavened." Converts are multiplied, yet their hopes and fears, their doctrines and their aims, are one.

The doctrines of the Gospel, with Christ crucified as the central point of attraction, become the basis of a new social and spiritual union. So it was in the beginning. "To whom shall we go? Thou hast the words of eternal life." After the ascension of Jesus, his disciples "all continued with one accord in prayer and supplication." "They that gladly received the word" of Peter, on the day of Pentecost, "continued steadfastly in the Apostles' doctrine and *fellowship*;" "all that believed were together," "continuing daily with one accord in the temple," "and the Lord added to the church daily such as should be saved." Here, then, is a church, as the natural fruit of

Christian doctrine. It has not officers, is not yet organized, has adopted no specific articles of compact, yet, inasmuch as its members are united in a holy covenant, it is a church of Christ. It is empowered to act in the name and authority of Christ, "for where two or three are gathered together in my name, there am I in the midst of them."

As the Scriptures plainly teach us that churches are composed of those only who have passed from death unto life by faith in the Saviour, it follows that doctrines preached, stand to churches in the relation of cause to effect; or as the seed to the plant which springs from it. Did the preaching of the Apostles produce churches? The same doctrines have produced churches in every subsequent age, and will continue to do so, whenever faithfully and fully preached, to the end of time.* Doctrines exist, and are true, and powerful, independently of the existence of any church; being contained in the written, infallible word of God. The belief, the mutual love, and the united desire to promulgate these, form the bond of church union. Doctrines, when received into the hearts of men, prepare the materials of which a church is made, and attract them towards each other. By the institution of the last Supper, the emblem of the cross, the great spiritual attraction, is set up in every church, so that before their eyes Jesus Christ had been evidently set forth, crucified among them.

"Either the church comes of faith, or faith comes of the church." The former part of the antithesis we maintain to be not only true, but to express a truth immensely important to the progress of religion; while the latter part, if it be true at all, is only so in a modified, and very restricted sense. Faith implanted in the hearts of men begets the church. The church

* "*The form has killed the substance*—here is the whole history of the Papacy and of false catholicism. *The substance vivifies the form*—here is the whole history of Evangelical Christianity, and of the true catholic church of Jesus Christ."—*Puseyism Examined.*

is formed of converted individuals, converted by the Word and Spirit of God.

As every true church is a fruit of faith, that is, of Christian truth received into hearts renewed by Divine grace, so its continued existence depends on the continuance of spiritual life in the souls of its members. When a church, as a body, ceases to believe and maintain the vital doctrines of the Gospel, it then ceases to be a church.

That a church which has become heretical, or corrupt, or lukewarm, may become extinct, or lose its existence as a church, we are clearly taught in the Scriptures. The Lord Jesus warned the churches in Ephesus and Laodicea of speedy extinction by his own visitation unless they repented. "I have somewhat against thee, because thou hast left thy first love. Remember, therefore, from whence thou art fallen, and repent, and do the first works; or else I will come unto thee quickly and will remove thy candlestick out of his place, except thou repent." "So, then, because thou art lukewarm, and neither cold nor hot, I will spew thee out of my mouth. Because thou sayest I am rich, and increased in goods, and have need of nothing; and knowest not that thou art wretched, and miserable, and poor, and blind, and naked." These awful threatenings were long ago executed, and, indeed, all those ancient churches which were gathered under the labors of the Apostles and their associates, having lost the principle of their perpetuity, have long ago ceased to be.

Some apostate churches have been swept away by outward calamities brought on by the Divine displeasure, as by war, or a popular tumult, or a revolution; others have been rent in pieces by internal dissensions, by confusion and division among their members; and others still, like Lot's wife, have been made the perpetual monuments of God's anger against apostasy; for though they retain a form and visible body, yet like the trees upon the shores of the Dead Sea, not prostrated by the winds nor shattered by the lightnings of heaven, but standing leafless and lifeless, instructive by their desolation and ruin, they are useful only for the sad and terrible lessons which they illustrate.

This, then, is manifest; that the preaching of Christian truth, attended by the influences of the Spirit of God, produces churches, as the seed, quickened into life by the warmth of the sun, produces the plants which grow from them. Churches are not formed by a power exerted from without, but developed from power working within.* As the first church, and the second, and indeed every one, whose origin is described in the New Testament, received its existence and form from the inherent force and working of the spiritual energies of Christianity, so should every church be formed. Wherever and by whatever means the truths of the Gospel are received in love, there all needful authority exists for the formation of a proper and valid church of Christ.

SECT. 5. *Gradual development of Principles.*

From the Scriptural account of the origin of churches, it is evident that the principles and doctrines which produced them were unfolded gradually, in such an order as to lead naturally to the formation of local associations, or congregations of believers, for the worship of God, and the administration of the ordinances of the Gospel. "So is the kingdom of God, . . . first the blade, then the ear, after that the full corn in the ear."

First, came the prophetic announcement of a new institution about to be established in the earth, with the high distinctive name, "kingdom of God," or "kingdom of heaven;" a name which would raise the expectation that its subjects would be separated from the mass of mankind. Our Saviour declared that he had come to establish this kingdom.

* Where the Spirit is, there is the church; this is the principle of the reform: where the church is, there is the Spirit, is the principle of Rome and Oxford; and it is also, though in a milder form, that of Lutheranism.—*D'Aubigné.*

But then he declared at the outset, that all the members of that kingdom must be so changed as to be radically different from other men; they must be made anew, or, in his expressive words, "must be born again." "Except a man be born of water and of the Spirit, he cannot enter into the kingdom of God." Here, then, is not only a new kingdom announced, but a new order of moral beings to compose it.

Significant of this spiritual change, a new, peculiar rite of admission is appointed, is honored by the obedience of Jesus Christ himself, that he might 'fulfil all righteousness,' and is then enjoined on all his followers. During his earthly ministry it is called "the baptism of repentance for the remission of sins," but after his ascension, is found also to be symbolic of his burial and resurrection, to impress on the hearts of believers their obligations to be dead unto sin, that they may walk in a new life.

This inward change and outward rite created a new bond of sympathy and union among the disciples, who now formed a family or community around the Saviour. Though permitted to exercise none of the powers or rights peculiar to a church, while the King in Zion was among them in person, yet they were united on the same voluntary principle of obedience to his commands.

As a first practical lesson, they were taught that the kingdom of God, of which they had become members, was to be extended by their efforts, made effectual by divine influence. "Ye are the light of the world." "Ye are the salt of the earth." "Pray ye the Lord of the harvest that he would send forth laborers into his harvest." Immediately, while the number of his disciples was yet small, he selected twelve whom he named Apostles, or *men sent*, to prosecute this work. Soon after he chose seventy others, and sent them forth as heralds of the kingdom of God.

Next, he now invites all who would find rest and safety to their souls to come to *him*. And although he addressed Jews who claimed that the oracle, the temple, the priesthood, and the mercy-seat, were exclusively with them, yet he uses the most decisive and unequivocal language: "Your fathers *did* eat manna in the wilderness and are dead: he that eateth of this bread—or believeth on me—shall live forever." "I am that bread of life." "If any man—Jew or Gentile—thirst, let him come unto *me* and drink." "Come unto me all ye that labor and are heavy laden and I will give you rest." And when an institution of the Old Testament comes in his way, he asserts his power to change it. "The Son of man is Lord also of the Sabbath." "Here is one greater than the temple." He came into the world clothed with authority to set aside any previously existing Divine institutions.

The assertion of this authority was speedily followed by no dubious intimations that the Jewish Theocracy would pass away, to give place for the Gospel. Knowing that nothing would so much enrage the Jews as the announcement of this truth, it was gradually made known to his confidential disciples. When Moses and Elias passed away before Jesus in the mount of transfiguration, he strictly commanded that they should tell the vision to no man till the Son of man be risen from the dead. So startling an announcement as that a new form of religious polity was soon to supersede and displace the old, was made with wise caution.

On the other hand, he assured his disciples that the open profession of faith in him which they were required to make, would excite against them the hatred and persecution of the world, especially of that portion who were zealous for an outward form of religion; so that their separation from all others for the purpose of uniting together would be an act of necessity as well as of duty.

When the time of his crucifixion drew near, he spoke with less reserve of the setting up of his kingdom, and the destruction of the existing religious institutions, till finally, as the King of Zion, in literal fulfilment of prophecy, he made his public entry into Jerusalem amid the allowed and justified acclamations of the multitude.

Immediately after this decided step, he foretold the utter destruction of the city of Jerusalem, and of the temple; the stay, the glory, and the hope of Judaism.

But quickly gathering his disciples around the Paschal table, now spread for the last time in its original significancy, he abolished that ancient feast which only pointed to himself, exchanged the bleeding, symbolic victim for the broken bread and the flowing wine, unfurled the cross for a rallying banner, and commanded, as one who had authority to legislate in Zion, "THIS DO in remembrance of ME."

Having abolished the greatest Jewish festival, he next changed the Sacred Day, of which he had declared himself the Lord. His resurrection, the greatest event which the world ever witnessed, occurred on the first day of the week; on that day he appeared to his disciples, and on that day they of course assembled to worship Him, and to celebrate that ordinance which was appointed to be the standing memorial of his death.

He continued on earth giving "commandments to the Apostles, whom he had chosen; to whom also he showed himself alive after his passion, by many infallible proofs, being seen of them forty days, and speaking of the things pertaining to the kingdom of God." What these "things" were, the inspired writers have not told us, yet one of the first things which the Apostles *did* was to lead the disciples to the choice of one to fill the place of the fallen Judas. If, therefore, their deeds are to be taken as evidence of his "commandments" to them on this occasion, he enacted as a general law, that after his departure persons were to be appointed to offices of labor and trust in the kingdom of heaven, or in the churches, by the suffrages of their members. This is evident from the choice of Matthias, and the manner of choosing the seven, of whom Stephen was the first.

Then followed the gift of the Holy Spirit upon the church;

as if one design had been to indicate the whole church, though many members, are to have one mind, and that the mind of Christ, in the setting apart of officers, and in all other things in which the welfare of his kingdom on earth and the salvation of men are concerned.

Hitherto the inspired historian speaks of one church only, "the church in Jerusalem," but now arose "a great persecution against THE CHURCH which was at Jerusalem, and they were all scattered abroad throughout the regions of Judea, and Samaria, except the Apostles;" and "they that were scattered abroad, went everywhere preaching the word." The Holy Spirit owned their preaching, and though no Apostles were with them, churches were constituted, and we are soon after told of "*the churches* through all Judea, and Galilee, and Samaria," and "*the churches* of the Gentiles."

That each and all of these churches possessed equal powers and rights; that each could lawfully perform any act involving the purity, order, and welfare of the kingdom of Christ; in short, that each church had the Divine sanction in doing anything which any other church, or number of churches could do, is next evident from the facts recorded of the church at Antioch. This church of Grecians, under the direction of the Holy Spirit, separated, ordained, and sent forth the first missionaries; and when these missionaries had performed their work, they made their report to the whole church from which they had received their commission. When the same missionaries were chosen by the church at Antioch to go to Jerusalem to the Apostles and Elders, on the question about circumcision, the answer was returned in the name of the "Apostles, Elders, and Brethren," who together composed the church. Thus it appears that a Gentile church, which was planted by men who were not Apostles, did, before any Apostle had visited them, set apart, commission, and ordain men, to do the same work which the Saviour commissioned his ministers to do.

We next find these churches addressed by Apostles, and

finally by our ascended Lord himself, as possessing in themselves the powers of organization, government, and discipline. The great principles on which they should proceed are unfolded, their duties are clearly pointed out, and commended to their attention. The principle that each church is a distinct, independent body, complete in itself for all the purposes of its visible union, is, in all these transactions, fully recognized, while the duty of mutual love, coöperation, and assistance is strongly urged upon them all.

Thus the principles which produced Christian churches were gradually developed, and brought effectually to bear on men whose religious belief, prepossessions, and habits were altogether adverse to them. It could not be expected that principles adapted and intended to elevate the mass of mankind to the dignity and responsibilities of men, and to humble the aspiring, would be immediately embraced, or their excellence appreciated; and therefore this gradual development is a striking proof of the wisdom of the Saviour.

SECT. 6. *Formation of a Church.*

In what way, then, does a company of disciples become a church of Christ? What power, or what act is necessary to constitute a church on Apostolic principles, after the materials are prepared? Or what is the formative, constituting element, in the organization of a church?

Men have a natural right to associate by mutual agreement for the accomplishment of any innocent or useful purpose. In this way civil government was first formed, for mutual protection, and God owned the institution as one of his own appointment. The disciples of Christ have the right to unite themselves together in churches, for the promotion of their piety and the spread of the Gospel, unless he has forbidden them in his revealed word. This he has not done. It is, therefore, from the nature of the case, proper that men should unite in a mutual, voluntary covenant for religious purposes. The objects in view are more important than those attained in the civil compact, in which men unite in a mutual covenant for a common benefit; and the act is as reasonable and as necessary in itself.

Nature also teaches us that man is a social and a religious being. We first open our eyes on a world of beings of the same image, sympathies, interests, and frailties with ourselves. We incline to their society, we feel a need of their aid, we soon see that none of us liveth to himself alone. Each, too, finds himself, in common with all others, endowed with capacities for the worship and service of the infinite Creator. If men, therefore, meet in the halls of science and legislation because it is agreeable to their nature as well as mutually advantageous so to do, the same is true of their religious concerns. And from the great strength of the social and religious feelings combined, when the latter are roused to action, men would feel inclined often to engage in acts of worship in company. The formation of churches, therefore, for united worship, is agreeable to reason, by supplying an obvious demand of human nature.

The reception of the doctrines of the Gospel, including the promised gift of the Holy Spirit, furnishes, as has been already shown, additional bonds of union, of the most sacred and affecting nature. None but believers can be sufficiently aware of the dreadful evil and danger of sin, of the desperate wickedness of the human heart, the infinite benevolence and compassion of God, the intense vicarious sufferings of the Redeemer, the worth and danger of the soul, and the incomparable superiority of the concerns of eternity to those of time. The Gospel, too, changes the hatred of men to love, their selfishness to benevolence, lifts their hearts from the sensual to the spiritual, and thus powerfully draws them together. Then the choicest promises of the Saviour are to united prayer, the most solemn vouchers of his presence to united worshippers. His own example sanctioned the principle of association, the solemn ordinance which commemorates his dying love, and the great transaction by which salvation was procured, must be observed by an associated company.

After the Gospel had been preached a few years, we find inspired epistles addressed to churches, implying their right to exercise the power of discipline and exclusion, explaining the principles on which it should be done, and exhorting them to its performance. The Saviour himself, by his servant John, directed separate epistles to each of the seven churches of Asia, through their Angels or Pastors, recognizing the complete church power of each, and exhorting each to the performance of duties which belong to the church regimen.

All the members of these churches became such by their own voluntary act. In other words, each entered freely into covenant with all the other members, and thus became a part of the church. The *faith* of an individual convert did not of itself constitute him a member of any particular church, nor did his baptism, which is the universal badge of the Christian profession, but his voluntary *covenant* to walk with that church in the commandments and ordinances of the Lord made him a member. Here, then, is the fundamental principle on which every true church was originally constituted; *the mutual covenant of baptized believers to unite in sustaining the worship, the doctrines, and the ordinances of the Lord, and that discipline among themselves which is according to godliness.* The light of nature, the influence of the Gospel, the example of the Saviour, the inspired references to churches, all sanction and confirm this view, and no precept or precedent can be found in the Scriptures in opposition to it.

From this view of the subject, it is evident that a suitable number of believers possess the right, at all times, in proper circumstances and from good motives, to unite themselves in mutual covenant to obey and execute the laws of Jesus Christ; and that, while they do so, they enjoy and exercise all the rights and authority which he has conferred on any visible church.

This may explain the reason why the Saviour did not, while

on earth, form any visibly organized church. Had he done so, that church might have claimed preëminence over others, as the mother church, the only true church, or even the holy catholic church. But the Saviour neither in person erected a church, nor made it any part of the special duty of the Apostles, nor even of ministers, in virtue of their office, to form churches. He enacted the principles and laws, and left his people at large to apply them by *forming themselves* into churches according to their circumstances, by a mutual covenant.

Thus the reason why the whole church is the judge of the claims of those who apply to be admitted as members, is also plain. Without this mutual consent to the admission of members, there could be no covenant; for a covenant must, from the nature of the case, be mutual and voluntary. Any other mode of admission to membership in a church, therefore, than by the free consent of the members, would destroy this essential element of its existence. It might still be a body of professed or real Christians, but it would not be a church of Christ according to the Scriptures.

CHAPTER II.

PRINCIPLES INVOLVED IN THE FUNCTIONS OF A CHURCH.

CHRISTIAN churches, like all other affiliated bodies, possess and exercise certain powers in virtue of their associated capacity. States and voluntary societies adopt written constitutions to define and determine the extent of their corporate powers, and the principles on which they shall be exercised. The constitution of a Christian church, on the contrary, is contained in the New Testament. To the model there sketched, by precept and by precedent, every church is under obligation to conform all its regulations and practices.

The principles on which the powers of an associated body proceed, depend on the nature and the objects of the association and the characters of its members. "If men were angels," says a distinguished civilian, "they would scarcely need the form of government, if they were devils, they must be bound in fetters of brass, and as they approximate to the one or the other so must their form of government and laws be modified." A prison cannot be governed on the same principles as a literary society, nor a company of soldiers by the rules of a parliamentary assembly. The objects of a church differ entirely from those of any other association of men. "My kingdom," says the Saviour to Pilate, "is not of this world;" and this he gave as the reason why he adopted a policy entirely different from every other king. It is evident, therefore, that an institution for objects diverse from all others, having nothing in common with worldly maxims or policy, must be governed on different principles.

But especially when it is recollected that a church, as has been shown, is composed of "a peculiar people," differing so entirely from all others that they are said to be "created in Christ Jesus to good works," "born again," to be "dead to the world" and "alive to God," to be branches of Christ, and "heirs of God," we should expect that when associated their constitutional powers would proceed on principles essentially different from those of all other human associations. Unlike civil society, it is no part of their object in forming this union to protect themselves from each other, nor to acquire any temporal advantage. Love to God, love to each other, and love to all mankind; love in its highest, holiest exercise, is to be the all-pervading element in which they are to live and move, and in which all their acts are to be performed. As "love is the fulfilling of the law," and is a far better guide to duty than rules and penalties, a church formed on the principle of love needs but a few plain indications of the will of Christ for its guidance, and such only he has given.

When brought to the tribunal of an earthly monarch our Saviour declared himself to be the king of truth. The realm of truth is his empire. Every church which is 'built on the foundation of the Apostles and Prophets, Jesus Christ the chief corner-stone,' is a part of this empire. The spirit of truth, whom earthly kingdoms cannot receive, dwells in it. The written will of Christ, and not the unwritten suggestions of nature, nor the enactments of men, is its supreme law; the promised Spirit of Christ, so long as sought by prayer, is its unerring and unfailing guide. The power of a church consists in understanding, obeying, and executing this law, the constituent elements of which are truth, holiness, and love.

SECT. 1. *The Powers of a Church.*

A church, therefore, being a peculiar institution, in respect to its origin, its objects, and the qualifications of its members, the question now arises, what powers does it possess? Or what may a church do in its collective capacity as a Gospel church, which individual Christians, or a company of Christians, not united in church fellowship and covenant, may not do? This question is of great practical importance in its bearings on the rights of individuals, and the prosperity of the kingdom of Christ.* It is necessary, therefore, to consider,

1. The source of church power. Is the power of a particular church derived from the church universal? If so, it will be necessary to prove that such an institution exists as a corporate body, that it has power to spare, and has a right to delegate it. As neither of these points can be proved, we must inquire after some other source. The Scriptures plainly teach us that the Lord Jesus is the source from whence his churches derive their power. Rev. 3 : 7. Isa. 9 : 6. This might be clearly

* Yes, I admit it--the church is the judge of controversies—*judex controversarium*. But what is the church? It is not the clergy, it is not the councils, still less is it the Pope. It is the Christian people, it is the faithful.—*D'Aubigné.*

inferred from the relation in which He stands to his people. He is called the "true light," the "bread of life," the vine, of which his people are the branches, the "good Shepherd who giveth his life for the sheep," and his people as "bought with a price," "purchased by the blood of Christ," as "redeemed by his blood and made kings and priests unto God." By bestowing these inestimable benefits on his people, He has acquired the right to govern and direct them, by bestowing and withholding such powers as he sees to be suitable or otherwise, and they have incurred the obligation to submit to him as their supreme and only legislator.

But the Scriptures have not left this truth to depend on even so plain an inference as this. They inform us that Christ came into the world with express and ample powers to be sole lawgiver in Zion. Prophecy had declared that the Messiah was to be the Son of God. At his baptismal consecration the Father spake from the Eternal throne as he never condescended to speak before in the ears of mortals, "This is my beloved Son; hear ye him:" and to crown the august scene, the Holy Spirit himself assumed a visible form, and "abode upon him." He himself declares soon after, "All power is given unto me, in heaven and in earth." He had power even when on earth to forgive sins. He is called "heir of all things," with "power to give eternal life to as many as God had given him." He is declared to be "the HEAD over all things TO THE CHURCH, which is his body." And "he is before all things, and by him all things consist: and he is the Head of the body, the church: who is the beginning, the first-born from the dead, that in *all things* HE *might have the preëminence.*"

As the procurer and the giver of everlasting life, the head or ruler of the people of God, and the heir of all things, He has full power to establish such principles of order and polity in the kingdom of saints as shall seem best to him. These principles he has, in great wisdom and mercy, revealed in his Word, for the guidance and edification of his saints, in sustaining united prayer and worship, and the holy ordinances of baptism and the breaking of bread. All the power, therefore, which any church may lawfully possess and exercise, must be derived from Jesus Christ, whose revealed will is in all things to be implicitly obeyed. "He openeth and no man shutteth; He shutteth and no man openeth."

This supreme power of the Saviour in and over his churches, may be expressed in several particulars, each of which is confirmed by the direct words of Scripture. As, 1. The sole power of making laws for all churches is in him, and is not transmitted to any other. James 4 : 12. The only power given to churches is to publish and execute his laws. Matt. 28 : 20. Being perfect and able to make the man of God *perfect to every good work*, 2 Tim. 3 : 17, they need no addition. 2. That He only can erect and establish the true church constitution. Heb. 3 : 3–6. No man has a right to set up a church except according to that frame or pattern. 3. All offices, ordinary and extraordinary, are established by him, and the authority belonging to them, Eph. 4 : 11. 1 Cor. 12 : 5–18, as well as all gifts of wisdom and grace to discharge the duties of every station in the church, Col 2 : 3–9, together with all spiritual efficiency to make these gifts and offices effectual for the perfecting of saints and the conversion of sinners. Matt. 28 : 20. Col. 1 : 29.

2. The nature of church power. A church is to learn, and then to execute its Lord's will. Its power is therefore exclusively spiritual. It has no right to the use of political power; nor to form any coalition with the civil state, and if it does so, it ceases to be a true church of Christ. Nor has a church the right to use force, either directly or indirectly, to accomplish its purposes. It may persuade, exhort, entreat, admonish, and rebuke, to produce obedience; but has no right to resort to corporal or pecuniary pains and penalties.*

* We reject all Christian discipline exercised by constables and soldiers; we lay aside all public force, retaining the power of vigilance, of charity, and of the Word of God.—*D'Aubigné.*

This spiritual power must be used in an executive sense only. The Saviour has revealed all the laws by which it is to be governed. He has delegated no legislative power to any church. The right of each to execute his laws among its members, implies the right to study those laws for itself, and to adopt that construction which the united wisdom of its members believe to be true.

It is highly important that the true nature of church power be thoroughly understood, because mistakes on this point have been fruitful in oppressions and corruptions. The rights, the comfort, and the spiritual prosperity of every church-member, and the interests of the Redeemer's kingdom depend, very much, on a correct understanding of this subject by the members at large. Church power is not the power of a majority, nor is it the power to do good in general, nor is it the power to declare in favor of everything which is good or right in itself. It is of the nature of the power of a church that it has regard solely to the spiritual welfare of men, as it is of the nature of the power of civil government to be applicable only to the protection of its subjects in the enjoyment of their temporal rights. There are many duties which belong to men as men, or as citizens, but not as church-members, nor to churches as churches.

3. The objects to be attained by the exercise of church power are those only for which the Saviour toiled and suffered, and to crown the whole, "gave himself for us, that he might redeem us from all iniquity, and purify to himself a peculiar people, zealous of good works." To accomplish this, he devoted himself exclusively to it, refusing to turn aside to oppose the exaction of an oppressive and unjust tribute, or to persuade a man to do a simple act of justice to his brother, even in the use of a moral influence. "Man, who made me a Ruler or a Divider over you?" This example of our Lord is a law to his churches. They were not called into the church state to attempt the accomplishment of general good, such as the promotion of science, morality, or philanthropy; but the particular good, of saving

men from their sins, and of preparing them for heaven. This being the sole purpose of Christian churches they have no right to use that power, authority, or influence, which they derive in virtue of being a church, for any other purpose.

The design of the church, as a visible society, is to train men for heaven. Does not reason teach us that this object is great enough to require, and good enough to be worthy of, all its strength? Such a cause as the spiritual salvation of men may justly claim *all* the power and influence of *one* form of association, surely. Is there as much danger that the temporal interests of men—even their dearest rights will suffer, if churches, as churches, take no care of them, as that their spiritual interests will suffer by dividing the attention and the efforts of churches? There is certainly very little danger that any church will be more exclusive and single, in confining its efforts to the salvation of souls, than were those which were under Apostolic guidance. The example of Jesus is the pattern for every church-member. Is it not, then, the duty of all churches to refrain from interference in any cause, however good, which may absorb their strength, or divert them in the least from their appropriate work?

4. The extent of the powers of a church. Like those of all other associated bodies, the powers of a church have a definite limit. And, first, they are limited to its own members. Over them it has the right to exercise the strictest watch-care, to call them to account for every neglect or violation of the Saviour's laws. It may admonish, censure, and expel the disobedient. It has the power to choose and set apart its proper officers. It may also, in obedience to its Lord's will, set apart members to the work of spreading the gospel in any portion of the earth, to which they are willing to go, and it may require all its members to do something to promote the work.

Second, the power of a church over its own members is limited by the right of private judgment and individual conscience. It is evident that in the Apostolic churches great freedom in private judgment was allowed. "Him that is weak in the faith receive ye, but not to doubtful disputations." His doctrinal knowledge or his Christian character may be defective, yet receive him, and make not slight errors the topic of dispute, for "Who art thou that judgest another man's servant? to his own Master he standeth or falleth." "But why dost thou judge thy brother? or why dost thou set at naught thy brother? for we shall all stand before the judgment-seat of Christ." "Let us not judge one another any more, but judge this rather, that no man put a stumbling-block, or an occasion to fall, in his brother's way." It was the glory of the Gospel then, as it should be now, that it could unite men of different theories, and dissimilar education, on the great principle of love. If Jew and Gentile could not harmonize in *opinions*, they could leave each other to their individual accountability to God, hold to what they had mutually attained, and love each other for Christ's sake. And they were cautioned against agitating "questions which minister strife, rather than godly edifying."

SECT. 2. *Reception of Church Power.*

Before a church can be formed, the materials must be prepared. These, as we have already seen, are baptized believers. To prepare such materials previously to the formation of churches, our Saviour instructed, commissioned, and sent forth the Apostles, and the seventy disciples, none of whom were, during his earthly ministry, either officers or members of any particular church. Of the converts made and baptized by them, churches were afterwards formed. How did these bodies of Christians obtain the powers of Christian churches? Or how does a body of baptized believers *now*, obtain the right to exercise those powers?

Two things are necessary. First, A *mutual covenant*, voluntarily entered into by all the members, to obey and execute the commands of Christ; and, second, A faithful adherence to the obligations thus assumed.

1. Without a mutual covenant on the part of believers to walk together in the duties and ordinances of the Gospel, no church could ever have been formed. There might be real Christians, unconnected, and recognizing no power of mutual watch, reproof, and discipline; but they could not be a church without entering into covenant for that purpose, and voluntarily assuming the obligations necessary to that relation.

In fact, there can be no enduring and obligatory unions among men except such as rest either on the laws of nature, or ultimately, on a voluntary covenant. Christian love in some sense unites believers in all lands, of all names, and of all the various shades of belief, but is not alone sufficient to unite any portion of them in the church relation. There are duties which the members of the same church owe to each other which they owe to no others. Christians not united in a church capacity have no right to call each other authoritatively to account for violating the laws of Christ. It is from the agreement of the members to watch over each other, and submit to the admonitions and censures of the body, that this power arises.

2. When a company of believers thus united take the law of Christ for their rule of action, and faithfully execute it, they possess all the power, rights, and authority, ever vested by him in any church on earth. This is evidently the import of the principle laid down in Matt. 18 : 20. After having revealed the law of discipline, and granted his disciples the power of binding and loosing, with the assurance that their acts, when they should be united in the church capacity and obedient to his will should be ratified in heaven, and having thus explained to them the sacredness of the church power with which they were to be invested, he adds : "For where two or three are gathered together in my name, there am I in the midst of them." "In my name," signifies, subject to his authority, and doing his will. This passage is often, and very properly mentioned in circles of Christians gathered for prayers, as a source of encouragement to united supplication. But it extends further. It applies with

full force only to a band of disciples pledged to each other and to the Saviour to honor and obey his commands. With such a company thus united, he has promised to be, and where Jesus is with his disciples approvingly, there is full church power.

This power or privilege comes directly from Christ the supreme Lawgiver to each church as a body of brethern thus united in covenant, and is not transmitted to them through any other hands. For, if they are not the first subject of their church power they must have derived it either through their ministry, or through other churches. They did not derive it from or through their ministers, because they have the right to choose their own ministers, who have no authority previously to such choice. Therefore the church had this power before they had ministers, and so could not derive it from or through them. They could not derive it from any other particular church, because all churches have equal powers, all of which are restricted within themselves, no one inferior or subordinate to another. They could not derive it from a combination of churches, because churches cannot increase their power by combination. It must, therefore, come to them directly from the Lord Jesus Christ.

That the vitality of a church consists in faithfulness to its covenant, that it is perpetuated by obedience, is further evident from the inspired declarations. Respecting the church at Ephesus we are informed, Acts 19 : 1–6, that when the Apostle first came to that city he found twelve men, called disciples, who had been baptized to John's baptism only, without a proper recognition of Jesus as their Lord, or the Holy Spirit as their Sanctifier. He, therefore, first instructs these men, then orders them to be baptized into the regular Gospel church state, and then commences his evangelical labors for the purpose of building up this church, in that city, where he continued preaching two years. A few years after, in writing to this church on important points, which they did not yet fully understand, this comprehensive language occurs. Eph. 2 : 19, 20. "Now, therefore, ye are no more strangers, but fellow-citizens with the saints, and of the household of God, and are built upon the foundation of the Apostles and Prophets, Jesus Christ himself being the chief corner-stone, in whom all the building fitly framed together groweth into an holy temple in the Lord; in whom ye also are builded together for an habitation of God through the Spirit."

From this passage we learn, that the church at Ephesus was at that time, "*an* habitation of God," that its members belonged to "the household of God," and that Jesus Christ was its head, or corner-stone. It was a household of God while it continued on "the foundation of the Apostles and Prophets, Jesus Christ the chief corner-stone;" when it removed from that foundation it would cease to be entitled to the name.

Now let us trace the history of this church still further onward, and examine carefully, a message sent to it, dictated by the Lord Jesus himself. After the Apostle Paul had been driven from Ephesus, he spent considerable time preaching in other places, and then returned to the neighboring town of Miletus, from which place he sent to Ephesus and called the elders of the church, and said to them, among other things: Acts 20: 28–30. "Take heed, therefore, to yourselves, and to all the flock, over which the Holy Ghost hath made you overseers, to feed the church of God, which he hath purchased with his own blood. For I know this, that after my departing shall grievous wolves enter in among you, not sparing the flock: also of your own selves [that is, from among them, the Elders,] shall men arise, speaking perverse things, to draw away disciples after them." For the manner in which this prophetic declaration came to pass, let us examine the description which the Lord Jesus gives of the condition of this church thirty-five years afterwards. "Unto the Angel of the church of Ephesus, write: These things, saith he, that holdeth the seven stars in his right hand, who walketh in the midst of the seven golden candlesticks: I know thy works, and thy labor, and thy patience, and how thou canst not bear them which are evil, and thou hast tried them which say they are Apostles, and are not, and hast found them liars; and hast borne, and hast patience, and for my name's sake hast labored, and hast not fainted. Nevertheless, I have somewhat against thee, because thou hast left thy first love. Remember, therefore, from whence thou art fallen, and repent, and do the first works, or else I will come unto thee quickly, and will remove thy candlestick out of his place, except thou repent." In this remarkable and instructive message, it is worth while to note at present, First, that the Lord Jesus commends the church for many excellent traits, especially for the exertion of that disciplinary power with which they, in common with every church, were invested, of trying the claims of pretended Apostles: Second, they are censured for having declined in love: Third, they are admonished to consider their fallen state, to repent and commence anew: and, Fourth, they are threatened with the repeal and withdrawal of all their powers, privileges, and rights as a church, unless they fulfil the obligations of that covenant by which they were constituted a church. This threatening was executed. While they continued to meet in his name, in faithful, sincere obedience, he was in the midst of them, sanctioning their doings; when they ceased to do so, he withdrew from them the sanction of his authority. They might still remain united as a visible society, they might call themselves, and be called, a church, as many organizations are, long after they have ceased to deserve the name, but they were no longer so in reality, when the approval and authority of the Lord Jesus was withdrawn. "I will remove thy candlestick out of his place," is threatening the church with utter extinction.

The proof is, therefore, complete, that the power which each and every church exercises is conferred directly by Christ, is continued on condition of obedience to his laws, and is withdrawn when that obedience ceases. It is also plain, that when a company of baptized believers assume these obligations in obedience to the plain will of their Master, and faithfully fulfil them, they become a church, authorized to perform all acts proper to a

Gospel church. No bishop, no council of ministers, nor delegation from other churches, nor sanction of the church universal, can impart to them the least degree of church power. The reasons why it is a duty, in most cases, to call in the assistance of neighboring churches and ministers when the formation of a new church is contemplated, is for mutual counsel and prayer; but they can impart no power to the new body, for they have none to spare; and what they possess is in its nature incommunicable by human agency. It must come from Christ alone.

It is also evident from the nature of the case, and from analogy, that a church could acquire and retain this power in no other way. It is absurd to suppose that the Lord Jesus would continue to sanction the acts of a corrupt church, and bind in heaven what an apostate body had bound on earth; but it is reasonable to believe that he would sanction the doings of a pure and faithful body. And we have no reason to believe that He will interpose any but the ordinary means to prevent any church from falling into apostasy. An illustration may assist to make these views still more plain. It had long been customary for companies of individuals to ask of the Legislature of Massachusetts certain powers to act in corporate capacity, so that their acts might be legal, and the collective body be responsible for them. The Legislature, when satisfied that the object was good, and the applicants trustworthy, granted powers and privileges of incorporation in each case as it occurred, by a special act or statute. But in 1833, general provisions respecting corporations were framed,* by conforming to which, any association of individuals whose object was a proper one, could, on application, receive corporate powers "to make by-laws and regulations, consistent with the laws of the Commonwealth, and for the due and orderly conducting of their affairs."

So the Christian Lawgiver has enacted "general provisions," of which every associated body of his disciples may avail them-

* See *Revised Statutes*, chap. 44.

selves "for the due and orderly conducting of their affairs" as a church, and when they do so, by complying with those provisions, they have full corporate powers from the Lord Jesus Christ to do anything which is proper for any church on earth to do. They hold "the keys of the kingdom of heaven," having the power to admit and expel members according to the law of Christ, to choose and ordain officers, in short, to exercise the highest ecclesiastical functions. On this principle the First Church in Providence, R. I., founded by Roger Williams, Ezekiel Holiman, and others, possessed all the authority ever invested in any church by the Divine Head, whether in England or in Rome, in Antioch or in Jerusalem. After the lapse of two hundred years, its soundness in the faith, its purity, spiritual vigor, thorough, Scriptural discipline, and uninterrupted prosperity, furnish a strong proof of the validity of its powers, and the approval of the Saviour. While it continues faithful to the covenant under which its corporate powers were obtained from its Divine Head, it will stand unshaken, when ecclesiastical hierarchies, and national religious establishments, with all their political power, their wealth, and titles, and orders of ministry, shall exist only among the records of history.

SECT. 3. *The Rights of a Church.*

All the rights which a church possesses in its collective capacity being derived from its conformity to the Saviour's revealed will, may be considered in respect to its own members, to other churches, to men of the world, as individuals, and to civil governments.

Over its own members a church has the right to exercise a very extensive and thorough, spiritual supervision. Its purity, its influence, its reputation, its efficiency, nay, its very existence, all depend on the conduct, public and private, of its members. It has, therefore, the right to investigate and judge of their belief and conduct, so far as these affect their religious or moral characters and standing. It has the right to require of all its members a punctual performance of all the duties prescribed in the church covenant and in the Word of God, and to call them to account for neglect or violation.

Every church has the right to adopt articles of faith according to its own conscientious, prayerful interpretation of the Word of God. No other church, or collection of churches has any right to prescribe articles of faith or rules of conduct for its observance. Nor is any church obliged to hold other churches, or the members of other churches, or of anything called a church, whether of the same denomination or not, in fellowship, unless it can conscientiously do so, nor is it bound to be associated nor to coöperate with them, unless in its judgment the law of Christ requires it. Membership in one church does not of itself give the right of membership in any other church, because each church has the right to judge of the qualifications of all applicants for its privileges, whatever credentials of standing in any other church they may possess. A letter of standing and recommendation is to be received as evidence, but never as a sole and sufficient title to admission.

Churches have a right to associate for mutual assistance, and for the advantages of union in efforts to evangelize the world. But a body composed of pastors and delegates from churches, possesses no power to legislate for the churches which its members represent; nor, indeed, any church power whatever. If invited to give an opinion on any question of church order or discipline, or to assist in settling difficulties in any church, their decisions can be binding on no church any further than that church believes them to be in accordance with the Scriptures.

It is usually the case that a number of unconverted men and their families meet with the church for public worship, assist in defraying the necessary expenses, and they are often proprietors in the house of worship. In the choice of a pastor the wishes of the members of the congregation should be considered; but the right of ultimate choice rests with the church.

This right is sacred. No society or congregation, however wealthy, intelligent, or respectable, may justly infringe upon it. Men, not members of the church, who contribute for the support of worship, should do so with the understanding that they are to hear such a preacher as the church may select.

Of civil government, a church claims nothing but the impartial protection of the laws, and such legal facilities for holding and managing its property as are common to other associated bodies. To these it has an undoubted right. Its members neither gain nor lose any civil rights or privileges by being members of the church. With the organization, doctrines, and discipline of churches, civil government has no right to interfere; nor has the church any right to ask its interference or support, nor to be in any manner allied to it.

Sect. 4. *The Duties of a Church.*

That the primitive churches maintained public worship on the Lord's day, is too obvious to require proof. That they were taught not to forsake the assembling of themselves together at other convenient times, for prayer, singing the praises of God, and for mutual exhortation, is also plain. They considered it to be the sacred duty of every church to meet for the worship of God, whether a minister was present or not. Worship was regarded as the primary and paramount object in their assemblies.

Yet every church ought to make all proper efforts to obtain a pastor possessing the Scriptural qualifications, and to provide for him an ample support, that he may devote himself wholly to his work. "Let him that is taught in the word communicate unto him that teacheth in all good things." "Even so hath the Lord ordained that they who preach the Gospel should live of the Gospel." The duty of churches to provide for the support of a faithful, efficient, and godly ministry, is very clearly taught in the Scriptures.

To provide a suitable place for public worship, to make arrangements for the convenient administration of the ordinance of baptism, and the frequent celebration of the Lord's Supper, to maintain a faithful, affectionate watch and discipline; to guard carefully against the admission of unrenewed persons to its membership; to use all vigilance to keep itself pure; to furnish pecuniary aid, if necessary, to its poor members; to provide for the religious education of the children, particularly those of its own members; to watch for all favorable opportunities to bring the unconverted under the influence of the Gospel, and to produce a wide-spread attention to the subject of religion, by multiplying meetings, and by all Scriptural efforts as the providence of God may seem to direct;—all these are to be the constant and cherished objects of every church, in its associate capacity.

It is the duty of every church to present constant encouragements to such young men as the Saviour may be designing to employ in the ministry to prepare themselves for the work, by seeking the advantages of a good education. It is the duty of every church to maintain fraternal relations with other churches; to pray and labor for their union, peace and prosperity; to unite with them in associations for mutual benefit and coöperation in spreading religion in the world; to be tender of each other's feelings; to assist each other, when invited to do so, by counsel and influence, and if necessary by pecuniary aid.

In short, while each church ought to guard its rights as a complete and distinct body, as respects its visible organization, perfectly independent of all earthly control, accountable only to Christ, the sole Head and Lawgiver of his people, it should yet regard itself the servant of all men, a "debtor both to the Greeks and to the Barbarians, to the wise and to the unwise," even as Christ, who was free from all, made himself the servant of all. The servant is not above his master, nor is the church above her Lord. All her members are created in Christ Jesus for good works, and they are to labor without fainting till death, in sending forth missionaries, training up ministers, in circulating the Scriptures, religious books, tracts, and periodicals, and in all judicious efforts for the salvation of men.

SECT. 5. *Each Church accountable directly to Christ.*

As a church is a spiritual society, composed, according to the Scriptures, of regenerated persons only, associated for purposes exclusively spiritual, its accountability must be of the same nature. While pursuing its appropriate line of duty, it is, therefore, in no sense, accountable to any power on earth. Its duties and pursuits as a church, all have reference to the interests of the soul, and to the concerns of eternity. As it receives all its power from Christ, and comes into possession of it by conforming to his will, it is accountable to him separately, directly, and exclusively, for all its ecclesiastical proceedings.

This principle is one of the strong safeguards of religious liberty, the bulwark of our defence against the encroachments of civil and ecclesiastical domination. The venerable fathers in our churches understood its value well; they guarded it as the apple of the eye, and were ready to shed their blood in its defence. Cleared from the dust and rubbish of ages, they have handed it down as a priceless legacy to us, to transmit untarnished and unencumbered, to posterity. As this is a principle of great importance, and one on which the views of writers on church polity are much divided, it is deserving a very careful examination. The question may be thus stated: Is each church separately, directly, and solely accountable to the Lord Jesus Christ for its doings, or to other churches, to the church universal, to a Conference, a General Assembly, a Consociation, a presiding Elder, a house of Bishops, or a Pope?

The presumptive argument is very clear, if not decisive of this question. For, if the first church that was ever formed,— the church in Jerusalem, was directly and solely accountable to Christ, as all admit, although it was not formed till after he had ascended to Heaven, there is no reason why any other church formed on the same principles, of the same sort of persons, and for the same object, should not possess the same privilege, and assume the same responsibility. One church possesses equal facilities, is quite as near to Christ, and can enjoy as ready access to him as another. If one has the revealed, written word, and the promise of his presence, so has the other. While one enjoys the instructions of inspired teachers, so does the other; when one is deprived of them the other is also. If Christ is the direct and only Head of one, he is also of the other. Unless the Scriptures teach the contrary doctrine, this argument alone settles the principle that each church is accountable directly to the Saviour, or in other words, is essentially and fully INDEPENDENT. What then saith the Scripture?

Many churches are mentioned in the New Testament besides the church in Jerusalem, such as the church at Antioch, the church in Ephesus, the church at Corinth, &c., but no hint is given that either of these churches was subordinate or accountable to the others. The churches located in a single province, as the churches in Macedonia, and the churches of Galatia, are addressed or referred to by the inspired writers in the same terms as "the church at Rome." Every form of allusion, or address, to these churches, fully implies that each separate company of believers, associated to obey the laws of Christ, was regarded as a church, complete in itself for all the purposes of such an institution.

But the Scriptures do not leave this question here. The brief addresses to the seven churches in Asia, Rev. 2 : 3 : are alone sufficient to set this question forever at rest. The Lord Jesus is there represented as walking among the churches—the golden candlesticks—minutely acquainted with all their circumstances. He holds the stars—the angels or pastors of the churches—in his hand, and causes them to rise or set, or to remove, at his pleasure. He addresses the churches through their pastors because the messages were written, and they were the authorized messengers of his Word, each to the church committed to his care. These addresses are various, according to the various circumstances of the churches. The church at Ephesus had declined in love; the church in Smyrna was suffering persecution; the church in Pergamos was lax in discipline, by suffering erroneous doctrines among its members; the church at Thyatira permitted a false teacher to disseminate corrupt doctrine; the church in Sardis was fast going into apostasy; the church in Philadelphia was zealous and faithful in severe trials; and the church of the Laodiceans was wealthy, proud, lukewarm, and graceless.

Now we cannot fail to observe that each of these churches was separately addressed, and commended, admonished, warned, or threatened, as accountable, solely, separately, and directly to Christ, for its condition and its doings. One church is not praised or censured for the doings of the others, nor the whole collectively, for the condition of any one. No mention is made of a "Bishop of Asia," through whose remissness in "visitation," or negligence in "confirmation," these evils had crept in. No charge is made against any such personage, for not "deposing" "corrupt and unruly clergy" in his "diocese;" but, on the contrary, one church is censured for not silencing a false teacher, which implies the power to do so, and another is praised for having tried those who claimed to be Apostles, and proved them liars. Nothing is said of the "diocese of Asia," or the "church of Asia," but the messages are, "to the *churches* IN Asia." Each one is addressed as completely accountable to Christ for the state of its zeal and love, its doctrines and discipline, and even the influence of its teachers, as though no other church or ministry existed on the earth. Not even the angels or pastors were held accountable; the responsibility is unalterably fixed on *the churches themselves.*

The proof of the soundness of this principle is complete. We have seen in what light the Lord Jesus regards his churches as accountable, and where he fixes the responsibility. It is impossible to reconcile these facts with the theory of an organized universal, or catholic church, a national church establishment, diocesan churches, or any theory of aggregation of churches. From this proof of the separate, independent character of each church it follows:

That to become a church-member is an act which involves the highest degree of responsibility to God and to man; and places every member under the most solemn obligations to study thoroughly the will of Christ, lest this liberty of ours become a cloak of maliciousness.

That to be independent, as a church, is by no means to be *not* accountable, since by the very terms of its independence a church assumes the greatest responsibility which any associated body on earth can sustain.

As each church is directly and separately accountable to the Lord Jesus for the correctness with which it interprets, and the spirit and manner in which it executes his laws, it must receive them directly from him; that is, *from the Scriptures as understood by itself.*

As in the matter of discipline each church is held answerable for the character and conduct of its own members only, it follows that no others have any valid *claim* to its privileges and communion. All invitations to its communion, extended beyond its own members, are matters of courtesy and convenience, solely; not of claim.

The independence of the churches should be scrupulously respected and vigilantly guarded, as the bulwark of religious liberty and doctrinal purity; and all interference with the terms of church fellowship by conventions, either of ministers or laymen, is unscriptural and dangerous.

As each church is bound to understand the will of Christ respecting church order, fellowship, and discipline, it should always, if possible, settle its own difficulties without calling in even the advice and influence of other churches.

The necessary expenses of all churches should be sustained

by voluntary contribution, without any help from the secular arm. Spiritual power only should be relied upon to accomplish all their purposes, and that power *is for edification purely, not for destruction.* If a member refuse to bear his just part of the common burdens, he may be subjected to admonition, censure, and even to excision, but not to litigation.*

"Inasmuch as they all stand in the same relation to Jesus

* That the churches continued to be independent of all earthly control, each being separately and directly accountable to the Lord Jesus Christ, throughout the first two centuries, and a part of the third, ecclesiastical history furnishes the most unequivocal proof. Gieseler says, vol. i. p. 56, "The new churches everywhere *formed themselves* on the model of the mother-church at Jerusalem. At the head of each were the Elders, (Presbyters or Bishops being the same,) as follows from Acts 20 : 17–28, all officially of equal rank." Again, p. 103, in the second century, after speaking of the influence of city churches over country churches which had grown up around them, he remarks : "With this exception, all the churches were alike independent." And he informs us that this independence was not materially encroached upon till the third century, and then by "the idea of a catholic church, beyond whose pale there could be no salvation."

Mosheim says, vol. i. p. 86, "All the churches in those primitive times, were *independent* bodies; or none of them subject to the jurisdiction of any other. It is clear as the noonday, that all Christian churches had equal rights, and were, in all respects, on a footing of equality.' Again, p. 82, "The assembled people did everything that is proper for those in whom the *supreme power* of the community is vested." In the second century, he says, p. 142, "During a great part of this century all the churches continued to be, as at first, *independent* of each other, or were connected by no consociations or confederations. Each church was a kind of little, independent republic, governed by its own laws, which were enacted, or at least sanctioned, by the people." And in the third century, p. 201, "Although the ancient mode of church government seemed, in general, to remain unaltered, yet there was a gradual deflection from its rules, and an approximation towards the form of a monarchy." After speaking of the encroachments of the bishops, he remarks, on the next page, "This change in the form of ecclesiastical government was followed by a corrupt state of the clergy." Let Christians read and beware.

Christ, their common legislator, they are all equal. No one has any right to assume any superiority over another. Nor is any one dependent on any other. Each contains, within itself, all the elements necessary to self-existence. Each one is a perfect and complete system. The decisions of one are not binding on another. Each one is at liberty to interpret the laws of Christ for itself, and to govern itself according to that interpretation. Each church is therefore as essentially independent of every other, as though each one were the only church in Christendom."*

Sect. 6. *Judicial Power vested in each Church.*

The power to expel a member from any associated body, being an essential counterpart of the power to admit to membership, both must necessarily be vested in the same hands, as well as the right to interpret the rule or law of admission and expulsion, and its application to particular cases as they arise. That the power of excommunication was vested with the collective body of believers in each of the primitive churches, is capable of the clearest proof.

In 1 Corinthians, 5th chapter, we have the instructions of an Inspired Apostle to the church at Corinth relative to the excommunication of an offending member, or in legal phrase, *rulings* from the court above, addressed to the church as a jury, in regard to applying the law of Christ. The Apostle does not pass the sentence himself, but as an inspired teacher he explains the law; and urges them to execute it, on the supposition that the reported offence be proved, a question which rested entirely with the church. "For I, verily, as absent in the body, but present in spirit, have judged already, as though I were present, [on the supposition that the offence be proved,] concerning him that hath so done this deed, in the name of our Lord Jesus Christ, [that is, acting by his authority,] when ye are gathered

* Wayland.

together, and my spirit, with the power of our Lord Jesus Christ, [which ye as a church are to exercise,] to deliver such a one to Satan for the destruction of the flesh." And again, verse 12, urging the responsibility of the church, "Do not *ye* judge them that are within?" that is, your own members. "But them that are without, [not members of your body,] God judgeth. Therefore, put away from *among yourselves* that wicked person." Here it is perfectly evident that this church was instructed by the Holy Spirit to perform the highest and most solemn act of church sovereignty.

But it appears that this act of exclusion was the means of bringing this incestuous man to repentance. Deeply affected, the Apostle writes to them the mind of Christ respecting his further treatment. 2 Cor. 2: 4–11. "Sufficient to such a man is this punishment, *which was inflicted of many*, [by vote of the church,] so that ye ought to forgive and comfort him." And, verse 8, "Wherefore I beseech you, that ye would confirm your love towards him," by restoring him to fellowship. The power of the church to act in the premises, is clearly recognized in these instructions, and all that the Apostle does, is, to explain the law of Christ, as taught him by the Holy Spirit, and afterwards "beseech" the church to see that law executed.

When the same Apostle, Acts 20: foretold the corruptions which would come into the church in Ephesus, he does not direct the overseers or bishops (*episcopous*) to adopt disciplinary measures, and thus cut off the "grievous wolves," but he exhorted *them* to "feed the church of God." The inference from which is, that they, as overseers, had the right to do the latter, but no right to do the former. That was the prerogative of the whole church.*

* That this power was exercised by the churches collectively for some time after the death of the Apostles, is undeniable. Mosheim says, vol. i. p. 82, "The assembled people . . . excluded profligate and lapsed brethren, and restored them; they decided the controversies and disputes that arose; they heard and determined the causes of presbyters and deacons."

The church in Pergamos is censured, Rev. 2 : 14, 15, for retaining among them those "that hold the doctrine of Balaam," and "them that hold the doctrine of the Nicolaitans," a fact which takes for granted that they had the power to exclude them, but did not use it. For this neglect they were censured.*

To the same point are the directions of our Saviour in Matt. 18 : 15–20, in regard to the course to be pursued in cases of private quarrels between brethren. The final resort is, "If he neglect to hear the church, let him be to thee as a heathen man and a publican." As the offence which subjects to excommunication is "neglecting to hear [that is, to obey] *the church*," the whole body of course, and not its officers, must pass the sentence. He connects the solemn assurance, "Whatsoever *ye* [the church,] shall bind on earth shall be bound in heaven." The righteous decisions of every church shall be ratified in heaven. And then, as if to forestall the inquiry, What is a church? he immediately adds, that it is a *company of believers*, however small, united in covenant to obey him: "For where two or three are gathered together *in my name*, there am I in the midst of them."

As it is certain that each church is invested by the Saviour with the highest ecclesiastical, disciplinary, and judicial power, it follows, necessarily, that each is an independent body, complete in itself for all the purposes of a church on earth. Although

* According to Gieseler, sect. 49, vol. i. the independence of the early churches was lost by laxity in discipline till heresies had crept in, and then by "the churches which held to the ancient faith making common cause" against the heretics. "Thus was developed the idea of a catholic [universal] church, as opposed to, and excluding all heretics; and this idea in its turn, as well as a common interest, led to a more intimate union." The result was, first, prelacy, with its worldliness and pride, and finally, papacy, with its legion of abominations. Let churches, then, beware of two things: *First*, of neglecting discipline by suffering persons who have adopted dangerous heresies to retain membership, and *Second*, of combining their power for any disciplinary purpose, however urgent or desirable.

this point has already been proved, yet this furnishes an independent proof of the same point. There can be no higher act of sovereignty performed by a nation, than that of expulsion from citizenship.

As the power to expel necessarily implies the power to admit members, it follows that this also is vested in the members of the church, who are to decide on the admission of each candidate by the rules of the Gospel. For no church could be held answerable for the state of its discipline, unless it had the sole power to admit or refuse applicants for membership, according to its judgment of their characters and fitness. The power to admit into, and the power to expel from, any society, must necessarily be vested in the same hands.

SECT. 7. *Obligations of Believers to join a Church.*

This obligation does not arise from the doctrine that there is no salvation without such membership, for the Scriptures teach no such doctrine. The penitent thief on the cross was a member of no visible church, enjoyed neither of the ordinances, yet he went to heaven. Salvation is not made to depend on connection with any church, nor is there a single promise in the Scriptures of which membership in a church is the condition of its fulfilment. "He that believeth and is baptized shall be saved," is its language. It is a sure mark of an apostate and corrupt church to exalt membership, or the acts of *its* ministry, above the ordinances of Christ.

Yet there are sacred obligations on every Christian to unite with the people of God in the church relation. The promotion of our own piety, and the spiritual welfare of our fellow-men, are best attained by uniting with the church. It is the effect of Christianity to produce a peculiar people, and to separate them from the world, and thus a necessity arises for uniting them in a society or church.

The Saviour's will is also clearly indicated in the institution.

of baptism, to be followed by "teaching" his doctrines and com mands, which implies association; of the Lord's Supper to be perpetually observed; and of the rule of discipline and exclusion; neither of which could be obeyed unless Christians were united in a visible organized society. "On this rock will I *build* my church," a form of expression indicating that as the different parts of a building are united to form the structure, so his followers are to be joined in a visible community.

The example of the Apostles under whose labors believers were formed into churches, in obedience to the Saviour's personal instructions to them, acting also under the guidance of immediate inspiration, fully settles the question that it is the sacred duty of believers to unite in visible church covenant and fellowship with the people of God.

An argument which should be conclusive with every child of God is, that by means of the church, Christ is glorified. The church "with one mind and one mouth," testify to his faithfulness. It is the candlestick from which the light of the Gospel is to shine over this dark world. The religious gifts, and the mental powers, are improved by association and exercise.

The very nature of the Christian life also requires it; and he who attempts to maintain a life of piety without a visible profession and union with a church of Christ, is sure to be disappointed. He will neither honor the Saviour, nor be happy himself, nor useful as a Christian to his fellow-men. Experience and observation amply confirm this.

It is manifest that a duty of this kind could not be the subject of a positive command, without great danger to the purity of churches, and to the salvation of individuals. The obligation is left, therefore, to rest on other grounds. Yet it by no means follows that the obligation does not exist. It seems too plainly involved in the nature of the case to require a command, especially in connection with the example of Christ, of the Apostles, and of the early converts. He that is joined to the Lord, will desire to be joined to His people. The obligation is

one to be felt, rather than to be described. It is addressed, first to the heart, then to the understanding.

SECT. 8. *Relations and mutual Duties of Churches.*

Having seen that every church is formed of believers, whose rights are equal, by a voluntary compact, in virtue of which they were endowed with church power; that one church is neither superior nor inferior to another in rights and authority; that all ecclesiastical authority comes directly from Christ, and not from, nor through, any particular church, or churches, or church officers; that each church is separately accountable to Him for the use or abuse of its power; that a suitable number of disciples may, for good cause, and in an orderly way, form themselves into a church by mutual covenant, and exercise the highest ecclesiastical power, without being connected with, or dependent upon, any other church; it is proper that we next examine the true relations of churches to each other, and the duties arising therefrom.

It has been supposed that an aggregation of churches by their representatives, in an association, consociation, synod, conference, diocess, presbytery, convention, or general assembly, has more power than a single church. But instead of this, such an assembly has no church power at all. No such body has any right to receive a single member to, or expel one from, any church; nor to dictate in the least degree in respect to the doctrine, discipline, or fellowship of any church. It is an error to suppose that churches can increase and concentrate their power by union. This error is the parent of high church doctrines, of prelacy and popery, as well as of every other form of ecclesiastical intolerance, with all their train of evils.

It should be remembered that the real bond of union in a church is love. It was love that first drew the members together—it is love that still holds them in union. This is the element in which they should live and move, and have their

being, as a church. The Saviour well knew that these principles of church order and government could not be carried into practice without love, directed by knowledge; nor, indeed, any other form of church government; for without love there could be no church at all. As he was about to leave his disciples, therefore, who were soon to be formed into churches without his visible presence, he said to them, "This is my commandment, that ye love one another." Says the Apostle to the Corinthian church, "Let all your things be done with charity," or in the exercise of love. "Let brotherly love continue." "Have fervent charity [love] among yourselves." In this respect the analogy between churches and civil governments entirely fails, for men form the latter to protect themselves against each other's selfishness, and nearly all the wisdom of statesmen, legislators, governors, judges, and civil tribunals, is directed to this end. Churches are formed on precisely the opposite principle—not at all for mutual protection against each other, or against the rest of mankind, but because mutual love draws the members together, and love to all men constrains them to labor for their salvation in obedience to their Lord's command.

Let this principle be kept in mind, and it will be seen that distinct churches have no occasion for combining their power. There can be no desire for it till they become selfish bodies, and when they do, the sooner they cease to be churches, or to be called such, the better. The church at Ephesus was threatened by the Lord Jesus with extinction, because it had left its *first love*—an awful threatening which was long since executed. "I will remove thy candlestick out of his place, except thou repent."

There is, therefore, no necessary bond of union between *churches* but fraternal love. In the exercise of this grace it was customary for the primitive churches to assist each other by pecuniary aid, by furnishing each other with teachers, and by advice in cases of difficulty. The modern custom of forming associations of churches for the cultivation of acquaintance and

mutual love, and for more unity of effort in the cause of human salvation, while the independence of each church is recognized, is in perfect accordance with this principle, and is of obvious utility. The only object for which one church should seek any form of union with others is, that of doing them good, or in connection with them, of doing good to the world.

The great principle which regulates the ralations and the mutual duties of churches is this : In design, in spirit, in doctrine, in love, in their purposes and desires, they are all one church; in visible organization, many. Consequently, what is injurious to one, is injurious to all; what is for the good of one is for the good of all. Each is, or ought to be, a type of the church above. They have no compulsory authority over each other, but they are bound to seek each other's welfare by every means in their power, and to pay respectful attention to each other's opinions, wishes and doings. The acts of coöperation mentioned in the Scriptures are,

I. Sending spiritual teachers to each other's help. Such were sent by the church in Jerusalem to the church in Antioch. Acts 11 : 22–27. 15 : 22–27. 18 : 27. Eph. 6 : 21. 1 Cor. 16 : 15–18.

II. Administering to each other's temporal necessities. 1 Cor. 16 : 1–3. 2 Cor. 8 : 1–4, 13–24. 9 : 1–15. In Rom. 15 : 26, this pecuniary assistance is called a *communion*, though translated *contribution ;* and in the next verse the duty of affording pecuniary aid is declared to be reciprocal with that of furnishing spiritual teachers.

III. Seeking and affording advice and assistance to each other in cases of divisions and contentions by which the peace of any church is disturbed and its prosperity endangered. The clearest case of this kind, in which the relations and the duties of churches in matters of this nature are most fully brought to view, is in Acts 15. We are there told, 1. That "no small dissension and disputation" had arisen in the church at Antioch respecting a very important question of doctrine and discipline.

Verses 1, 2. 2. That the church sent ministers and brethren, probably from both parties, to Jerusalem for advice and assistance. Verses 2, 3. 3. That these messengers "were received by the church, and the Apostles, and elders" in Jerusalem. Verse 4. 4. That the question was publicly discussed by the Apostles and others. Verses 5–11. 5. That opportunity was given to the delegates from the church at Antioch to state the facts in the case. Verse 12. 6. That the opinion given by the church in Jerusalem was in the name of the "Apostles, elders, and brethren;" which was transmitted to the church in Antioch in writing. Verses 23–29. 7. That "the Apostles and elders, with the whole church," chose and sent men of their own number to accompany the delegates from Antioch, "to tell the same things by mouth." Verses 22, 27.

This example illustrates very fully the duty of seeking the advice and aid of sister churches in cases of difficulty and division; the duty of rendering it promptly and affectionately when desired; and the nature of it when given. It was not dictation which was sought, but instruction and advice, which were given and made pleasing by kindness, and effective by moral influence. And it is worthy of special remark, as illustrative of true church independence, that although the question was a far-reaching and all-important one, and although inspired Apostles were present, yet they do not attempt to settle it by interposing their official authority. They resort to a clear statement of facts, and to argument founded upon them, to procure a decision of the "whole church," so that the advice comes to the church at Antioch in the name of the whole church at Jerusalem.

IV. It is plain that the principle of coöperation in the general spread of the Gospel and the gathering of new churches, was recognized by the Apostles and the primitive churches. The church in Antioch first engaged as a church in this work, Acts 13 : 2, 3; but it is evident that Paul and Barnabas, and others, received their support in part from other churches. 2 Cor. 11 : 8. 12 : 13, 18. Phil. 6 : 10–18. Such were the poverty and the persecutions which pressed down the primitive churches that they could do little else than establish the principle, which it belongs to more favored churches to carry out fully.

It is evident, therefore, that churches sustain to each other most sacred and enduring relations. Their separate independence is in itself no barrier to their cordial, extensive, and useful coöperation; and ought never to be so regarded. On the contrary, it is a strong argument in favor of such coöperation; for no services are so pleasant, or mutually profitable, as those which are freely given. Independent completeness in visible organization—in corporate rights and functions—involves no separation, in purpose or in spirit. So that, were ten thousand churches, formed on these principles, to act consistently with their obvious design, they would, for all the purposes of their existence, be as truly ONE CHURCH as they could possibly be, if consolidated into one organized body under the oversight of a bench of prelates, or a pope.

CHAPTER III.

PRINCIPLES OF ORGANIZATION.

A CHURCH, therefore, may exist, with full powers, without officers; though a Scriptural organization is necessary to its prosperous existence and usefulness. Officers, or ministers, are to a church what hands and feet are to a man. Every society must have its officers, whose duties are defined in its constitution and laws. Civil government could not accomplish its purposes without officers, or public servants, appointed to the discharge of specific duties. Neither can a church, although its constituent elements, and its objects, are so entirely different.

The opinions of men, however, differ widely in regard to the principles on which civil governments should be organized, and their officers be appointed. Some advocate the "divine right of kings," disobedience to whose authority is treason against God. This right to rule, *jure divino*, they maintain, existed previously to all civil compacts, and all municipal law. Others believe that men are endowed with all the necessary capabilities for self-government, and possess the inherent right to choose, or elect, their civil officers. In like manner some maintain that prelatic bishops have the sole right "to rule the church, to ordain other clergy, and to transmit their power to successors;" that to them, all men should yield spiritual obedience, the refusal of which is "most grievous sin." No ordinances can be valid or beneficial, according to these views, without their sanction.

The main object of this chapter is to show in what light the Scriptures place this subject. For although they contain no such specific form of organization for Christian churches as that given to Moses in reference to the Jewish priesthood—for the *manner* of the New Testament in reference to this and kindred topics is entirely different from that of the Old—yet precepts and precedents may be found which indicate, with sufficient clearness to the obedient spirit, the *principles* by which the people of God should be guided in the organization of churches.

It is obvious that the principles of church organization must be in harmony with the nature and design of churches. As one design is to humble the pride of the human heart, to purge out the love of power, of rank, and distinction, it is certain that no mode of organization which fosters these passions, is of Divine origin. The Saviour enjoined his disciples to call no man on earth Master, or Father; because they have one Master, Christ; and one Father, God. He prohibited them from seeking any preëminence over each other. "Whosoever will be great among you, shall be your minister; and whosoever of you will be the chief, shall be servant of all." The offices in the church, therefore, are not titles of rank, and means of exaltation but posts of service.

SECT. 1. *The Power of appointing Church Officers.*

Christian churches, like every other associated body, have the natural right to elect their own officers, unless that right has been taken from them by their divine Founder; for no earthly power may take it away. If Christ has taken away that right, we may expect to find the fact clearly revealed, and some other method of obtaining church officers plainly prescribed. Officers must be appointed in one of three ways: either, first, by a lineal transmission of office from father to son, as in the case of a hereditary monarchy, or of the Aaronic priesthood; or second, by the incumbents appointing their successors, for which no precedent can be found except in the case of the Budhist priesthoods, the succession of the grand Lama, a few tyrannical civil governments, and the Papal and Episcopal hierarchies; or third, by election of the members of the body at large. For the two former methods, no precept nor precedent can be found in the New Testament certainly; the second, especially, is altogether repugnant to its spirit.

The presumptive argument on this point is plain, since no reason can be given from the nature of the case, why a church should not choose its own officers, like any other associated body. There is nothing in the nature and objects of a church which should deprive it of its natural right, and certainly nothing in the character of its members, who are required to be spiritually enlightened; to be regenerated persons, who act from principle and not from impulse and passion; who, if their profession be true, govern themselves by the precepts of the Holy Scriptures. It is strange logic to maintain that unregenerated men are capable of governing themselves by choosing their civil officers, and yet that Christians, sanctified in Christ Jesus, are incapable of exercising this natural prerogative! But here, too, we have positive Scriptural precedents, sufficiently clear to determine this point.

The first case that occurs, or could occur, is recorded in Acts 1 : 15–26; and though not the election of an officer in a particular church, is pertinent in its application to the principle under consideration. Up to that time all officers in Christ's visible kingdom had been appointed by him, in person, though no church had yet been formed and no church officers appointed; now, although his will was to be sought by prayer and obeyed, in appointments to office, as in all other acts, yet it must be made known in some other way than by personal, oral communication, as before. A principle was then to be settled as to the manner in which his will should be communicated and executed in the selection of men to be officers in his kingdom on earth, in all future ages. By a careful examination of this account we observe: 1. That the election of Matthias was made by the *whole body* of the disciples. 2. That Peter, in leading them to a choice, acted under Divine direction respecting the manner of effecting it, the qualifications for, and the duties pertaining to, the office. 3. That the special object of this appointment to the duties "of this ministry and apostleship" was, that he might be a witness with the Apostles of Christ's resurrection. 4. That they next proceeded to elect two as candidates. 5. That they then prayed to Christ to decide between them. 6. That when the case was decided by lot,* and Matthias was chosen, he was not called an Apostle, but "was *numbered with* the eleven Apostles."

Now if the inspired writer did not intend to be understood that in making this election, the whole body acted, why should he say, immediately after mentioning all the eleven Apostles

* Mosheim and others understand the expression ἐδωχαν χλῆρουσ αὐτῶν, to mean, *they cast their votes.* To express the casting of lots the verb βαλλειν is used; Matt. 27 : 35, Mark 15 : 24, Luke 23 : 34, John 19 : 24. The word χλῆρος, he maintains, is used in the sense of ψῆφος, a *suffrage*, or *ballot*, so that the meaning, according to this writer, is, "they gave their votes, and the choice fell upon Matthias,"&c. But without insisting on this interpretation, it is certain that the transaction was a subject of consultation and of action in the whole assembly of the disciples.

by name, "in those days Peter stood up *in the midst of the disciples* (the number [multitude] of the names together were about a hundred and twenty,") "and *they* [the whole company of disciples] appointed," "and *they* prayed," "and *they* gave forth the lots?" Who did all this, but the one hundred and twenty disciples, led to a choice by Peter? If a part only acted, which part? The conclusion from this precedent in favor of an election by the whole body of disciples, cannot be evaded.

The next precedent is recorded in Acts 6 : 1–6, and is the more in point as the disciples had now become a church. Circumstances rendered a new office in the church necessary, and as in the preceding case, inspired men "called the multitude of the disciples" together, and told them it was their duty and privilege to elect suitable persons to perform its duties. They did so, and the Apostles gave the solemn sanction of the imposition of hands, accompanied with prayer, to the choice. These examples show the manner of electing men to both the permanent offices in a Christian church.

We find also, that persons entrusted by the churches with any important service, not a part of the regular duties of either of the permanent church offices, were elected by vote. The companion of Paul, who was associated with Titus in taking charge of the benefactions of the poor saints, 2 Cor. 8 : 19, was CHOSEN *by the churches* to travel, &c.; and in verse 23, he and another, are called "the messengers of the churches;" while Titus is called the "partner and fellow-helper" of the Apostle. These precedents,* in the entire absence of any precept or pre-

* The expression in Acts 14 : 23, has by one class of writers, been appealed to as proving that elders were elected by vote of the church, and the interpretation has been as strenuously opposed by others. The word there translated *ordained*, from χειροτονεῖν, properly signifies, both according to its etymology and its prevalent use in the classics, *to stretch forth the hand for the purpose of voting.* One of the ways in which the people of Athens voted, when convened in general assembly,

cedent in opposition to the obvious inference which must be drawn from them, are quite sufficient to place beyond reasonable dispute a principle which nature and common sense so clearly teach, that churches have the right to elect all persons who are to perform any permanent or transient service for them, or to be placed in any office of trust or responsibility in their behalf.

was, by raising the hand; and this is the proper word for denoting that form of suffrage. Suidas, in his Lexicon, illustrates this mode of voting, as it was practised on certain judicial occasions. The herald said: "Whoever thinks that the accused is guilty, let him lift up his hand." Then those who thought so stretched forth their hands. Then the herald said again: "Whoever thinks that the accused is not guilty, let him lift up his hand;" and those who were of this opinion stretched forth their hands. The number of hands was counted each time by the herald; and the president, upon the herald's report, declared on which side the majority voted. From this specific meaning it came to be employed to denote the result without reference to the mode, that is, *to elect, choose*, in general. This word is used in 2 Cor. 8 : 19, above referred to, with the undoubted meaning, *to elect* by general suffrage; but as, in the passage under consideration, Paul and Barnabas are its nominative agents, the question arises whether it can denote the *taking* of the hand vote, as well as the action of *voting by stretching forth the hand.* It can hardly be supposed that these two men would have gone from church to church *electing* them elders by raising *their own hands*, and if the writer had intended to inform us simply that they appointed these officers without the suffrage of the churches, some other word would have been used. The word is never used with the signification to consecrate, set apart, or ordain, by the laying on of hands; so that the evidence, so far as it goes, is in favor of a general suffrage by the members of the churches. It cannot be doubted that the choice was made, as everything was done in the primitive churches, by the united voice of the Apostles and brethren.

The author would here acknowledge his obligations to the Rev. Professor Hackett, of Newton Theological Institution, for a valuable critical note on this word, and refer the reader who wishes to see the whole subject treated more at large, to Coleman's "*Apostolical and Primitive Church*," chap. 4; also to the work before mentioned by Chancellor King, and to Neander's *Church History.*

From these considerations it is clear that the power of choosing church officers was left with the churches collectively.* Among all the instructions, warnings, and rebukes, administered by the Apostles, speaking in the name of Christ and in all their acts, not one can be found which conflicts with the right of every church to choose its own officers and teachers. And this accounts for the fact that no class of church officers, ordinary or extraordinary, was commanded to perpetuate their order or their office—a fact which can be accounted for in no other way; for if they were not to be elected, how was the office or order to be perpetuated?

SECT. 2. *The Scriptural Officers in a Church.*

The Scriptural officers in a church are bishops, or pastors, and deacons.† During the Apostolic age there were others of special or miraculous appointment, but there is no proof that they were designed to be permanent like these. The church

* "The assembled people," says Mosheim, vol. i. p. 82, "elected their own rulers and teachers, or by their authoritative consent received them when nominated to them."

For several centuries, at least, the pastors or bishops of the churches were chosen by the suffrages of the people, and ordained by the neighboring pastors *plebi suffragio ac cleri ordinato.* Thus Cornelius was placed over the church in Rome, and Alexander over the church in Jerusalem. Euseb. lib. 7, c. 11. Cyprian speaks of his own election to the charge of the church at Carthage, as *judicio Dei et plebis favore;* and again, Epist. 55 : 7, *populi universi suffragio* "by vote of all the people." Clement, of Rome, brings forward the Apostolic rule for appointment to church offices "*with the consent of the whole church.*"

† "In those primitive times," says Mosheim, vol. i. p. 81, after laying down the sound principle that "that form of the primitive churches, which was derived from the church of Jerusalem, erected and organized by the Apostles themselves, must be accounted *divine,*" he adds, "each Christian church was composed of the *people,* the *presiding officers,* and the *assistants* or *deacons.* The highest authority was in the *people,* or the whole body of Christians."

at Philippi, it appears, was very dear to the Apostle Paul because united and obedient in all respects to the Word of God, and very generous to him, their spiritual father. Twelve years after its origin, as recorded in Acts 16 : 9–40, he thus commences his epistle to them. Phil. 1 : 1. "Paul and Timothy, the servants of Jesus Christ, to all the saints in Christ Jesus, which are at Philippi, with the Bishops* and Deacons." The reason why he uses this particular form of address to this church seems to be, because it was now correctly and perfectly organized, according to the Scriptural pattern, by the choice of these two kinds of officers.

The epistles to Timothy are, as all admit, the instructions of an inspired Apostle, or in other words, the commands of God, directed to an evangelist, who held no office in any particular church; in regard to the doctrines and church order which he and all others should teach and observe. The necessary qualifications of church officers are described in 1 Tim. 3. They are Bishops and Deacons only. It is evident that these epistles were not written for Timothy's private perusal only, but to be exhibited if occasion required, as his Divine commission, and to stand written in the Inspired Volume for the guidance of churches to the end of time.† Now as we cannot suppose that God would give directions respecting the qualifications of a part of the officers in a church only, or that an inspired man would forget or neglect to record them, we must conclude that the Holy Spirit intended to teach us that these were the only permanent

* It would be well for those who contend that bishops are prelates, each having the oversight of several "inferior clergy," with their congregations, to inform us how many such the single city of Philippi in Macedonia, probably contained at this time.

† Clement, of Rome, in his first epistle to the Corinthians, says: "In the villages and cities where the Apostles preached, they ordained the first converts to be bishops and deacons." And, again, a few pages after: "The Apostles foreknew, through our Lord Jesus Christ, that contention would arise about the name of bishop, and, therefore, being endued with perfect foreknowledge, appointed these offices."

church officers. So that whatever offices existed during the life time of the Apostles, originating in spiritual gifts which have now ceased, it is plain that they were not intended to be permanent.

And, finally, the two classes of duties appropriate to these two offices are the only ones referred to in the Scriptures, or needful to the welfare of churches. Those of a pastor or bishop are, to "take heed to all the flock," "to feed the church of God," and to "give himself continually to prayer and to the ministry of the Word." For this reason "a bishop must be apt to teach," "able by sound doctrine, both to exhort and convince the gain-sayers." The duties of this office are therefore to teach religion, and to look after the spiritual welfare of the church. The other class of duties is of a temporal nature, requiring not aptness to teach, but eminent piety, honesty, sobriety, good sense, and business habits. These are provided for in the office of deacon, whose duties may be inferred from the word *diaconus;* waiting servant, from the circumstances in which the office originated, and from the requisite qualifications. 1 Tim. 3 : 8–13. The wants of churches are all provided for in these two offices. They have no more occasion for the services of prelates, or diocesan bishops, to govern churches, ordain ministers, and administer discipline, than a civil state has for those of an autocrat, or a dictator.

SECT. 3. *All Pastors or Bishops equal in rank.*

As churches have equal powers and rights, so their pastors are entirely equal in ministerial rank and power. This point, however, is capable of independent proof from Scripture, and as it is a disputed, though by no means a difficult one, the proof will be briefly exhibited.

1. *Apostles.* The choice of the Twelve is recorded in Matt. 10 : 1–4, Mark 3 : 13–19, Luke 6 : 12–19 ; the occasion of sending them forth, in Matt. 9 : 36–38 ; they are instructed and

sent forth, Matt. 10 : 5–42, Mark 6 : 7–11, Luke 9 : 1–5. They are endowed with miraculous power—are commanded to go two and two, without purse and scrip—to preach the Gospel—heal the sick, &c. with promises of Divine support. It appears then, 1. That the Apostles were chosen, instructed, commissioned, and sent forth, by our Lord personally, and on His sole authority. 2. They were endowed with miraculous powers. 3. They were infallible in their teachings, at least after the Day of Pentecost. The reasons for their appointment, as far as the Scriptures inform us, were, 1. To preach the Gospel before churches could be raised up to designate them to the work and sustain them in it. 2. That they might be witnesses of the life and resurrection of Christ. 3. To provide infallible teachers of religion and accredited organs of the will of Christ after his ascension, till the Scriptural canon should be completed, and the disciples organized into regular churches with appropriate officers. Hence their Apostolic power in respect to churches, had these two peculiarities : That each Apostle might exercise, as occasion required, the ministerial functions of all the officers in a church, ordinary and extraordinary. In virtue of their Apostolic office they were prophets ; Acts 20 : 25–29 ; 2 Thess. 2 : 1–17, missionary evangelists ; Matt. 28 : 19 ; Acts 10 : 19–48 ; 20 : 1–38 ; Rom. 1 : 14–15, teachers ; 1 Tim. 2 : 7, presbyters, or elders ; 1 Pet. 5 : 1, they might preside and baptize as pastors or bishops ; Acts 1 : 15 ; 6 : 2 ; 1 Cor. 1 : 14–16, receive and distribute the bounties of the church as deacons ; Acts 4 : 35 ; 1 Cor. 8 : 4–20, as well as declare the will of the Lord respecting particular questions in doctrine and discipline ; 1 Cor. 2 : 16 ; 5 : 3–7, and in the infliction of special judgments ; Acts 5 : 1–11 ; 13 : 11 ; 1 Tim. 1 : 20. The other peculiarity was, that this power extended to all churches alike. They discharged these offices in particular churches as the messengers of God to all Christians and to all churches.*

* Or in the words of old John Cotton, in his "*Power of the Keyes of the Kingdom of Heaven*," "This Apostolicall power, centring all church

No provision is made for the continuance of the Apostolic office, nor is any hint given that it was intended to be permanent. On the contrary, Apostles are in 1 Cor. 12 : 28, numbered among those extraordinary "spiritual gifts" which we know have passed away. "First, Apostles ; secondarily, prophets ; thirdly, teachers ; after that miracles, then gifts of healing, helps, governments, diversities of tongues." The word *Apostle*, signifies, simply, *sent*, and is never a term expressive of office, except when applied to the ORIGINAL TWELVE, and to PAUL, who was also called and sent by our Lord personally, though after his ascension. This is evident from the manner in which the word is used in 2 Cor. 8 : 23, "or our brethren be inquired of, they are the messengers [apostles] of the churches, and the glory of Christ," and in Phil. 2 : 25, "Epaphroditus my brother and companion in labor, and fellow-soldier, but your messenger [apostle]." The Apostles, therefore, neither had, nor could have, any successors in office, since each must be appointed by our Lord personally ; their Apostleship ceased with their lives, and contained in it no warrant for appointing nor for ordaining successors,* nor made any provision for transmitting or perpetuating the Apostolic office. They were not officers *in*, or

power into one man, and extending itself forth to the circumference of all churches, as the Apostles were the first subject of it, so they were also the last ; neverthelesse that ample and universall latitude of power, which was conjoyned in them, is now divided even by themselves amongst all the churches, and all the officers of the churches respectively, the officers of each church attending the charge of the particular church committed to them, by vertue of their office, and yet none of them neglecting the good of other churches, so far as they may be mutually helpful to one another in the Lord."

* Successors in the Apostolic office, the Apostles have none. As *witnesses* of the resurrection,—as *dispensers* of miraculous gifts,—as *inspired oracles* of Divine revelation,—they have no successors. But as *members*,—as *ministers*,—as *governors*,—of Christian communities, their successors are the regularly admitted members,—the lawfully ordained ministers,—the regular and recognized governors of a regularly subsisting Christian church.—*Whately*.

of, any church; they do not in their official epistles style themselves *the* Apostles or bishops of any church, or churches, or diocese, nor "Right Reverend Father in God," but simply "Apostle of Jesus Christ," and "servant of Jesus Christ." They never appoint any one to office, nor interfere with the internal affairs of any church, but simply assert their right to declare the infallible will of Christ, as his inspired messengers, requiring obedience of faith from all in every age, whether bishops, deacons, or private Christians.

2. *The Seventy Disciples.* In Luke 10 : 1–16, is the account of the sending out of seventy disciples on a similar mission. The occasion of their mission was the same, verse 2, and they received similar instructions. Their mission was solely to the Jewish nation. They likewise soon after returned and made a similar report of their doings and their success. When they had fulfilled their commission, their office, like that of the Apostles, ceased.*

3. *Prophets.* This term is especially applied to those who foretold future events. That such an order of men existed in the first churches is admitted by all. See Acts 13 : 1. 15 : 32. 11 : 27. 21 : 10. 1 Cor. 12 : 28. 14 : 32. Eph. 4 : 11, &c. This order of men has also ceased, as all admit.

4. *Teachers.* This term is often applied to our Saviour,

* The appointment by the Lord Jesus of the particular numbers, *twelve*, to be Apostles, and *seventy* to go on a special mission to the Jews, has been thought to be significant. From his own words, Matt. 19 : 28 ; Luke 22 : 30, it appears that the number of Apostles had some reference to the number of the tribes of Israel. Its adoption might have been intended to indicate to them that He was their Lord and Saviour. An earthly sovereign would appoint a ruler or judge to each tribe; as their spiritual king He *sent* the same number of messengers to them. The Sanhedrim, or grand council of the nation, was composed of *seventy*. A temporary mission of seventy disciples was well adapted to indicate the approaching end of their religious authority, and that Jesus was king in Zion. See Mosheim, Ecc. Hist., vol. i. p. 51. Also Ripley's Notes on Matt. 19 : 28.

where it is usually translated *Master*, and it often occurs in the book of Acts, and in the Epistles. It is not used to designate any particular office in a church, but simply to denote that the person to whom it is applied is engaged in teaching religious truth. The office is in its nature perpetual, although that special order of teachers raised up by spiritual gifts to meet the emergencies of the times, while churches were in the process of formation, has ceased.

5. *Elders.* The Greek word, translated elder, is *Presbyter.* Its primary meaning may be seen in the phrases, "now his *elder* son was in the field," or, "likewise ye younger submit yourselves to the *elder*," &c. The term, and the customs to which it alludes, are of Hebrew origin. The first churches were composed of Jews, among whom the term elder was already in common use, denoting age and wisdom.

Although so much has been written on the office of presbyters, yet as far as the Scriptures are concerned, it is plain that this is a term, not of any particular office, but of age, standing, and influence, or of office generally. If the use of the term proves anything respecting ministerial office in the Apostolic churches, it proves that the elders in the church at Ephesus were bishops, and that the Apostles, Peter and John, were also elders, or presbyters. 1 Pet. 5 : 1. 2 John 1. 3 John 1. It is undoubtedly often applied to church officers, both pastors and deacons, as well as to Apostles and others, who held no office whatever in the churches. Any aged, exemplary, and judicious brother in the church may with propriety be called an elder, and is entitled to all the deference and authority which was accorded to presbyters in the Apostolic churches.

6. *Minister.* This word is in the original *servant*, and is of course, a general term, not appropriated to any particular office. It is applied indiscriminately to deacons, bishops, evangelists, and Apostles, and even to Christ himself. This application of the term doubtless originated in His instructions and example: "Whosoever of you will be chief, shall be *servant* of all. For

even the Son of Man came not to be ***ministered unto*** but to *minister*." Every church officer is a servant of the church, and in that sense a minister.

7. *Evangelist.* This word signifies literally a messenger of good tidings, or a preacher of the Gospel. Philip, "one of the seven," is mentioned, Acts 21 : 8, as an evangelist, and so is Timothy. 2 Tim. 4 : 5. They are mentioned also, Eph. 4 : 11, as among the gifts of Christ to his people. An evangelist was not, and of course, could not be, a church officer: his work was that of a missionary to the destitute.

8. *Bishop.* This word is a translation of the Greek *Episcopos.** In Acts 20 : 28, it is translated literally, *overseer.* It is also found in three other passages referring to men, and once, 1 Pet. 2 : 25, referring to Christ. It was not a favorite term with the Apostles, who never once assume it, or demand its prerogatives, like those who claim to be their successors; though they often call themselves servants. It is now universally admitted that the term, bishop, is never applied in the Scriptures to a prelate, nor is there the least proof that any church officer existed in the Apostolic churches superior in rank or authority to a pastor or bishop of a single church.†

* This word from *ἐπισκοπέω, to inspect, to oversee,* was employed by the Athenians according to Suidas, to designate an officer whose duty it was to preserve order in the city, and was used interchangeably with *φύγᾶκος*, a keeper. The Lacedemonians called this officer *ἁρμοστὴς*, one who had charge of the public morals. According to Dionysius Halicarnassus it was applied to a sentinel or city watch.

† Mosheim says, vol. i. p. 85—"Whoever supposes that the bishops of the first and golden age of the church, corresponded with the bishops of the following centuries, must blend and confound characters that are very different. For in this century and the next, a bishop had charge of a *single* church, which might ordinarily be contained in a private house; nor was he its *lord*, but was in reality its *minister* or *servant;* he instructed the people, conducted all parts of public worship, and attended on the sick and the necessitous in person; and what he was unable thus to perform, he committed to the care of the presbyters (elders); but without the power to ordain or determine anything, except

9. *Pastor.* This word, signifying ***shepherd***, occurs in Eph. 4 : 11, and in 1 Pet. 5 : 1–4, where the original word is used as synonymous with elder, and is translated *shepherd*. Our Saviour often called himself a shepherd, or pastor; and the associations which it recalls are pleasant, John 10 : 1–18. He is called "the chief shepherd" in 1 Pet. 5 : 4.

10. *Angel.* This term is applied in Rev. 2 : 3, to the pastors or bishops of the seven churches in Asia. Why this term was chosen we do not know, though it comports well with the symbolic language employed in that book. That the pastors, or those who had the charge of giving religious instruction and the general oversight of the churches are intended, is evident.

All the terms appropriated in the New Testament to religious teachers, or church officers, have now been examined; and we find two only, those of Pastor and Bishop, which in a literal sense are applied to the first officers in a church. Pastors or Bishops are all spoken of as of equal rank, and authority.*

The office of bishop is, therefore, identical with that of pastor. Either title may with propriety be applied to him who is chosen to minister to any church as its spiritual teacher and guide, or overseer. A pastor or bishop may also properly be called an elder, who is also a bishop or pastor, whenever he is chosen to be the spiritual overseer in any church.

Sect. 4. *The Authority of Pastors.*

Office necessarily implies authority. The pastor, though the servant of Christ, and in another sense, of the church, is yet an officer, and must possess some authority. He speaks in the

with the concurrence of the presbyters and the brotherhood." Lord King fully sustains these views of the office and work of a bishop during the first three centuries.

* Gieseler informs us, vol. i. p. 65, how this order was gradually broken up by the encroachments of prelacy, and papacy: "After the death of the Apostles, to whom the general direction of the churches had always been conceded, some one among the presbyters of each

name of God, and is to the church the appointed expounder of the Saviour's will. "Obey them that have the rule over you, and submit yourselves: for they watch for your souls, as they that must give account; that they may do it with joy, and not with grief: for that is unprofitable for you." Here is the precept "obey" and "submit," with the grounds of it, the accountability of pastors.

This passage certainly forbids all dictatorial, persevering opposition to the pastor's measures. His brethren may advise and remonstrate with him respectfully, but they have no right to set themselves in obstinate, persevering opposition to him. If his measures are oppressive and palpably unreasonable, it may be their duty to seek a speedy and peaceable termination of his pastorship, in a regular and quiet way. And it inculcates on private members the duty of treating with deferential modesty and submission, what ought to be the better judgment of the pastor. He is accountable in a sense, and to an extent, which no private member can be, and has better means of forming correct opinions. Respecting the nature of this obedience, and the spirit in which it should be rendered, these instructions are given. "We beseech you, brethren, to KNOW them which labor among you, and are over you in the Lord, and admonish you: and to esteem them very highly in love, for the works' sake." "To know," is to recognize their just authority. It is obedience, growing out of esteem and love, which is enjoined. It is evident, therefore, that when a church elect a man to be their pastor, they ought to attend diligently to his instructions, that they have no right to put another in his place, as a public teacher, contrary to his wishes, while he remains in office, that all the members should faithfully coöperate with him in the cause of religion; that they be scrupulously careful of his repu-

church was suffered gradually to take the lead in its affairs. In the same irregular way the title of *episcopos* (bishop) was appropriated to this first presbyter. Hence the different accounts of the order of the first bishops in the church at Rome."

tation and his influence: that they honor him as the ambassador of God, and submit to his Scriptural authority, as a sacred duty.

The pastor has no mysterious or superstitious power. He can inflict no temporal nor spiritual chastisements, nor can he, by the exercise of his prerogative, displace any member of the church, nor in the least degree abridge the rights or privileges of any member. His authority extends only to the duties of his office.

The authority and the honor belong to the office, not merely to the man who fills it. It is the authority of Christ as represented in the person of his ambassador. As the church is the organ or medium through which the will of Christ was expressed to invest the pastor with his office and authority, so when he abuses, or becomes unworthy of it, by the same medium it should be withdrawn. But while it continues, it cannot be abridged nor intruded upon without guilt and evil consequences.

Sect. 5. *Ordination.*

As it has been shown that every church has the right to elect its officers, the only remaining question respecting the foundation of their office and the validity of their acts is, What constitutes ordination, or consecration to the office and work of the Christian ministry, with full powers to preach the word, preside in the church, and administer the two ordinances or sacraments of the Lord's house, Baptism and the Lord's Supper? What power, gift, or influence, is conferred in ordination, who can confer it, and in what manner should it be conferred?

The word *ordain*, from the Latin word *ordino*, occurs in various forms *twenty-one* times in the English New Testament, as a translation of *thirteen* different Greek words; but in only three or four of these passages does it refer to the placing of an individual in the Christian ministry, nor even in these to anything done, or conveyed to, the candidate by other ministers, nor to any influence, gift, or authority, imparted by, or through them, to him. The same words which are translated *ordain*, are used in other passages with the meaning, to set, or place, to enact, to command, to be, to mark out, to judge, to arrange, to record, to choose by hand vote, &c. There are other passages in which the laying on of hands is mentioned as a token of the setting apart and consecrating of candidates to the Christian ministry, or to some special service connected with that office, but the laying on of hands is not the ordination, nor is it declared to be essential to the validity of ordination, nor is it enjoined, like baptism and the Lord's Supper, for perpetual observance.

To ordain, is simply *to place in order.* When a person is regularly put into the ministry, he is ordained; whether the act proceed from the people, or the ministers, or from the concurrent voice of both. In so far as ministers do anything to introduce a man to the ministry, they ordain him; in so far as the people do it, they ordain him. So far as the proper use of the word is concerned, it may be applied with equal correctness to the acts of the people, or of the ministry, or of both united.

The purpose to be accomplished in ordination is, to appoint to the ministry those whom God has inwardly called by His Spirit—to set apart, before the world, those whom He has already set apart by His grace. This is not the place to inquire what constitutes an inward call to the ministry, it is sufficient to premise here, that no one has a right to enter it unless he solemnly believes that he is called to do so by the Spirit of God, nor unless his character and life are consistent with such belief. Among such men only, has a church the right of election, in which they are bound to act simply as the organ, or medium of expressing the Lord's will, whose gift pastors and teachers are declared to be. Eph. 4 : 11. It is for them to inquire, by fervent prayer in the vigilant exercise of their rational, discerning faculties, whom He has chosen and qualified to be their pastor or missionary.

The essence of ordination, as a public act, is, *the hearty consent and approval of the Christian people, and the Christian ministry, to invest with its sacred functions one whom they believe God has called to that ministry.*

Ordination, then, consists in two things: First, the election by the church of one to be their pastor, or to perform some ministerial service in their behalf, either to them, or as an evangelist, to the destitute. Second, his solemn induction, or inauguration, in which the ministry publicly recognize him as one of their number, welcome him to their brotherhood, and, by the consent, and acting in behalf of, their respective churches, pledge to him the fellowship, confidence, and affection of the ministry and churches. The first is the essential act, without which no one could properly be invested with the office and functions of a Christian minister.

The question whether a church, after it has elected a man to be its pastor and teacher, is competent, in and of itself, without the aid or intervention of other churches, or their ministers, to ordain or consecrate him fully to the office, has been much debated. It is evident that the right to consecrate, is involved in the right to elect; and this right, as we have seen, the Lord Jesus Christ has vested in each church. All questions, therefore, respecting the *validity* of any ordination, must be settled by reference to this cardinal principle: *the choice or election of a man to the ministry, is a greater act than that of consecration or induction into office;* consequently the church which is competent to do the greater, must possess in itself all inherent power essential to the valid performance of the less. The church, —not the ministers,—is the body of Christ, the organ of his will on the earth.

It is manifest, however, that the right of each church to ordain its own ministers, is an ultimate, and not an ordinary right. Though inherent in every church, and essential to its completeness as the representative body of Christ, yet the occasions and mode of exercising this prerogative are modified and restricted by its relations to other churches, and to their ministers. From these most endearing and sacred relations, important duties arise—duties not involving subordination, nor any restrictions on the just exercise of ministerial rights, or of church independence. A man living alone on an uninhabited island possesses ultimate or extreme rights which cease when the island becomes inhabited. Were a church so situated that it sustained no intimate, fraternal relations to other churches, or to their ministers, being consequently under no obligation to respect the feelings nor to seek the fraternal counsel, sympathy, and coöperation of any other church, it properly might, and necessarily must, perform all ecclesiastical acts by, and from itself alone.* Or, if all surrounding churches should become heretical, or corrupt, a church might properly proceed to consecrate its ministry, relying on the direct authority and guidance of Christ alone; but should they do so under the influence of prejudice and passion, they must expect His blighting displeasure.

It is evident, moreover, that a minister, chosen and set apart by one church alone, would have no right or claim to be received as a minister in any other church. The just exercise of his office would be limited to the church which had invested him with the office. While the Scriptures give no support to the popish doctrine that the power to ordain church officers is vested entirely in the ministers, independently of the churches, —a doctrine subversive of all proper church authority and independence, as well as of ministerial liberty, and so manifestly invented to serve the designs of an ambitious prelacy,—they do place the churches under sacred moral obligations, growing out of their relations to each other, to treat each other with high

* "If any pious laymen were banished to a desert, and having no regularly consecrated priest among them, were to agree to choose for that office one of their number, this man would be as truly a priest as if he had been consecrated by all the bishops in the world. Augustine, Ambrose, and Cyprian, were chosen in this manner."—*Luther, as quoted by D'Aubigné.*

deference and respect. The instructions to churches in these matters, are like those to individual members: "Brethren, we have been called unto liberty; only use not liberty as an occasion to the flesh, but by love serve one another." No church liveth to itself alone.

The reason why a presbytery, as a representative council of the ministry and churches, should be called for the purpose of completing the ordination of a minister already chosen by a church is, that he ought to be recognized as a minister of Christ by all other churches and their ministers. For this purpose he must give them satisfactory proof that he is worthy of such a public pledge of confidence and fellowship, by submitting himself to their examination in respect to the evidences of his spiritual hope, of his internal call to the ministry, and his views of Christian doctrine and of ministerial duty. While it is plain, therefore, that ordination services are no more essential to the *validity* of the minister's office than inauguration services are to that of President of the United States, yet it is appropriate and desirable as a public acknowledgment and testimonial that he is worthy of that office, and a solemn benediction on his induction into it.

The laying on of hands is a very ancient custom, and was practised with various significations. Jacob laid his hands on his grandsons, the sons of Joseph, when he gave them his last blessing. The Israelites when they presented their sin-offerings at the tabernacle, laid their hands on them while they confessed their sins, and the High Priest laid his hands on the head of the Scape Goat when he confessed the sins of the people, to signify that the sins of the people were thus transferred to the goat, to be borne off into the wilderness. Our Saviour laid his hands on children when he blessed them, Matt. 19 : 15; on the sick when he healed them, Mark 6 : 5; Luke 4 : 40; 13 : 13; and the Holy Ghost was given to those who were baptized, in the laying on of the hands of the Apostles, Acts 8 : 17; 19 : 6; though a different action was employed by the Saviour to signify the same thing, John 20 : 22. Like baptism, it is a symbolic action, often signifying the setting apart from a common to a sacred use, as in the case of a victim for sacrifice. Lev. 1 : 4. The Levites were set apart and consecrated to the service of God by the laying on of the hands of the children of Israel at large, in presence of the whole assembly. Num. 8 : 10. It was also practised at the consecration of Christian ministers, Acts 6 : 6; 13 : 3; 1 Tim. 4 : 14; 5 : 22; 2 Tim. 1 : 6, as a symbolic act, like baptism, or the breaking of bread, to signify that they are separated and set apart from the ordinary lawful pursuits and business of this life, to the work of God in the ministry of the Gospel.

The laying on of hands, therefore, is a circumstance connected with ordination by Apostolic example, and should be perpetuated; not as essential to its validity, nor as conveying any grace, virtue, or influence, but for the same reason for which the Apostles practised it—because the teaching of nature, and the example of good men in all ages concur with the Divine sanction of this act under the Mosaic dispensation, as an act appropriate to so solemn an occasion. The legitimate use of the practice is its public moral influence. It is fit and proper, that the ministers present, acting in behalf of all the ministry and of the churches, should, by some significant, outward act, as well as by words, express their hearty approval and consent to the induction of one to this sacred office; and this is done in the solemn act of laying on of hands.

This investigation of the subject brings us to the following conclusions.

1. That no mysterious or peculiar gift, or influence, is conferred in ordination. No Apostolic *virtue*, no sacred clerical *fluid*, is transferred from one person to another. A minister is the same physically, intellectually, and spiritually, after ordination, as before. His relations and obligations, only, are changed. All that is conferred in any part of ordination may, from its nature, come from private Christians as well as from

ministers, for no minister can impart his own ordination, or the essence of it, in any sense, to another minister. The notion that the presence or agency of an ordained minister is necessary to impart sanctity or validity to the ordination of another, *by virtue of his own ordination*, is unsupported by Scripture, and is absurd. Ordination can no more propagate or perpetuate ordination, than conversion can propagate conversion; or than one man chosen to be President, can impart his office, or the virtue of it, to another.

2. That the ministry proceeds from the church, not the church from the ministry; that the ministry is for the church, and not the church for the ministry; that the ministry of each church holds authority *in* the church, and not that the whole ministry, as a body, is to *rule over* all the churches.

3. That the benefits or the validity of preaching, or of the ordinances, baptism and the Lord's Supper, are in no sense dependent on the validity, or even on the regularity of the administrator's ordination. Neither Scripture nor reason teaches that there is any such connection between these institutions, as that any irregularity in one, destroys the validity, or prevents the benefits of the others. If a man has been irregularly introduced into the ministry, the blame rests with him, or with the church, or the ministers concerned in the act, or on them all, and they must meet the consequences; and not the innocent and unsuspecting disciples to whom he may have preached, or administered the sacraments of the Gospel.*

* The lengths to which prelatical pride and ecclesiastical fanaticism have gone in desperate attempts to convince the world that "there can be no church without a bishop," nor valid or beneficial ordinances except those administered by prelates, or clergymen ordained by prelates, will scarcely be credited. All, except those who have received the sacraments at the hands of Episcopally ordained ministers, are declared by the High Church writers to be "unbaptized," and "out of the pale of the church." "They and their children," says Palmer, "are as the heathen." "Neither the preaching nor the ordinances administered by men not Episcopally ordained," they assert, "can be of the least spirit-

4. That the vows assumed, and the pledges given, in ordination, by the candidate, the church, and the presbytery, are of the most solemn character, requiring the utmost caution, prayerfulness, and sincerity, on the part of all concerned. No minister is obliged to consent to the ordination of a person whom he deems unworthy, nor to take part in the public services after a council has voted it; and it is an act of presumptuous wickedness to assist in vesting with the sacred functions of the ministry one of whose worthiness he is not fully convinced. 1 Tim. 5 : 22.

5. That the dogma of the necessity of a historical succession of ministers from the Apostles downward in order to give validity to ordination, is without foundation either in reason or Scripture.

All questions relative to the validity or sufficiency of ordination performed by other religious bodies, must be settled by reference to the principles above established : viz., whether the individual has received the call or election of a properly constituted church and the public recognition of the ministry and presbytery of such churches; and whether he has assumed ordination vows to practise and promote the form of church order, doctrine, ordinances, worship, and government, which the

ual benefit." And all these consequences, they pretend, follow because the ministers have not been ordained by a prelate in "Apostolic succession." Yet the principle above stated, is held to be sound in civil law. A marriage contract, the most solemn and sacred of all, is not vitiated by any official defect on the part of the officiating functionary.

"No marriage, solemnized before any person professing to be a justice of the peace, or minister of the gospel, shall be deemed or adjudged to be void, nor shall the validity thereof be in any way affected on account of any want of jurisdiction or authority in such supposed justice or minister, or on account of any omission or informality in the manner of entering the intention of marriage, or in the publication of the bans; provided that the marriage be in other respects lawful, and be consummated with a full belief, on the part of the persons so married, or of either of them, that they have been lawfully joined in marriage." —*Revised Statutes of Mass., Part II. Tit. 7, Chap. 75, Sect. 24.*

churches to whom he proposes to minister have received as of Divine appointment. If he has received the election of such a church, and the sanction of such a ministry, to preach the doctrines, perform the ordinances, and sustain the church order maintained by such churches and ministry, he ought to be received as a regularly ordained minister of the Gospel; otherwise he has no claim to be so received, and should be ordained to the ministry as though no such service had taken place. This conclusion, it will be seen, is arrived at irrespective of any questions whether the churches or the ministers of the religious body to which the candidate previously belonged are true churches, or a true ministry; since it is manifest that a man is not ordained to do that which he did not agree to do when the alleged ordination was performed. If his views of church polity, ordinances, and government, are changed, so that he desires to sustain those which he before opposed, he should give a public pledge and receive public testimonials accordingly.

SECT. 6. *Summary of Principles.*

The reader who has thus far patiently and attentively followed this investigation of the fundamental principles on which churches are constituted, according to the Scriptures, will now be gratified to see the results arrived at, in a condensed form; for convenient reference. Those principles of polity, which are essential to the existence, the functions, and the lawful organization of a true and Scriptural church of our Lord Jesus Christ may be thus briefly summed up.

The Holy Scriptures, being a revelation of the will of God, of supreme authority in doctrine, morals, church order, discipline, and ordinances, are addressed to the reason and consciences of men, who consequently have the right to take them for their guide, and in obedience to their instructions, any competent number of believers may form themselves into a distinct church; to profess and promulgate what they unitedly believe to be the teachings of the Scriptures, and to maintain Christian worship.

It is the duty of every person to repent, believe the Gospel, be baptized, seek religious instruction and Christian fellowship, connect himself with a gospel church, and partake of the Lord's Supper.

Persons who profess to believe in and obey the Lord Jesus Christ, and whose lives conform to that profession, should be admitted as church-members; and no others.

The holy catholic church, more properly called "the kingdom of Christ," is composed of all the truly regenerated on earth; who being known to Him only who searcheth the heart, it cannot be a visibly organized body.

A church is a company of baptized believers, voluntarily associated in a sacred covenant to obey and execute the commands of Christ.*

The formative union, or incorporation of believers into a church, is made by a voluntary covenant, or agreement, expressed or implied.

It is the right and duty of every church to declare what it considers the will of Christ to be, in respect to ordinances, moral and Christian duties, the terms of communion, and church order and to govern all its members accordingly.

Every church derives its ecclesiastical power immediately from the Lord Jesus Christ, comes into possession of it by con-

* Since this work was written, the author has met with the following definition, by that profound scholar and thinker, as well as unrivalled poet, John Milton; in his "*Treatise on Christian Doctrine, compiled from the Holy Scriptures alone.*"

"*The visible church* is either *universal* or *particular.*

"*The universal visible church* is the whole multitude of those who are *called,* in every part of the world, and who openly worship God the Father through Christ, in any place whatever, either individually or in conjunction with others.

"*A particular church* is a society of persons professing the faith, *united by a special bond of brotherhood,* and so ordered as may best promote the ends of edification, and mutual communion of the saints."

forming to his will, and is accountable directly to him for its rightful exercise.

Church power cannot be delegated, nor can it be increased by an aggregation of churches, or a denominational league, since each church is complete for all the purposes of its formation, and may perform the highest acts of judicial power.

A church properly consists of no more members, including all who usually assemble with them, than may conveniently meet in one place for worship.

Churches are independent of each other, and of all others, so far as authoritative interference or control is concerned; yet they sustain an intimate relationship, and are bound to watch over each other in love.

The power to receive persons to the fellowship and privileges of the church, and to censure or expel offenders, in accordance with the laws of Christ, is vested in the whole body.

The members of a church have the right to choose their own officers, and this election is the essential part of ordination; though the relations of churches and ministers, as well as Apostolic example, render a public recognition or ordination under the hands of the presbytery, highly proper, and in ordinary cases a duty.

The permanent Scriptural officers in a church are bishops, or pastors, and deacons.

The members of a church, acting as such, in an assembled capacity, and not the officers, have the power to receive others to their fellowship, by judging of their spiritual state according to the Word of God, and to expel offenders.

The disciplinary power of a church, which extends to its own members only, is wholly spiritual; having exclusive reference to the religious character and relations of the subjects of it, and a church has no right to resort to temporal penalties, or civil inflictions.

Pastors or bishops are all of equal rank, and possess equal rights, and authority.

Baptism, church fellowship, and the Lord's Supper, should be granted to believers only, the former in all cases preceding the other two in the order of time.

The Scriptural principles of church polity have now been exhibited, with brief references to the proofs on which they rest. Baptists believe and advocate those principles because they are of Divine authority, not as the products of their own wisdom, or the mere deductions of their own reason, though they approve themselves strongly to their reason and common sense. We believe that all Christians are sacredly bound to be governed by these principles, in their church capacity. And while we do not suppose that the practice of them, or of any other principles of church polity is essential to personal salvation; nor consider membership in a Baptist church, or any other church, the unfailing test of Christian character, yet we are deeply convinced that all departure from these principles will be attended with injury to the cause of Christ, and to individual Christians. We profess to be actuated by higher motives in all our religious duties, than the mercenary spirit of doing and of believing nothing except what is absolutely necessary to a comfortable prospect of heaven.

It is no part of the design of this book to controvert the views or the practices of others, nor to exhibit the various ecclesiastical systems which now prevail, in disparaging contrast with others. Nor would any other systems be mentioned, or even referred to, but for the sake of presenting the principles here advocated with greater clearness by exhibiting those points in which they differ respectively. For this purpose only, some of the prominent points of difference from other existing theories and systems will be pointed out.

First, then, the system of church order embraced by Baptists, differs from all *national or state religious establishments*, as they exist in Italy, Germany, Denmark, and England; and generally throughout Europe and the East; in maintaining that churches should not be incorporated with the state, that civil magistrates have no right to control religious opinions, rites, or forms of worship; and that the pecuniary expenses of churches should be sustained by voluntary contribution, not by compulsory taxation.

Second, it differs from all systems of *ecclesiastical catholicism*, papal, episcopal, and presbyterial; in maintaining that a Scripturally organized church is an assembly of baptized believers, who meet in one place for worship, for administering ordinances, and the trial of offenders. It allows of the existence of no such body as a universal, national, or provincial church, nor of any form of extensive aggregation or concentration of church power.

Third, it differs from papacy, and from every form of prelacy, whether ancient like the Oriental; more recent as the English; or modern like the Wesleyan, by the principle, that all church officers are selected and chosen by the Christian people, that ministers are all of equal rank, and that they have no official authority except in the particular church which selects them to office.

Fourth, it is distinguished from these systems by the principle that all church power is in the church as a body, not in its ministers; that it comes to each church directly from the Lord Jesus Christ according to his promise, by virtue of the union of its members in the church relation, and is not transmitted by succession from any previously existing body; and that it is the right and the duty of each church to interpret and apply the laws of Christ for itself to its own members, and to them only.

Fifth, by the principle that churches are properly executive, and not legislative bodies; that they have no right to adopt any terms of membership except those laid down in the Scriptures, nor to change the form or the subjects of church ordinances.

Sixth, it differs from all these systems in maintaining that no person can be *born* into a Christian church, nor be made a member by any act of parents in infancy, but that to become a member in any church must be a *personal, voluntary* act on the part of each individual; that the new birth, or personal piety, is the qualification for membership; and that the assembled church is the divinely appointed organ of expressing Christ's will in the reception of members.

Seventh, it differs from all pedobaptist systems, whether Papal, Episcopal, Lutheran, Moravian, Presbyterian, Methodist, and Congregational, in admitting no persons except professed and credible believers to either of the ordinances of the church, of which baptism, in the Scriptural meaning of the term, is always to precede admission to the Lord's table; by distinguishing between spiritual and natural or political relationships; by recognizing no church relation to the children of believers any more than of others till they give evidence of piety, and at their own desire are baptized into the fellowship of the church.

PART II.

DOCTRINES.

THE principles on which churches should be constituted, and their relations to each other having been explained, the next inquiry relates to the doctrines* which they are to believe and teach. For it is plain that God has, in the Scriptures, commanded every church to believe, and through its ministry and members to teach, the Gospel to the world. The duty of teaching, implies that doctrines are to be explained, and, of course, understood by the teacher. The duty of understanding Christian doctrine is by no means confined to ministers of the Gospel; it is strongly enjoined, in the word of God, on all Christians. Private Christians are censured for their slow progress in knowledge, and churches as collective bodies, for suffering false and corrupt doctrines among their members.

It is the right and the duty of every Christian to take the Scriptures, and with such helps as he can obtain, in prayerful reliance on the Spirit of God, to determine for himself what doctrines he ought to believe and promote; and while he does so peaceably, and without infringing the rights of others, no earthly power, civil or ecclesiastical, has any right to molest

* The word *doctrine,* in its most extended signification, is used to denote *whatever is taught.* In this sense it would include Parts I. and III. which unfold the constitution and government of churches. It is here applied in its more common acceptation, to those Scriptural truths which form the substance of the creed, or the confession of faith of churches, and church-members.

him. It is likewise the duty of every church to decide for itself what doctrines the Scriptures reveal; and having done so, these doctrines form its creed. These the church agrees to maintain. If an individual adopts views of doctrine radically different, he ought not to be injured therefor in person or estate, yet he ought not to be admitted to the church; or if a member of the church has renounced its creed, he has deprived himself of the right to continue in its membership.

As to *written confessions of faith*, each church follows its own views of propriety. This is a necessary result of their strictly independent character. If a church has no written articles, it is liable to be annoyed by members, who, having adopted dangerous errors, declare that they understood such to be the doctrines of the church when they became members, that they can maintain their views from the Bible,—the only creed of the church,—and thus deny the right of the church to censure or exclude them. To prevent such troubles and promote unity and peace, it is customary for churches to have their articles of faith and covenant printed, and to furnish each candidate for membership with a copy, and if afterwards he shall see fit to renounce it, he cannot complain if the church withdraw from him their fellowship. A creed so formed and used, does not fetter the church, nor oppress the conscience of any member, for it is in the hands of all the members for daily comparison with the Scriptures, and can be altered by the church when necessary, with far more propriety when reduced to clear, written propositions, than if entrusted to the fallible memory of men. A written creed, then, may be useful to the sound, consistent, and quiet members of a church, and is inconvenient to none but such as wish to remain in it while they reject its doctrines, and wantonly destroy its peace.

Articles of faith should be limited to those fundamental points of doctrine, and practice, which lie on the very face of the Scriptures. Minute specifications would render them difficult to be remembered, and needlessly multiply questions of discipline. It is unwise to require exact uniformity of opinion on every theological question. Private judgment should have as much scope as may consist with peace; while vital truths must be held firm by all the members, or they cannot be associated in church fellowship with comfort or advantage: but with these, united to consistent practice, elevated piety, vigilant discipline, and brotherly love, no trouble will arise from differences of opinion on other points.

In presenting the following outline of Christian doctrines, the author may be permitted to say, that he has made use of such language as appeared to him least liable to misconstruction. It is no part of the design of this book to furnish a creed or articles of faith for general adoption, nor to disseminate new or peculiar doctrines among the churches. After comparing the articles of faith adopted by a great number of Baptist churches in all parts of the United States, and in England, no one was found to be adapted, *in form*, to the plan of this work. Without setting up any claim to originality, therefore, the author preferred this plan, which, so far as it extends, includes the substance of those leading doctrines which our churches have received as of Scriptural authority. This harmony of doctrinal views among so many independent bodies, so widely scattered, each of whom is at liberty to frame and adopt its own creed, is remarkable; and happily illustrates the safety of intrusting the matter to their own judgment. And it is far more important to the purity, the peace, and the usefulness of the churches, that we all clearly understand, firmly believe, and ardently love those leading doctrines and vital truths of the Gospel in which we agree, than to dispute about those respecting which we do not agree.

CHAPTER I.

OF GOD, AND DIVINE REVELATION.

Sect. 1. *The Scriptures.*

The Holy Scriptures of the Old and New Testaments are a revelation from God, written by men divinely inspired. A book or writing may be true, yet not inspired; though it cannot be inspired without being true. The truth of a book cannot prove its inspiration, yet it must be proved to be true, and the authentic production of its professed writer before it can be proved to be inspired. The proper method to arrive at the proof of the inspiration of the Scriptures, therefore, is first to seek for the proof that they are authentic and true.

It is not necessary to discuss at large the means by which the authenticity and truth of ancient records in general are proved. Those which have the following marks of genuineness, have commanded the unanimous confidence of mankind.

1. The general consent of tradition. The fact that an ancient book has for many hundreds or thousands of years been ascribed to a certain individual, as its author, is a strong proof of its genuineness, because it is impossible to conceive how such a belief became prevalent unless it was originally established by known and undoubted proofs.

2. The correctness of its references to known cotemporaneous events, to persons living at the time when it professes to have been written, and the correctness of its geographical and astronomical references.

3. The testimony of cotemporary historians and other writers.

That the books of the New Testament are the genuine, authentic writings of the men whose names they bear, is capable of the clearest proof. Any one who is willing to investigate the subject thoroughly, may have every doubt removed, by evidence of the most satisfactory character. A few considerations, only, will be submitted.

1. Authors, not Christians, but opposers of Christianity, pagans and Jews, who lived at the same time with the Apostles, testify that during the reign of Nero, Christians were multiplying in Judea, where they tell us that Christianity originated, that they were rapidly extending into other countries, and that they used sacred writings peculiar to themselves, and different from those of the Jews. The most eminent and approved historians of the Roman empire testify to these facts, which are further illustrated and placed beyond doubt, by the corresponding testimony of official state documents from the highest civil officers, and the writings of Josephus, the great Jewish historian of his time. The same sacred books are referred to by heathen writers in their attacks upon Christianity, in the second and third centuries, and the references are such as to leave no doubt that they are the books of the New Testament.

2. Christian writers, from the first century onward, some of whom had been conversant with the Apostles, refer to various books of the New Testament as the genuine writings of the men to whom they are ascribed, and often quote their language, so as to leave no doubt that they are the same books which have come down to us. Some of these writers were hearers of the Apostle John, others were well acquainted with all the writings and other testimony, extant in their day; they were eminent for learning and virtue; some of them wrote extensively in defence of Christianity, and they all bear abundant testimony to the genuineness of most of the books of the New Testament, as undisputed by friends or foes.

3. There were early heretics, who bitterly opposed some of the generally received doctrines of Christianity, to whose interest the authority of these writings was destructive; yet they did not undertake to dispute their genuineness, but their manner of quoting, and referring to them, and the methods by which they undertook to evade the force of those passages which most

plainly opposed their views, prove, beyond a doubt, that the genuineness and authenticity of the books were so universally admitted, that to call it in question would be destructive to their cause.

4. None of the motives which actuate wicked and designing men, can, by any probability, be ascribed to the writers of the New Testament. These writings contain the purest and most salutary precepts of virtue, justice, self-denial, and religion, ever presented to the human mind. It is absurd, in the last degree, to suppose that such writings could be the forgeries of bad men; if they are not the forgeries of bad men, they are authentic and true.

5. That the writers of the New Testament would not practise deception if they could, is plain from their upright and truthful characters; from their simplicity, most of them belonging to the humble classes of society; from their impartiality in recording their own faults; from the artlessness of their narrations, which often appear contradictory, but on examination are found to be wonderfully harmonious, though written without concert, and at different times and places; and from the fact, that instead of aggrandizement, they expected, and actually suffered, poverty, reproach, toil, scourging, imprisonment, and death, for adhering to the truth of their writings. That they could not if they would, is evident from the nature of their narrations. The life, the teachings, the miracles, the trial and crucifixion of Jesus Christ, were all public, and so were the lives and ministry of the Apostles. Such accounts as are recorded in the four Gospels, and the Acts of the Apostles, could never have gained credence unless they were the true records of fact, as any one who has read cotemporaneous history, and the researches of modern travellers and geographers, must admit. In short, there never were writings, which, if false, could have been so easily detected; none have been subjected to so many sharp-sighted and searching scrutinies by friends and foes; yet

no false statement has ever been discovered in them—a satisfactory proof that they are authentic and true.

6. Viewed, therefore, as historical compositions, the internal and external proofs that they are the genuine writings of the men to whom they are ascribed, and a true record of facts, are so abundant, that to deny it would betray the greatest ignorance, presumption, and folly. It would be calling in question all the rules of historical evidence, and the truth of all history. There are no ancient writings extant, whose genuineness, authenticity, and truth, are sustained by so many clear and incontestable proofs.

The proof that the Scriptures are divinely inspired, is closely interwoven with that of their authenticity; though it is in some respects even more triumphantly satisfactory. They reveal a religion, which enlightened reason, and conscience declare must be from God; so that most persons become thoroughly convinced that they are Divine, before examining the evidence that they are authentic; yet it seems more correct to show that they possess entire historical credibility, before proceeding to show that they have the higher claim of being the infallible words of God.

That the Holy Scriptures are a complete revelation of the will of God to men, free from all error, and without any omission, is capable of the most satisfactory proof.*

1. It is abundantly evident that mankind need, and have always needed, a revelation from God. The condition and doom

* The design and limits of this work admit of a mere outline only, of the arguments for the authenticity and inspiration of the Holy Scriptures. The following are a few of the works in which the various questions connected with this subject are discussed at length; *Alexander on the Canon*; *Campbell's Preliminary Dissertations; Watson's Apology for the Bible; Jenyns's Internal Evidence of the Christian Religion; Paley's Evidences of Christianity; Leslie's Short Method; Hug's introduction to the New Testament; Robinson's Researches in Palestine; Horne's Introduction; Gaussen's Theopneustia, translated from the French, by Rev. E. N. Kirk; Neander's Church History, etc.*

of the antediluvian world, the darkness and wretchedness of the heathen nations who have not yet received it, and the superior intelligence, the social and political elevation of those who have enjoyed its benefits, show that mankind greatly need a revelation from God.

2. It is not unreasonable to believe that God would give a revelation of his will to men. For without it, the highest capabilities of the human race could not be attained. The superior intelligence, bodily comfort, social order, and moral elevation of those nations, and communities, where the revelations of the Bible form the basis of their systems of mental culture, and of civil compact, contrasted with those nations which have not received the Bible as a revelation from the almighty Creator of the world, abundantly prove this to be true of man in the present life. And it is obvious that man needs a revelation from God, to enable him to prepare for the life that is to come.

3. It is reasonable to believe that God would cause this revelation to be committed to writing. That he can communicate the instructions which he desires to promulgate among men, to the mind of a man, so that it shall be recorded in "the words which the Holy Ghost teacheth," is as reasonable to believe; as that he first created the human mind, and gave to men the power of conception, of memory, and of expression. As it could not be transmitted from place to place, and from age to age, without being written, we should expect that it would be committed to writing, together with the proofs of its Divine origin.

4. As the inspiration of a man to speak or write the infallible words of God is an *invisible* miracle, the certainty of which can be known only to him who professes to be inspired, the proper proof, before the world, of his inspiration, must be some *visible* miracle, or miracles: such as healing the sick, raising the dead, or giving sight to the blind, with a word; and in such circumstances as to make it plain that the miracles were special acts of Divine power, exerted by God himself, to attest the claim of

the message to be received as the testimony of God. The New Testament was written by men who performed miracles, and uttered prophecies as proofs of their Divine commission. They declare that they wrote the Scriptures under the same influence as that by which they healed the sick, raised the dead, and foretold future events. They claimed that their *works*—evidently the direct, special product of Divine power—should be received as proofs of the Divine infallibility of their *words*.

5. The excellence of the Scriptures, the great superiority of their moral precepts, the purity and elevation of their doctrines, the perfect harmony of the writers, though they wrote without concert, and in different ages and places, and with great variety of style, their powerful and continually increasing influence to check sin, to promote holiness in men, to purify society, to increase intelligence, sustain justice, benevolence and public spirit, in short, to promote every interest dear to men in the present world, or cheering to their prospects in the world to come, prove that the Scriptures are not the forgeries of men, but are a revelation from God.

6. The four Gospels delineate a perfect, sinless character. Four different writers, each from his own point of view, have severally described Jesus Christ as a man who made no mistake, committed no fault, accomplished all he undertook. No such being had ever appeared on the earth before, no one has appeared since. The four Evangelists have either presented the character of Jesus Christ truly, or they have invented a fictitious one, with the intention to deceive. But it is impossible for imperfect men to invent a perfect character. In every effort to do so, they have left traces of their own imperfection. But the character of Jesus Christ, delineated by the Evangelists, is either a true and real one, or it is a forgery, perpetrated with a base, dishonest intention to deceive! Reason and common sense pronounce this to be impossible. The character of Christ, as there exhibited, is alone a sufficient proof of the truth of the description, unless we can believe so manifest an absurdity, as

that dishonest men, with a dishonest intention, would invent, and hold up to the admiration of the world, a sinless and perfect character. This argument alone, for the Divine origin of the four Gospels, is unanswerable.

7. The Lord Jesus Christ testified most fully and clearly to the Divine inspiration of the Old Testament. He called it "the Word of God." Mark 7 : 13; Luke 4 : 4; John 10 : 35. He declared it to be infallible, and that in the minutest degree. Matt. 5 : 18; Mark 14 : 49; John 10 : 35. He appeals to it on all occasions, as a perfect, unerring record, given by God. Matt. 7 : 12; 11 : 10, 13; Mark 9 : 12; 14 : 21, 27; Luke 7 : 27; 10 : 26; 16 : 16, 29; 20 : 17; 24 : 25, 27, 44. He refers to the greater part of the books by name, as written by Prophets, and by those to whom they are ascribed, and he quotes their words as the infallible words of God.

8. The fulfilment of the prophecies proves the Scriptures to be inspired. Many of them foretold events the most improbable at the time they were written, which have since received an exact, and most wonderful fulfilment. Those which relate to the posterity of Esau, and Jacob, to the condition of the Jews, to Nineveh, to Babylon, to Tyre, to Egypt, to the four great empires of the world, to the time of Christ's appearance, and many others, form a most unexceptionable and convincing proof, through every age, that the Prophets wrote the unerring words of the Most High.

9. Finally, the Scriptures, whose authenticity and truth are sustained by the most triumphant proofs, declare that they are divinely inspired, and should be received as the unmingled, infallible, and perfect words of God. "The prophecy came *not* in old time by *the will of man*, but holy men of God spoke as they were moved (*borne along*) by the Holy Ghost." 2 Pet. 1 : 21. This refers particularly to the writings of the Prophets. They declare the same things of themselves, and of each other. A few instances will be given. Isaiah 1 : 2, 10, 18; 2 : 1; 3 : 16; 6 : 1–13; 7 : 3–9; 8 : 1, 5; 43 : 1–28; 50 : 1; 56 : 1;

Jer. 1 : 2, 3, 7, 11 ; 2 : 1 ; 3 : 6 ; 4 : 1 ; 7 : 1 ; Ez. 1 : 3 ; 3 : 4 ; Hos. 1 : 1 ; Joel 1 : 1. David says, "the Spirit of the Lord spake by me, and *his word* was in *my tongue.*" 2 Sam. 23 : 2. And Peter, "this Scripture must needs have been fulfilled, which the *Holy Ghost by the mouth of David spake.*" Acts 1 : 16. Peter, also, confirms the inspiration of "all the epistles" of Paul, placing them, in this respect, on a level with "the other Scriptures." 2 Peter 3 : 15, 16. And by the hand of Paul we have the Divine declaration that *all* the Scriptures are "given by inspiration of God." 2 Tim. 3 : 16. See, also, Heb. 1 : 1, 2 ; Acts 28 : 25 ; 1 Cor. 14 : 37 ; 1 Thess. 2 : 13 ; 4 : 8 1 Pet. 1 : 10, 11 ; Matt. 28 : 19, 20 ; 10 : 20 ; Mark 13 : 11 Luke 12 : 12 ; 21 : 14, 15 ; Acts 1 : 8.

These passages are but specimens of the testimony which the Scriptures uniformly bear to the great truth, that they are from God. By inspiration, therefore, is not meant that all the persons whose words and actions are recorded in the Bible, were inspired when they did and said those things, not that their conduct was right, because recorded in the Scriptures ; but that the men who *wrote* the Scriptures, were so instructed, moved, guided, and restrained by the Spirit of God, that they recorded, truly and correctly, those things which ought to be recorded, and nothing more, free from the least error or omission. The inspired writers wrote the very words, and all the words, which God intended they should write in the sacred Scriptures, and no others. They ought, therefore, to be received as the *perfect, infallible words of God,* to be interpreted according to the laws of language, and every truth which they reveal, every doctrine they teach, every positive institution they enjoin, every duty which they inculcate, ought to be implicitly believed and obeyed.

SECT. 2. *Of God's Existence and Attributes.*

The Scriptures teach that there is one God ; Gen. 1 : 1 ; Ex. 3 : 14 ; Deut. 6 : 4 ; 32 : 39 ; and one only ; Is. 44 : 6, 8 ;

Mark 12 : 29; 1 Cor. 8 : 4, 6; 1 Tim. 2 : 5; who is eternal; Deut. 32 : 40; 33 : 27; Psalms 90 : 2; 102 : 26, 27; Dan. 12 : 7; Rom. 1 : 20; Rev. 10 : 6; the maker and creator of all things, and of all other beings; Gen. 1 : — 2 : 7; Neh. 9 : 6; Ps. 33 : 6, 9; Heb. 2 : 10; 3 : 4; Rom. 11 : 36; Col. 1 : 16; almighty; Gen. 18 : 14; 17 : 1; Matt. 19 : 26; Rev. 19 : 6; invisible; John 1 : 18; Col. 1 : 15; 1 Tim. 6 : 16; Heb. 11 : 27; everywhere present; Ps. 139 :—Prov. 15 : 3; Jer. 23 : 24; Eph. 1 : 23; perfect in knowledge of everything, great and small, past and future, visible and invisible; Ps. 147 : 5; Prov. 15 : 11; Acts 15 : 18; Matt. 10 : 29, 30; 1 John 3 : 20; Ps. 139 : 1–15; infinitely benevolent; Ex. 34 : 6; Ps. 145 : 9; Luke 6 : 35; 1 John 4 : 8–11; holy; Lev. 19 : 2; Is. 6 : 3; wise; Rom. 11 : 33; Col. 2 : 3; Is. 40 : 28; of perfect justice; Rom. 2 : 5, 6; Ps. 5 : 4–6; Rev. 15 : 3; and veracity; Deut. 32 : 4; Num. 23 : 19; John 3 : 33; 17 : 17; gracious and merciful; Ps. 51 : 1; 103 : 13; John 3 : 16; Tit. 3 : 4; Eph. 2 : 4, 5; immutable in his being and purposes; Ps. 102 : 24, 27; Mal. 3 : 6; James 1 : 17; Ps. 33 : 11; Acts 2 : 23; whose existence is manifest from the works of creation; Rom. 1 : 20; Ps. 14 : 1; 19 : 1–6; and the workings of the human conscience; Rom. 2 : 13–15.

The works of creation, also, are full of clear and undisputable proofs of the existence of God, as well as of most of his attributes, as revealed in the Scriptures. But natural theology is little understood, and very little studied, except when it is preceded and illustrated by the theology of revelation.

Sect. 3. *Of God as Father, Son, and Holy Ghost.*

The One only living and true God, infinite in every natural and moral perfection, has revealed itself in the Scriptures as the Father, and the Son, and the Holy Spirit.

1. The Divinity of Christ. The Scriptures teach us that Jesus Christ, through whose agency, and for whom God created all things; Eph. 3 : 9; Col. 1 : 16; Heb. 1 : 2; through whose

mediation, and for whose sake, believers will be saved; Eph. 1 : 3–5; 2 : 7–10; 2 Tim. 1 : 9; John 1 : 12; 14 : 6; 1 John 4 : 9; 1 Thess. 5 : 9, 10; Col. 3 : 4; John 17 : 2; is not a mere man, but possessed a twofold nature; John 6 : 62; 16 : 28; 8 : 14; 3 : 11, 13; compare John 6 : 33, 35, 38, 40, 46, and 8 : 23, with 1 Cor. 15 : 47; Acts 9 : 3–5; that he existed before his human birth, and appearance in the flesh; John 8 : 58; 1 : 15; before the beginning of the world; John 17 : 5, 24; Col. 1 : 17; and they declare his existence to be eternal; 1 John 1 : 1, 2; Heb. 1 : 10–12; Rev. 1 : 11; 2 : 8; 22 : 13; 1 John 5 : 20; Is. 9 : 6. Divine attributes, as omnipotence; Phil. 3 : 21, compare John 10 : 28–30; 2 : 19; 2 Peter 1 : 3; and omniscience; Rev. 2 : 23; Matt. 11 : 27; John 2 : 24, 25; 6 : 64; with that adoration in praise and prayer, which is due to these perfections; John 5 : 23; 14 : 1, 13; 1 Cor. 1 : 2; 2 Cor. 12 : 8; 1 Thess. 3 : 11; Acts 7 : 59; Heb. 1 : 6; Phil. 2 : 10, 11; and which can properly be paid only to the Divine Being; Is. 42 : 8; Jer. 17 : 5; Matt. 4 : 10; are ascribed to Christ; from which we learn, that he is called God; John 1 : 1, compare verse 14; 20 : 28; Rom. 9 : 5; 1 John 5 : 20; Heb. 1 : 8; in such a sense that it can be said he possesses power to do whatever God can do; and that all the perfections of the Divine nature can be predicated of him, and all adoration, obedience, trust, and love, claimed by the Divine Being, should be paid to him; Ps. 2 : 12; Matt. 28 : 9; Luke 24 : 52; John 5 : 23; Acts 7 : 59; Rev. 5 : 11–14.

It is evident, therefore, that independently of the union of the Son, or the Word, with the man Jesus, there is a real and an eternal distinction between Him and the Father. The Scriptures teach that the Son is God, in the same sense as the Father, yet there is but one God, and the very same, and the entire Divine perfection which belongs to the Father, belongs also to the Son.

2. Divinity of the Holy Spirit. The Scriptures further teach us to pay equal and undivided honor to the Holy Ghost, with

the Father, and the Son; Matt. 28 : 19; 2 Cor. 13 : 13; 1 Cor. 12 : 4–6; both in the formula of baptism, which is to be administered in the name (or in honor) of the Holy Ghost, equally with the Son and the Father; and in the Apostolic benediction, inasmuch as their united, co-equal agency, is employed in the salvation of every redeemed soul. Compare 1 Pet. 1 : 2, with Jude 20, 21. See, also, Matt. 12 : 32.

And while he is represented as in the closest union with the Father and the Son; John 15 : 26; 16 : 13–15; compare Matt. 10 : 20; Rom. 8 : 9, 11, with Gal. 4 : 6; he is also clearly distinguished from both; John 14 : 16; 1 John 5 : 7; is often called God; 1 Cor. 3 : 16; 6 : 19, 20; Acts 5 : 3, 4; unlimited power is ascribed to him; 1 Cor. 12 : 8, 9, 11; as well as knowledge of future things; John 16 : 13; of the secret purposes of God; 1 Cor. 2 : 10; and Divine works; such as the conviction of sin, the conversion and sanctification of the soul, bestowing miraculous gifts, and the inspiration of the Scriptures; Eph. 4 : 30; Mark 12 : 36; Luke 1 : 35; 2 : 26; 3 : 22; Acts 1 : 2, 16; 13 : 2; 15 : 28; 20 : 28; 21 : 11; 28 : 25; 1 Cor. 2 : 13; Heb. 2 : 4; 3 : 7; 2 Peter 3 : 21.

Thus clearly and fully do the Scriptures teach us the doctrine of the Divine Trinity in Unity. They offer no explanation of the mode of God's mysterious existence as three in one sense, and yet but one; they only reveal it as a fact. As such it is our duty, humbly, heartily, and joyfully to believe it. It is not contrary to reason; if it were, it should be rejected. It is above the power of reason to comprehend, and so are the eternity, the self-existence, the omniscience and omnipresence of God, and the existence of spirits; to say nothing of thousands of unexplained things which lie in our path every day. The infallible Word of God has taught it, together with many other mysteries as great, therefore it is to be believed.

SECT. 4. *Of God as the Creator and Ruler of the World.*

1. God created all things, animate and inanimate, visible and invisible, the heavens and the earth, with all their inhabitants. Gen. 1 : 1 ; Ps. 121 : 2 ; 146 : 6 ; Neh. 9 : 6. Compare Rev. 10 : 6 ; 14 : 7 ; Jer. 10 : 11, 12 ; Acts 17 : 24 ; Col. 1 : 16 ; John 1 : 3.

2. This he did without the intervention of means, or the employment of materials ; in other words, he brought into existence, by an act of his will, that which before had no existence, and which began to exist solely because he willed it. Ps. 33 : 6, 9 ; Is. 48 : 13. Compare Heb. 11 : 3 ; Gen. 1 : 3, 6, 9, 15, 20, 24.

3. He who created, also governs the world, and overrules the operation of natural causes, and the actions of his creatures. It is evident that God would not create a world, nor creatures, which he could not fully govern and control, and it is evident that he would exert his power to do this in the way which he sees best. Ps. 66 : 7 ; Eph. 1 : 11 ; Matt. 10 : 29 ; Luke 12 : 7.

4. It follows, therefore, that all things must take place in accordance with his pleasure. For, as nothing can occur without his knowledge and foresight, it is clear that whatever takes place according to what appears the course of nature, is so, not on that account merely, but because God sees it to be in accordance with his wise and benevolent purposes, for otherwise he would have specially interfered to bring about a different event. Ps. 139 : 16 ; Gen. 50 : 20 ; Amos 3 : 6 ; Is. 10 : 5, 7, 12, 15 ; Luke 19 : 42–44.

5. A firm confidence in the providence of God does not conflict with any just views of human freedom and accountability, nor encourage indolence or presumption ; but is fitted to tranquillize the mind, inspire courage, and animate us to holy and persevering effort. 1 Pet. 5 : 7 ; Matt. 4 : 5–7 ; Acts 27 : 23–25, compare with verses 31, 44.

CHAPTER II.

CHARACTER AND STATE OF MAN.

SECT. 1. *Of Man in his Original State.*

GOD created Adam and Eve; Gen. 1 : 27; 2 : 7, 21, 22; to be the progenitors of the whole human family; Gen. 1 : 28; Acts 17 : 26; perfect; Gen. 1 : 31; and like himself, holy; Gen. 1 : 26, 27; 5 : 1; Eccl. 7 : 29; and consequently happy. They were required to keep the whole moral law; Gal. 3 : 12; Luke 10 : 28; Mark 12 : 30, 31; Luke 10 : 27, 28; the essence and sum of which, consists in implicit obedience, growing out of supreme love to God, to prove which, an outward test was added, which was a command to abstain from the fruit of one tree; Gen. 2 : 17; in the garden which they were "to dress and keep," under the penalty of death; Gen. 2 : 17; or all that ensued—the painful dissolution of the body; Rom. 5 : 12; loss of innocence and happiness; Gen. 3 : 7, 8, 10, 16, 17; alienation and separation from God; Gen. 6 : 3, 5, 6; and condemnation to eternal misery; Rom. 6 : 23; 8 : 6, 7; Gal. 6 : 8; Heb. 12 : 14.

Our first parents were, in their primitive state, under a covenant of works. They might have been justified, and confirmed in holiness and happiness by their own efforts alone, had they never sinned. No other human beings were ever placed in this condition. Their innocence, holiness, and free communion with God, would have continued forever, the source and sure foundation of perfect felicity, had they perfectly obeyed the whole moral law. This is the standard of duty to all men, but not the condition of salvation to any, except to our first parents while in their state of innocence, before the fall.

Sect. 2. *Introduction of Sin.*

Eve being deceived, 1 Tim. 2 : 14; by the temptation of Satan, Gen. 3 : 1–5, compare Rev. 12 : 9; and by her persuasion Adam, also, ate of the forbidden fruit, Gen. 3 : 6; by which disobedience they became conscious of guilt, and shame, Gen. 3 : 7–13; their bodies became mortal, verse 19; 1 Cor. 15 : 21, 22; they were driven from the garden, Gen. 3 : 23, 24; condemned to hard toil for their subsistence, verse 19; and the earth was cursed, and made sterile on their account, verses 17, 18. In consequence of this single transgression—such is the law of God, and the nature of man—they became wholly sinners, James 2 : 10; and of course inclined to all forms of transgression, which sinful disposition was propagated to their immediate descendants, Gen. 5 : 3; and to the whole human family, Rom. 5 : 12; coextensive with death; so that all human beings are born with dispositions inclined to sin, John 3 : 6; Ps. 51 : 6.

Thus the whole law of God was represented in this prohibition of the fruit of the tree of knowledge of good and evil. By transgression of this one prohibition, they fell from that perfect love which is the fulfilling of the law, and became selfish, carnal, and depraved, in their affections. The question whether the human race should be born with holy, or with sinful natures, was suspended, by the will of God, on the conduct of Adam, in respect to this one prohibition. He is, therefore, the only man who ever was, or could be, guilty of *original* sin. The personal *guilt* of that *original* sin is not transferred to his posterity; but a depraved nature, which is a consequence of that sin, is inherited by them all. No one of Adam's posterity is born into the world with the same physical constitution, the same moral disposition, nor sustaining the same relations to God, or to the rest of the human race, as Adam in his state of original purity and rectitude.

SECT. 3. *The Depravity of Man.*

It is plain, from experience and from Scripture, that all human beings show a preference for sin as soon as they become capable of moral action. This fact proves the innate depravity of the whole race to be such, that they naturally incline to evil, and voluntarily prefer the pleasures of sense, which is opposition to God; Rom. 8 : 7; and incline to selfishness, which is the essence of all sin, and a violation of the whole law of God; Matt. 22 : 36–40; Mark 15 : 30, 31; so that it is uniformly true, that when the law is made known to them, they do but sin the more, Rom. 7 : 5, 8.

The Scriptural explanation of the origin of this universal, innate depravity, that "by no man sin entered into the world," is the most reasonable, though we may not be able to comprehend the connection between the original sin of Adam, and the corruption of his posterity. We know that children do inherit bodily and mental diseases, and peculiarities from their parents. Adam, by sinning, spread disorder through his whole nature, and analogy leads us to suppose that he would propagate beings like himself. This inherent inclination to evil is no excuse for any act of disobedience, or neglect of duty, because every sin is a voluntary act, in opposition to the law of nature, to conscience, and to the revealed will of God, and because every sinner has all the natural powers and faculties necessary for obeying God.

The character of man, then, is that of a voluntary rebel against his Maker. He prefers sin, is wholly destitute of love to God, and in this voluntary rebellion, love of self, and enmity to God, consists his total depravity.

The actual ruin of man is, consequently, twofold. 1. He has violated the law of God, and must suffer its penalty unless that penalty can be averted. 2. He is depraved, he so loves sin, and hates God, that unless his heart is changed he cannot hold happy intercourse with God. Such is the ruined, guilty, and miserable condition of man, from which no being but God could bring him deliverance.

Sect. 4. *The Condemnation of Man.*

In addition to the evils which have come upon the human race in the present life, and the sentence of mortality in consequence of their depravity, occasioned by the transgression of Adam, they are all, Rom. 3 : 23 ; children of wrath, Eph. 2 : 3 ; and under sentence of condemnation, Rom 5 : 16, 18 ; to most awful sufferings, Luke 16 : 24 ; Mark 9 : 48 ; in the future world, Matt. 25 : 31–46 ; Luke 16 : 22, 23 ; including separation from God, and from all holy beings, Luke 16 : 26 ; 13 : 28 ; Matt. 13 : 41–49 ; and a union with wicked spirits, Matt. 25 : 41 ; Rev. 21 : 8 ; in "the place of torment," which is described in the most terrific language, as "outer darkness," "furnace of fire," "where their worm dieth not, and the fire is not quenched," "blackness of darkness," and "lake of fire," from which there is no escape ; Luke 16 : 26 ; so that the sufferings of those who die in this state of depravity and condemnation, will never terminate throughout all eternity, Dan. 12 : 2 ; Matt. 18 : 8 ; 25 : 41 ; Mark 9 : 43–45 ; 2 Thess. 1 : 9.

Sect. 5. *The Agency of Created Spirits.*

The Scriptures also teach us the existence, Matt. 22 : 30 ; compare Acts 23 : 8 ; of a vast number, Matt. 26 : 53 ; Heb. 12 : 22 ; of created, Col. 1 : 16 ; rational beings, superior to men, 2 Pet. 2 : 11 ; Mark 13 : 32 ; Luke 9 : 26 ; of various ranks, Jude 9 ; 1 Thess. 4 : 16 ; who are employed, as their name indicates, as the *messengers*, and "ministers" of God, Heb. 1 : 14 ; Ps. 103 : 20 ; particularly to the saints, Luke 16 : 22 ; Acts 5 : 19 ; 12 : 7 ; and who are not to be worshipped ; Rev. 19 : 10 ; 22 : 4 ; Matt. 4 : 10 ; that some of them sinned, and left their original state, 2 Pet. 2 : 4 ; Jude 6 ; and drew everlasting misery upon themselves, Matt. 25 : 41; 2 Pet. 2 : 4; Jude 6; that they have a leader or prince, called the devil, satan, tempter, adversary, prince of the air, and of darkness, god of this world, Rev. 12 : 9; 1 Pet. 5 : 8; John 12 : 31; Eph. 2 : 2; who is crafty and malicious, 2 Cor. 11 : 14; Eph. 6 : 11; 1 Pet. 5 : 8; practicing wiles to seduce men into sin, John 13 : 2, 27; Acts 5 : 3; whose duty it is to resist him, James 4 : 7; and thus be secure against his machinations, 1 John 5 : 18; Eph. 6 : 11–18

CHAPTER III.

THE WAY OF SALVATION.

As all men became partakers of a sinful nature, and were involved in misery by the sin of one man, God was in mercy pleased to provide a way of salvation for all men, by one man, Jesus Christ. Rom. 5 : 12–19. The human race have lived, therefore, not under a legal, but a remedial dispensation, or covenant of grace; in which the pardon of sin, and the renewal of man's depraved nature, is promised to all who thankfully avail themselves of its provisions.

SECT. 1. *The Saviour.*

Jesus Christ, who is truly a man, though begotten not by a human father, but by an immediate act of the power of God, that he might be free from all depravity, and truly God, by an incomprehensible and inseparable union of his human nature with "the Word;" is the Redeemer and the Saviour of men, by having suffered the just penalty of the Divine law in their stead on earth, from which humiliation he is exalted to be the Judge of the world, governing all things with Divine power, the object of everlasting admiration and love, as "the Lamb slain from the foundation of the world." 1 Tim. 1 : 15 ; 2 : 5 ; 3 : 16 ; Luke 1 : 34–37 ; Matt. 1 : 18, 20 ; 25 : 31 ; Heb. 1 : 2, 3 ; 7 : 26 ; 10 : 10 ; John 1 : 1, 14 ; 4 : 42 ; 8 : 40 ; Col. 2 : 9 ; Is. 41 : 14 ; 43 : 11 ; 59 : 20 ; 60 : 16 ; Luke 2 : 11 ; Acts 5 : 13 ; Tit. 1 : 3, 4 ; 1 Pet. 1 : 1, 11 ; Gal. 3 : 13 ; Phil. 2 : 5–11 ; 2 Cor. 5 : 10 ; Eph. 1 : 20–22 ; Rev. 5 : 12, 13.

Sect. 2. *Atonement.*

The word *atonement*, though found but once in the New Testament, (Rom. 5 : 11,) is of frequent occurrence in the Old, denoting a propitiation effected on behalf of an offender, by some sacrifice or substitute for him. Thus, "he [the offender] shall put his hand upon the head of the [animal presented for a] burnt-offering, and it shall be accepted for him, to make *atonement* for him." Lev. 1 : 4. Christ, in like manner, by the sacrifice of himself, made an atonement which removes the obstacle arising from the justice of God to the pardon of sinners, so that all who repent and believe in Christ, are freely forgiven for his sake. Rom. 3 : 25, 26 ; Is. 53 : 4–7 ; 2 Cor. 5 : 15, 21 ; Heb. 9 : 14, 28 ; 1 Pet. 1 : 18, 19 ; John 1 : 29 ; 10 : 15 ; Matt. 20 : 28 ; Acts 20 : 28 ; Eph. 1 : 7 ; Rev. 5 : 9.

Sect. 3. *Regeneration.*

Regeneration is that change which is effected in the soul by the Holy Spirit, through the instrumentality of Gospel truth. Its confers no new power on men, but consists in a change of the affections, from the love of sin to the holy exercise of love to God, and pure, disinterested benevolence to all creatures. Ezek. 36 : 26 ; John 1 : 13 ; 3 : 3–8 ; Rom. 8 : 2 ; 1 Cor. 2 . 14 ; 2 Cor. 5 : 17 ; Gal. 6 : 15 ; Tit. 3 : 5 ; 1 John 4 : 7.

SECT. 4. *Love.*

As selfishness is the essence of all sin, so love—unconditional, impartial, disinterested love—to God, to truth and righteousness, including benevolence towards all creatures, is the essence of holiness, and is the first fruit of the Spirit in the regeneration or conversion of a sinner. 1 John 4 : 7, 8, 16, 20; Matt. 5 : 46–48; 22 : 37–40; Rom. 5 : 5; 8 : 28; 13 : 8, 10; Gal. 5 : 6, 22; Luke 11 : 42; 6 : 27–36; 1 Cor. 13 :—

SECT. 5. *Repentance.*

The next manifestation of that change which is produced in the soul by the Spirit, in regeneration, after the exercise of holy love, is repentance; which includes regret and humiliation for sin, because offensive to God, who is infinitely holy and good, a sincere and sustained resolve to forsake all sin, and approval of the law of God, springing from love to Christ, manifested in dying for sinners on the cross. 2 Cor. 7 : 10; 2 Tim. 2 : 25; Ps. 51 : 17; Prov. 28 : 13; Ezek. 16 : 63; 18 : 30; 33 : 11; 36 : 31; Jer. 31 : 18, 19; Mark 1 : 15; Luke 15 : 17–19; 24 : 47; Acts 2 : 38; 11 : 18; 17 : 30; 20 : 21.

SECT. 6. *Faith.*

Faith, which is an exercise of the soul, always joined with repentance in regeneration, includes both believing in Jesus Christ as the Son of God, believing his words, and a cordial trust in Him, as the only and the all-sufficient Saviour of sinners, to whom the same love, honor, and obedience are due as to the Father. This faith in God, the Scripture commands all men to exercise, with the promise of eternal life to those who believe, and the threatening of eternal misery to those who believe not. Rom. 1 : 16; 3 : 28; 4 : 16; 5 : 1; 16 : 26;

Mark 16 : 16; John 1 : 12; 3 : 16; 6 : 47; Acts 8 : 37; 16 : 31; Gal. 2 : 20; Heb. 10 : 22; 11 : 1, 6; 12 : 2; 1 John 5 : 10.

SECT. 7. *Justification.*

When a sinner exercises faith in Christ, he is pardoned and treated as though perfectly innocent and righteous in the sight of God, for the sake of what Christ has done and suffered in his behalf. This is Gospel justification, which signifies, not as in legal phrase, "to find and declare one *innocent*," but to declare him, though guilty, *wholly forgiven.* Rom. 3 : 24, 28; 4 : 5–8; 5 : 1, 16–19; 8 : 30; Acts 13 : 38, 39; 1 Cor. 6 : 11; 2 Cor. 5 : 19, 21; Gal. 2 : 16; 3 : 11, 24; Phil. 3 : 9; Tit. 3 : 7.

SECT. 8. *Obedience.*

It is the duty of all believers to render voluntary obedience to every command of God, from love to Him, as a motive; not as works of merit, or a means of justification, but as manifesting the work of the Spirit in regeneration; in which obedience and faith are so inseparably joined, that both must exist, or perish together. 1 Pet. 1 : 2, 22; 2 Pet. 1 : 5–11; Rom. 3 : 28; compare James 2 : 14–26; Gal. 5 : 6, 22, 24; Phil. 2 : 12, 13; Matt. 7 : 25–27; 10 : 41, 42; 11 : 29; 12 : 50; John 12 : 26; 15 : 4–8, 10, 14.

SECT. 9. *Sanctification.*

Those who are born of God are further sanctified through obedience, and His paternal chastisements, applied by the Spirit, by which the influence of sin over the soul and body is destroyed, the several lusts are weakened and subdued, and gracious affections are strengthened, so that by faithful efforts till death, and the constant supply of the Spirit of Christ, the saints grow in grace, perfecting holiness in the fear of God. John 17 : 17, 19;

compare Heb. 13 : 12; 1 Kings 8 : 46; Eccl. 7 : 20; Phil. 1 : 6, 9; 1 Pet. 1 : 22; 2 Pet. 1 : 5–11; 3 : 18; Heb. 12 : 11; Eph. 3 : 16–19; 1 Thess. 3 : 12, 13; 5 : 23; 2 Thess. 2 : 13; Ps. 17 : 15; Prov. 4 : 18; 1 John 3 : 2, 3, 6, 8, 9; Jude 21 :—

Sect. 10. *Perseverance.*

All who are regenerated by the Spirit, will persevere in obedience and holiness unto the end; for being kept by the mighty power of God, through faith unto salvation, nothing can separate them from His love. Compare John 5 : 24, with Matt. 10 : 22; compare John 6 : 37 with 15 : 6; compare 3 : 15, 16, 18, 36, with 8 : 31; 15 : 9; Rev. 2 : 7, 11, 17; 3 : 5, 12, 21; 21 : 7; See, John 10 : 28–30; 17 : 2, 3; 4 : 14; 1 John 3 : 9; Rom. 8 : 35–39; Phil. 1 : 6; 1 Pet. 1 : 5.

Sect. 11. *Assurance.*

A full assurance of personal interest in the grace and salvation of Christ is not always the immediate consequence of saving faith, yet as it is an inestimable blessing enjoyed by many, and as others may, without extraordinary revelation, in the right use of ordinary means, attain thereto, it is the duty of believers to give all diligence to make their calling and election sure, that their hearts may be enlarged with love and confidence, and strengthened to all holy obedience. Compare Col. 2 : 2 with Heb. 10 : 22, and 6 : 11; Rom. 5 : 2; 8 : 16; Job 19 : 25; 2 Cor. 5 : 1; Eph. 3 : 19; 2 Tim. 1 : 12; 2 Pet. 1 : 10; 1 John 2 : 3–5; 3 : 2, 14, 19; 4 : 13, 18; 5 : 10, 13.

Sect. 12. *Election.*

As God does, in fact, regenerate, justify, and save one, and not another, it is plain that He intended to do it, according to His gracious purpose, from all eternity; so that all who have ever been, or who will hereafter be, brought to exercise love, repentance, and faith, were from the beginning chosen in Him to salvation, through sanctification of the Spirit, and belief of the truth; and in consequence of the everlasting love of God to them, through the great atonement, the Holy Spirit is sent down to effect the work of regeneration in their hearts, without whose influence none would ever repent or believe; and this election of grace is the foundation of Christian assurance, and of perseverance in holiness. 2 Thess. 2 : 13; 1 Pet. 1 : 2; Eph. 1 : 3–6; compare John 17 : 1, 2, 6, 9, with Is. 53 : 10–12; Jer. 31 : 3; John 15 : 16; Acts 2 : 47; 13 : 48; 17 : 10; Rom. 8 : 28–30; 2 Tim. 1 : 9; Tit. 3 : 3–7.

SECT. 13. *The Offers of Salvation.*

Salvation is freely offered to all men in the Gospel; repentance and faith in Christ being the terms of reconciliation with God, by means of which men may be delivered from their lost state, and raised to everlasting life. Is. 55 : 1, 7; Ezek. 33 : 11; Matt. 11 : 28; Mark 6 : 12; 16 : 16; John 7 : 37; compare 5 : 40; 20 : 31; Acts 2 : 21; 3 : 19; 10 : 43; 16 : 30, 31; 26 : 20; Rom. 10 : 8–12; Rev. 21 : 6; 22 : 17.

CHAPTER IV.

THE FUTURE WORLD.

THE death of the body is one of the consequences of sin, appointed to all men, as the dividing line between the present and the unseen world—between the season of grace and that of justice—between probationary and retributive existence; introducing the soul immediately into that state of joy or of sorrow, for which it is prepared by the actions of this life. Gen.

3 : 19; Eccl. 12 : 7; Heb. 9 : 27; Matt. 13 : 39, 49; Luke 16 : 22–24.

All that science and philosophy can prove respecting death, is, that it interrupts the present form of man's physical organic existence. Setting Scripture aside, the final destruction of the body could by no means be proved from anything which is known of death, much less the extinction of the soul. But it is from the Scriptures alone, that certain knowledge can be obtained of the condition of men after death.

Sect. 1. *Resurrection.*

At the end of the world all the dead will be raised by a special exertion of the power of God. The righteous will come forth with incorruptible, because spiritual, bodies, glorious like that of Christ. 1 Thess. 4 : 15–17; Job 19 : 26, 27; Matt. 12 : 26; John 5 : 28, 29; Acts 24 : 15; 1 Cor. 15 : *passim;* Phil. 3 : 21.

All things are possible with God. It is as reasonable to believe in the possibility of a resurrection as in the actual existence of men now, of the world, or of spiritual beings. It is easy to see that the same Power who gave them one form of existence, can also give them another. It is true in science that no particle of matter is annihilated; the account of the creation, and all miracles, show that changes in matter entirely beyond the power and the comprehension of men, are produced by the immediate exertion of the will of God. Gen. 1 : 3, 11, &c., John 2 : 9. So in the operations of nature, the kernel of wheat dies, and from its death a plant springs up to life; the insect produces an egg, the egg becomes a caterpillar, the caterpillar a chrysalis, and the chrysalis an insect. None but Almighty Power could do this; the same power can raise the dead, or change a natural to a spiritual body—can cause this mortal to put on immortality.

Sect. 2. *The Judgment.*

When all the dead shall have been raised, and the living changed, they will be brought before the judgment-seat of Christ, who will declare on each and every individual of the human race, a sentence according to his character and actions in this world, which will then be consumed by fire. 1 Cor. 15 : 51; Eccl. 12 : 14; Matt. 12 : 36, 37; 25 : 31–46; Acts 17 : 31; Rom. 2 : 12, 16; 14 : 10, 12; 2 Cor. 5 : 10; 2 Pet. 3 : 7, 10–12; Rev. 20 : 12, 13.

Although the characters of all men are always perfectly known to God, and although at death their state is unchangeably fixed, yet the Scriptures speak of the judgment as the last day, in which God will bring the affairs of this world to a close, exhibit the righteousness of his dealings with his creatures by making known to men and to angels his decisions, and by making a discovery of men's true characters to one another, and to the universe.

The Scriptures also inform us that a full and final separation from the wicked will take place at the last judgment. Matt. 25 : 31–46. This truth is illustrated by the treatment of the fallen angels. 2 Pet. 2 : 4.

Sect. 3. *Future State of the Righteous.*

The saints, or believers in Christ, will be received into heaven, where they will dwell forever, freed from all sin, pain, sorrow, and death; being perfectly holy and happy in the presence of God, and the society of holy beings. Ps. 16 : 11; 17 : 15; Dan. 12 : 2; Matt. 25 : 34, 46; John 14 : 2, 3; 17 : 24; 2 Cor. 5 : 1; 1 Thess. 4 : 17; Rev. 7 : 15–17.

Of the nature, the certainty, and the eternity of the future happiness of the righteous, several views may be taken. As, 1. They are far more happy in the present life, with all their trials, persecutions, and self-denials, than the unconverted. 2. Their happiness is, from its nature, durable; while the pleasures of sin are transient. The certainty of it rests on experience which cannot deceive, and on the veracity of God, who cannot lie. 4. The immensity of it is evident from the striking figures in which the Scriptures speak of it, and from the fact that they declare it cannot be described in human language, nor conceived of by men. 5. The sufferings and death of the Son of God to procure it, prove the certainty, and the inconceivable greatness of the eternal bliss of the redeemed.

The language of the Scriptures authorizes the expectation that the number who will enjoy the bliss of heaven, surpasses human power to compute. What proportion it will bear to the number who will be lost, we are not authorized to inquire. Luke 13 : 23–30.

Sect. 4. *Future State of the Wicked.*

All who die impenitent, having never been born of the Spirit, will be shut out of heaven, and be banished from God into the place of torment, from which there can be no escape, where their sufferings will be inconceivably great, and will never end; yet those who shall be found guilty of rejecting Christ will be punished with much greater severity. See Sect. 4, chap. 2; Luke 13 : 3; John 8 : 21, 24, 44, 47; 3 : 5, 18, 36; Rev. 21 : 27; 2 Thess. 1 : 9; Luke 16 : 23, 26; Mark 3 : 29; Jude 7; Luke 12 : 47; compare Heb. 10 : 28–31; Matt. 26 : 24.

Texts which declare that the sin against the Holy Ghost will never be forgiven. Matt. 12 : 31, 32; Mark 3 : 29; Luke 12 : 10; 1 John 5 : 16; Heb. 6 : 4–6; 10 : 26, 27.

Passages in which the eternity of heaven and hell are contrasted. Dan. 12 : 2; Matt. 25 : 46.

Those which declare the eternity of future punishment negatively, by denying that they will have an end. Mark 9 : 43–48.

An unshaken confidence in the truth and righteousness of

this doctrine, is an essential part of Christian character. To reject it, is to deny the plain testimony of God, turn the Gospel into a fable, and the toils and sufferings of Prophets, Apostles, and even of Jesus Christ himself, into contempt.

No inference can be drawn from the endless punishment of the wicked against the infinite goodness of God; for we know from experience, that sin and suffering are permitted in this world, and must, therefore, in the future world, be consistent with the Divine benevolence. "Shall not the Judge of all the earth do right?"

Nor can any inference be drawn from the Scriptural doctrine that God is love, against this doctrine; because transgressions of the moral, and even of the natural laws, are punished with great severity in this world; and it is reasonable to believe that neglect of Christ would be punished with greater severity than any other sin.

CHAPTER V.

POSITIVE INSTITUTIONS.

"MORAL *precepts*," says Butler, "are precepts, the reasons of which we see; positive *precepts* are precepts, the reasons of which we do not see. Moral *duties* arise out of the nature of the case itself, prior to external command. Positive *duties* do not arise out of the nature of the case, but from external command. Moral and positive precepts are in some respects alike, in other respects different. So far as they are alike, we discern the reasons of both; so far as they are different, we discover the reasons of the former, but not of the latter."*

This distinction is very just. The obligation to love and worship our Creator is a *moral* duty, arising from the nature of the

* Analogy, Part II, Chapter I.

case; but whether we ought to devote one day in seven to this duty, or more, or less, we could not know without a positive, or revealed command. That we ought to consecrate ourselves to God, is a reasonable *moral* duty; but whether we ought to do it by baptism, or in some other way, we could not have known without a *positive* command from God. After the command is given, and the form of obedience prescribed, we may be able to discover some of the reasons for it, as well as the appropriateness of the form to teach some spiritual truth, yet our obligation to obey, does not depend at all on our own discovery of the reasons for the command, nor the fitness of the action, but on the proof that the command is from God.

Positive duties are necessarily matter of revelation purely, while moral duties are not only made the subjects of revealed command, but are also written upon the human conscience, and are taught by the light of nature. Should circumstances render obedience either to a positive institution, or the performance of a moral duty impossible, the latter is always to be preferred to the former; as, when the healing of the sick, or the satisfying of hunger, conflicts with the strict command respecting the observance of the Sabbath, our Saviour has decided in favor of moral duties. "I will have mercy, and not sacrifice." Obedience to positive precepts is sometimes rendered impossible by outward circumstances, as in the case of the penitent thief, who, while on the cross, believed in the Saviour, but was not baptized; because obedience to that ordinance was rendered impossible, by the fact that his body was nailed to the cross.

Yet we should be exceedingly thoughtless and wicked, to take occasion from these facts to neglect any positive institution of religion. We are not appointed to be judges of the relative value and importance of the various duties which God has enjoined. For, to use the language of the same judicious writer and profound thinker, "our obligations to obey all God's commands whatever, are absolute and indispensable; and commands merely positive, admitted to be from Him, lay us under a moral obligation to obey them; an obligation moral in the strictest and most proper sense."

The Mosaic Dispensation was a positive institution, founded, chiefly, on mutable relations and circumstances, which existed in the condition and wants of the human race at that time. It was, therefore, of such a nature that it might be repealed when it had fulfilled its purposes. Accordingly, we are taught that it was done away when the Christian Dispensation commenced. Heb. 10 : 9; 2 Cor. 3 : 7–11; Gal. 3 : 19, 24, 25; Eph. 2 : 14–16. But moral laws, founded in the nature of things, or on immutable relations between God and his creatures, or between man and man, are immutable, and cannot be abrogated. But while the Mosaic Dispensation was in force, obedience to every part of it was a sacred and indispensable duty.

It must not be forgotten, that disobedience of a positive precept of God to Adam, brought death into the world, and all our woe. So the way and the conditions of salvation come to us much in the form of positive, revealed commands of God. "Repent ye, and believe the Gospel." "Believe on the Lord Jesus Christ and thou shalt be saved." "Repent and be baptized every one of you, in the name of Jesus Christ." And salvation is promised on condition of obedience to both these commands. "He that believeth and is baptized shall be saved." God has not informed us which is the more important to be obeyed, the command to believe, or to be baptized, when both are equally in our power; and for us to disparage either is unwarrantable presumption.

As the obligation to obey a positive institution rests entirely on the revealed command of God, and not on our own perceptions of its appropriateness, or of the general fitness of things; it requires *literal*, as well as *sincere* obedience. No authority but that of the Supreme Lawgiver, can change the form of an ordinance, or positive institution of religion, in the smallest particular. The power to change a positive institution involves the power to abrogate entirely. God, only, possesses this power. It has never been delegated to any of his creatures.

Obedience to a positive institution of God, therefore, consists in two things: First, the *spirit* of sincere obedience; in which the understanding, the conscience, and the heart, unite their full assent. It is the province of the understanding to determine whether the command is from God, and in what form obedience is required, but not to inquire into the propriety of the action enjoined, nor whether some other act or form will not do as well; it is the province of conscience to recognize the supreme authority of the Lawgiver, and to impel implicit obedience; while the heart, moved by ardent love to Christ, consecrates the whole. Second, the *literal doing* of the specific *action* which is enjoined. Some other action than that commanded, or some other form observed as a substitute, on the ground that no mere outward form can be, in itself, essential to salvation, is not, and from the nature of the case cannot be, obedience to a positive institution of Christ. Sincere obedience, growing out of love, and the literal performance of the thing commanded, are both essential.

SECT. 1. *The Sabbath.*

1. At the creation, God blessed, sanctified, and set apart one day in seven, to be observed by the whole human race as a day of rest from labor, and to be devoted to religious duties. Gen. 2 : 1–3, compare Ex. 31 : 17. The necessity of one day in seven as a day of rest is also illustrated by experience; so that the principle seems to be founded in the nature of things, though revealed as a positive command.

2. The precept for the observance of the Sabbath is incorporated in the moral law, all the precepts of which are binding on all men, at all times. Ex. 26 : 8–11; Lev. 23 : 3, compare Acts 15 : 21; Neh. 13 : 15–21; Is. 56 : 2–6. Jer. 17 : 24, 25. It is therefore, of perpetual force.

3. At the resurrection of our Saviour, the particular day on which the Sabbath is to be kept, was changed, in such a way, that, while the design in its observance is the same, the obligation to keep it holy is rendered still more impressive. Concerning this change it may be observed, 1. Christ possessed, and claimed, authority to regulate the observance of the Sabbath, in all respects, as he saw fit. Mark 2 : 28 ; Luke 6 : 5. 2. His example, and the grounds of his defences against the charge of violating the Sabbath, prove that he had no intention to abolish, but to vindicate it from superstitious abuses, and restore it to its original design. 3. The resurrection of Christ from the dead, is incomparably the greatest event connected with the history of this world. If the finishing of the work of creation was worthy to be commemorated by a Sabbath, surely the resurrection of Christ, the finishing act in the great work of redemption, was much more so. 4. His example in meeting his disciples for religious instruction on the first, instead of the seventh day, as before, plainly indicates his purpose to change the day. Matt. 28 : 9 ; Luke 24 : 34, 18 ; John 20 : 19, 26. 5. On this day, at the festival of Pentecost, the Spirit was poured out in so remarkable a manner and degree. Acts 2 : 1–21. 6. It is evident that the Apostles knew the day to be changed, for they met the disciples for worship, and to celebrate the Lord's Supper on the first day of the week. 1 Cor. 16 : 1, 2 ; Acts 20 : 7 ; Rev. 1 : 10. As they were Jews, it is evident they would have met on the seventh day for these solemn observances, had not the Lord Jesus instructed them to meet on the first day. They also taught that the disciples were not under obligation to keep the seventh day. Col. 2 : 16, 17.

The sum of the teaching of the Scriptures, respecting this positive institution of religion, appears to be : 1. God has, from the beginning of the world, required men to devote one-seventh part of the time to religious purposes. 2. The particular day first fixed upon—the seventh—was selected as commemorative of the completion of the work of creation, particularly that of man, the last and noblest of all, then sinless and holy. 3. The institution was reaffirmed before the giving of the law, showing that it was intended for the whole race of *fallen* men. 4. The observance of the Sabbath on the *seventh day* was enjoined on the Jews, in the most solemn manner, in the ten commandments. 5. In other parts of the Jewish law, some special observances were enjoined on that people respecting the manner of keeping the day, which were intended for no other people. 6. In our Saviour's time the Jews had greatly perverted the institution, by self-righteous and superstitious additions. 7. Christ possessed full power to change the day, or the manner of keeping it, or to abolish the Sabbath altogether. 8. In the exercise of His supreme authority, He, while on earth, abolished a part of that law of the Sabbath which was given to Moses, but confirmed and perpetuated the original institution. 9. After his resurrection, instead of meeting his disciples on the seventh day for religious purposes, as he had done before, he met them on the first day. 10. The Apostles met for worship, and to break bread, on the first day. 11. They called it the "Lord's day." 12. They were evidently instructed by our Lord himself to do so. 13. They teach us that the Jewish, or seventh day Sabbath, is abolished. 14. They evidently intended to transmit the resurrection day of Jesus, as the true sacred day to Christians.

It is the duty, therefore, of all persons to abstain from labor, either by themselves, or those under their care; and from pleasure on the Lord's day, the first day of the week, and to devote it sacredly and entirely to religious improvement and worship. "God sanctified it," that is, set it apart from a common to a sacred use. 'Remember to keep it holy,' or to consecrate it all to the service and worship of God. The example of our Lord, and his Apostles shows that the public worship of God formed an essential and important part of the duties of this day.

Sect. 2. *Baptism.*

There are two symbolic ordinances, or sacraments, in the kingdom of Christ, which are of universal and perpetual obligation on all believers, and Christian churches. These are, Baptism, and the Lord's Supper. Both are positive institutions; the obligation to obedience arising from the fact that they are of Divine appointment. The proof that they are so, must, from the nature of the case, be derived from the Scriptures alone.

I. The nature of baptism. We find, by comparing Luke 3 : 2, 3 with John 1 : 33, that baptism was instituted by John the Baptist, in obedience to the express command of God, then first revealed to him. It was confirmed by the example, Matt. 3 : 13–17; Mark 1 : 9–11; Luke 3 : 21; John 4 : 1; and command, Matt. 28 : 19; Mark 16 : 16; of the Lord Jesus Christ; and thus established to be a standing ordinance of Christianity to the end of time. Being a positive institution, it requires literal, as well as sincere obedience. A specific duty is enjoined on the believer. The obligation to perform it, arises, not from our discovery of its fitness, or significancy, or its utility, but from the plain, express command of Christ alone. To substitute any other action in the place of that which is commanded, is to impugn the wisdom, and to set aside the authority of the Supreme Lawgiver. No other action, or outward rite, than the one which is commanded, whatever that is, can be baptism; because the command to believers to be baptized, always has for its object the performance of a certain specific *action;* which action, and nothing else, constitutes baptism. The power to substitute some other act, form, or rite, involves the power to abolish the ordinance entirely.

Baptism, the first of the two Christian sacraments, is the prescribed form of that public vow, or oath of consecration to Christ, which is enjoined on every believer. A Christian sacrament is a silent language of symbols; or of actions expressive of the leading facts, and fundamental truths, in the way of salvation by Christ. Unlike any written or spoken language, it is in its nature universal and unchangeable; while the meaning of *words*, written or spoken, is limited to one nation or tribe of men, and is ever changing. Had the prescribed vow of public consecration to Christ, been enjoined in words only, the meaning would have been plain to but one people, and by the constant changes of language, would soon have ceased to convey the original meaning even to them. But the meaning of a symbolic action, not only remains unchanged by the mutations of language—the symbol speaks a *universal language;* and conveys the same meaning to people of all nations and tongues, and of every age.

Actions, too, speak the feelings of the heart in a *plainer* language than words; even when the latter are fully intelligible. Solemnly impressive and deeply instructive as the *words* of Christ are, his ACTIONS are much more so. The most important and affecting of these are, "that Christ *died* for our sins, according to the Scriptures, that he was *buried*, and that he *rose again*, the third day, according to the Scriptures."—1 Cor. 15 : 3, 4.

These actions of the Saviour, the Scriptures teach us, are symbolized in baptism. Rom. 6 : 4; Col. 2 : 12. Whenever and wherever this ordinance is administered, it is designed to proclaim to the world the sublime and joyful truth, that Jesus died for our sins, was buried, and rose again. These, his actions, are also of infinitely more importance to the world than his words; for, without them, the words of the Prophets would have been falsified, and his own teachings rendered of no avail. It is fitting and necessary that the actions of Christ, on which the fulfilment of Scripture and the salvation of men depended, should be symbolized and their memory perpetuated by an expressive corresponding action on the part of believers, to the end of time.

A certain specific and definite outward *action*, therefore, belongs to the nature of baptism. The thing which is essential to its validity—that which constitutes it baptism, and without which there can be no baptism—is, THE ACTION, sincerely performed; and not the quality of the administrator, or of the liquid employed. The utility of baptism, as a public ordinance of religion, consists in its power to symbolize, and to exhibit impressively the great facts and truths in the plan of redemption by Christ; consequently if the outward form, or action, be changed, something else than baptism is substituted in its place, and it is no longer baptism.

The Scriptures further teach us, respecting the nature of baptism, that it is not only symbolic of what Christ *is* to them, and has done for them, in his own person, but of what believers are themselves to *be*, and to *do*. As he has died for their sins, and is risen again for their justification, so they are required to be dead to sin, and to rise to a new and holy life. This they solemnly profess in baptism; and this, baptism is designed and adapted to express. Rom. 6 : 4; Col. 2 : 12. These passages teach us that baptism symbolizes the death, burial, and resurrection of the believer; corresponding by an expressive emblem, to the literal death, burial, and resurrection, of the Son of God. In these two things consists its nature, as an ordinance, or positive institution, of Christ.

Baptism is, then, the divinely appointed form of ratifying God's covenant of grace with every believer. Christ is the real baptizer; for although he never administered baptism with his own hands, yet as the ordinance is performed by his servants, acting in his behalf, in obedience to his command, and in imitation of his example, it is Christ's act, John 4 : 1, 2, compare 3 : 22; and is in its nature a pledge, on his part, of spiritual blessings to the believer who sincerely assumes, and faithfully fulfils the conditions of this covenant, or enactment of grace: on the part of the recipient, it is a solemn assent to every part of that covenant, expressing more forcibly than words could do, the feelings of a penitent, in receiving free forgiveness, spiritual cleansing, life, and the hope of heaven. It is then,

ON THE PART OF THE SAVIOUR.

1. A sovereign command, ordinance, or enacted law. He gave it as "Head over all things to the church," and as possessing, and exercising supreme Divine authority. Matt. 28 : 18, 19; 11 : 27; Eph. 1 : 22; Col. 1 : 16–18. He joined obedience to this command with the promise of salvation; Mark 16 : 16; Acts 2 : 37, 38; and what God "hath joined, let no man put asunder." Baptism, presented to the mind of the convert simply as a test of submission and obedience to Christ's authority, with no other assigned reason, is well adapted to impress the truth that he is King, and Lord of all.

2. The appointed token, and pledge of the *remission* of sin. Mark 1 : 4. As baptism is, on the part of the believer, a confession of sin, and as forgiveness is promised to those only who confess their sins in Christ's appointed way, 1 John 1 : 9, 10; it is spoken of in the Scriptures as the specific act of outward public obedience, in connection with which the forgiveness of the believer is promised and declared. Acts 2 : 38.

3. It represents, and impressively illustrates the Divine agency employed in cleansing, renewing, and sanctifying, guilty, but penitent sinners. As water cleanses the body from defilement, and was

ON THE PART OF THE BELIEVER.

1. An acknowledgment of the rightful mastership, the universal, unlimited authority of the Lord Jesus Christ; of his perfect right to require any and every form of obedience which he pleases. The faith of Abraham was made perfect by simple, uninquiring, unhesitating obedience to a known command of God, even when he was not only unable to see any reason for it, but when many against it must have occurred to his mind. Gen. 32 : 1–14; Rom. 4 : 18–22. It is obedience to the ordinance of baptism, in the same spirit which renders it "the answer of a good conscience toward God." 1 Pet. 3 : 21.

2. A public, solemn *confession* of sin. Matt. 3 : 6, 8; Mark 1 : 5; Luke 3 : 3, compare Lev. 4 : 4, 15, 24, 29, 33. In the expressive symbolic action of baptism, the penitent sinner sets forth before the world the deplorable truth of his sinfulness before God, of which he has become deeply convicted, is sincerely sorry, and which he earnestly desires to break off by repentance, and that he hopes to be forgiven. Acts 13 : 24, 38.

3. A full admission, and clear recognition of the grand Scriptural doctrine, that the sins of the soul are the things which really defile a man. Compare Mark 7 : 20–23, with Lev. 10 : 10; 15 : 31. By

appointed to symbolize the cleansing from the spiritual defilements represented under the ceremonies of the Mosaic law, Ex. 29 : 4; Lev. 11 : 32; 17 : 16, etc., compare Acts 22 : 16; Heb, 6 : 2; 9 : 10; the believer is baptized in water, to denote that cleansing of the soul which is effected by the Holy Spirit, and is promised in connection with baptism, Acts 2 : 38; 19 : 5, 6; through the efficiency of the great atonement made by Christ, to which all the typical cleansings and purifications under the law had ultimate reference, and which imparted to them all their value and significancy. Heb. 10 : 4, 9, 14, 22; 9 : 11–14.

4. It represents the *entireness* of that spiritual cleansing, co-extensive with the total pollution of the sinner, which is promised to the obedient believer in Christ in that covenant of which baptism is the visible sign and ratifying pledge. The Saviour gave a solemn promise to his disciples of a baptism in the Holy Spirit, of which that received by the disciples of John in Jordan was an emblem; Matt. 3 : 11; Mark 1 : 8; Acts 1 : 5; which promise was literally fulfilled, Acts 2 : 2–4, compare 10 : 44; 11 : 15.

5. It is the symbol of the raising up to a new, innocent, holy life, the penitent believer who was before dead *in* sin, but is now dead *to* sin; in doing which, by the hand of his minister, the Saviour illustrating and enforcing this impressive truth, "the law was our schoolmaster to bring us to Christ;" and accordingly we find, that when the Lord in a vision sent Ananias to Saul, he came to him and said, "Arise, and be baptized, and wash away thy sins:" a form of speech forcible in itself, but especially so to men so intimately acquainted with Hebrew customs, and with those Scriptures with which the same idea is closely interwoven. By his baptism, Saul confessed, that notwithstanding his scrupulous observance of the law, Acts 22 : 3; 23 : 1; Phil. 3 : 6; he was still defiled with sin, till cleansed by Christ.

4. It is a confession by the believer of the humiliating truth also taught in the Scriptures, that this sinful defilement is *total*, having infected soul and body, from the crown of the head to the sole of the foot,—Ex. 29 : 20. *See above*, Chap. 2, Sect. 3. Rom. 8 : 7, 8, Compare Deut. 27 : 26, with James 2 : 10. As the sinfulness of men is total, so must be its confession; when that confession is made by means of a symbolic action, the action must be such as will represent the total sinfulness which is confessed.

5. As baptism is a figure of the overwhelming sufferings of Christ, Matt. 20 : 22; Luke 12 : 50; and of his burial in the grave, Rom. 6 : 3, 4; after his death for sinners, the believer, in the act of baptism,

gives this as the token of reprieve from the condemnation to eternal death, in which sin had involved him. Col. 2 : 12 ; Rom. 6 : 8, 9, 10. As He has in this impressive ordinance raised the believer's body from the image of *literal* death, in which it was while buried beneath the baptismal waters; he has ordained baptism to be the token and promise of spiritual grace, to enable the believer to "walk in newness of life."

6. Baptism presents to the believer the sufferings and death of an atoning Saviour, as his only ground of hope for acceptance with God, in the form of a visible pledge that his sins shall never be mentioned to his shame, nor be remembered for his condemnation, at the final judgment.—Mark 16 : 16 ; John 5 : 24 ; 6 : 40.

7. It is the appointed act of obedience in which the sincere believer is assured of the gift of the Holy Spirit to subdue his sinful affections, to quicken his faith and love, that he may overcome the world, grow in grace, and in the knowledge of Christ, and adorn his profession by a holy life. Acts 2 : 38 ; 16 : 34.

acknowledges that he deserves all from which that death delivers him —the overwhelming sorrows of eternal death ; Rom. 5 : 9 ; 1 Thess. 1 : 10 ; and in being raised up, signifies his faith in the resurrection of Christ from the dead, in His ability to deliver him from the power of spiritual death, and to enable him to live a new life of obedience, righteousness, and true holiness. Phil. 3 : 10 ; 2 Cor. 5 : 14, 15, 17, 21.

6. It is a public profession of faith in Jesus Christ, as the Son of God, the only Saviour of sinners, who by his perfect obedience, and vicarious death, has met all the demands of eternal justice, obtained forgiveness of sins, and the gift of eternal life for every believer. Gal. 3 : 24–27 ; Acts 2 : 41 ; 8 : 12, 37 ; 18 : 8 ; 1 Pet. 2 : 24 ; 3 : 18.

7. It is a solemn form of consecration to Christ, to love, serve, and trust in him, to forsake all sin, to live soberly, righteously, and godly, in confident expectation of perfect holiness and felicity when He shall appear the second time, "to be glorified in his saints, and to be admired by all them that believe." Rom. 6 : 1–14 ; 1 Cor. 12 : 13.

Being thus in its nature a spiritual service intended for and adapted to those only who are born of the Spirit, it conveys no benefit to others. As it is the initiatory ordinance into the kingdom of Christ, and a public assumption of the obligations of Christianity, it introduces the recipient into some Christian church. Performed by a pastor, pursuant to a vote of the church, baptism is the introductory rite to its fellowship, privileges, and duties. Performed by an evangelist or missionary, where no church exists, its initiatory obligations and meaning, equally strong, are prospective. It prepares, and lays the recipient under obligation to enter into church covenant relation, with others who may in like manner be prepared to enter with him into that relation.

II. Subjects. The nature of baptism requires that the subjects of the rite be persons capable of intelligent and responsible action. Being enjoined as an act of obedience, it is of course binding on those only who can perceive and feel the obligation to obey. There is no command to bring, carry, or force, any class of persons to be baptized; no one class, not even ministers, much less parents, are held responsible for the baptism of any other class. There is no command, to *any one* to *carry* infants to be baptized, nor any example of it in the Scriptures. The command which creates obligation to be baptized, is in all cases directed to those whose duty it is to *receive* the rite. The Scriptures contain but one passage which commands even ministers themselves to baptize, and then it is expressly limited to those who have previously been made disciples, and who, if obedient, would request to be admitted to the ordinance. Matt. 28 : 19.

It is further evident, from the plain declarations of Scripture, that none but believers in Christ should be baptized.

1. From the Saviour's commission to his ministers in Matt. 28 : 19; Mark 16 : 15, 16. This authorizes the baptism of believers, and of no others. The minister who goes beyond this violates, and forfeits his commission.

2. The numerous examples of baptism in the New Testament. John the Baptist required repentance and faith in the coming Messiah, as qualifications for baptism. Matt. 3 : 5–17; Luke 3 : 3–9; Acts 19 : 4. On the day of Pentecost, "They that *gladly received his word*, were baptized." Acts 2 : 41. At

Samaria, "When they *believed* Philip preaching the things concerning the kingdom of God, and the name of Jesus Christ, they were baptized, both *men* and *women*."—8 : 12. "What doth hinder me to be baptized? If thou *believest* with all thy heart thou mayest."—8 : 37. Other examples of the same kind might be cited, but these are sufficient.

3. The Scriptures contain no precept or example which authorizes the baptism of any persons but believers. This is fully admitted by the most eminent theological writers, in all religious bodies. This fact alone, is sufficient to prohibit ministers from baptizing any other class of persons. There is no command prohibiting the baptism of bells and animals, as the papists do, nor is any needed by obedient Christians.

The account of the baptism of certain households, Acts 16: has been cited as implying the baptism of some who were not believers. Were a household composed entirely of believers an impossibility, this argument would be valid. But it should be remembered that four or five believing families are mentioned in the New Testament; while only three, those of Lydia, Stephanas, and the Philippian jailer, are declared to have been all baptized, and two of these are expressly mentioned as composed entirely of believers. What inference, then, is to be drawn from the circumstance that *one* family is said to have been baptized; though it is not also expressly recorded in that one case, that *all* were believers? Simply, that the latter fact is omitted; as we infer that the believing families were baptized, in those cases where this circumstance is not recorded. The commission authorized the baptism of believers only; we are to infer, therefore, that all the members of this family became believers, unless plainly told that they were not, or unless the thing be in itself impossible.*

* There were eight baptized families belonging to the Karen Baptist mission before it was as old as the Apostolic mission, at the time when the family of Lydia was baptized. The Christian Watchman, of Jan. 29, 1841, presents authentic proof of the existence, at that time, of up-

III. Objects. No spiritual grace or virtue, is conferred or transmitted by the mere ceremony of baptism. Yet it has important objects, when it is administered according to the Divine command, and received in the spirit of a true disciple, and teaches weighty lessons. The believer is baptized "in the name of the Father, and of the Son, and of the Holy Ghost;" or, by the authority, in honor of, and dedicatory to, the Creator, the Redeemer, and the Sanctifier of men. The objects are,

1. To set forth to the world, in a solemn, public act, the sovereign claims of God, to any, and to every form of obedience, submission, and love, on the part of His creatures, which He may see fit to enjoin.

2. To separate, and set apart the followers of Christ, from the world.

3. To exhibit the leading facts and doctrines in the plan of redemption, by the mediation of the Son of God.

4. To assure believers of their personal interest in the Divine promises.

5. To ratify their individual covenant with God.

6. To enable all believers, of every language, and of no language, learned and unlearned, to testify to the world their faith in a crucified, buried, and risen Saviour.

7. To form the initiating token, and visible badge of church fellowship.

IV. Administrator. The commission to baptize was given to the first teachers of the Gospel, as such; Matt. 28 : 19; and was exercised by them, whether Apostles or evangelists. 1 Cor. 1 : 14; Acts 8 : 12, 38; 9 : 17, 18; 10 : 48. No instance of baptism by any person, not a minister of the Gospel, is given in the New Testament; nor is there any precept which determines the qualifications of an administrator of the rite. It is, therefore, Scriptural and proper, that the ordinance be performed by the

wards of *fifty baptized households,* connected with Baptist churches, *every member* of whom was baptized on profession of faith, and added to the church.

regular ministers of the Gospel, in all cases, if possible. Yet, if no minister can be obtained, or in places where there is a general departure from the true form, a pious layman, acting with the approbation and in behalf of the church, might, as a matter of necessity, baptize. The *essence* of baptism is, the immersion of a believer, in the name of the Father, and of the Son, and of the Holy Ghost, performed in all decency, and good sincerity, as an act of obedience to Christ. The character of the administrator cannot invalidate baptism, where these essential requisites unite.

It is, therefore, customary with our churches, to receive to membership, persons who have been baptized, on a profession of faith, by ministers who are considered unbaptized. If these persons received the rite in good faith, as an act of obedience to Christ, there is no cause for repeating it. If they were not baptized *as believers*, and if it is doubtful whether they were believers or not, and they are not satisfied with their baptism, they should receive the ordinance as if no such ceremony had taken place. But if they have been baptized as believers, on a profession of their faith, the rite should not be repeated.

V. Circumstances. Every church should have a convenient place for baptizing, provided with a sufficient quantity of pure water. In large cities, baptisteries within the houses of worship, are necessary; but in places where a river, pond, or canal, is easy of access, it is customary to resort to them. Regard should be had to the convenience of spectators, and to every circumstance which affects the solemnity and impressiveness of the scene.

Singing, and prayer, with an address to the spectators, if convenient, should form a part of the services, all of which should be in the highest degree solemn and devotional.

The length of time which should intervene between conversion and baptism, depends on the circumstances in the case of each individual. A reasonable time should be taken to obtain satisfactory evidence that the candidate is a true convert. This satisfaction might, in some cases, be obtained very soon;

in others, where the candidate is little known to the minister, or to the members of the church, or if his moral character has previously been bad, more time is required. In all cases it should be kept distinctly in mind, that the delay is not to ascertain how well the candidate can serve God out of the church, but to give the church time to be satisfied that he is a true convert, renewed by the Spirit of God.

SECT. 3. *Proof that Baptism is Immersion.*

That some one specific, bodily act, is enjoined on the believer, as baptism, is plain; the doing of which act, in the spirit of sincere obedience to the Lord Jesus Christ, constitutes Christian baptism. It cannot be an indefinite use of water, as a religious rite, because the command to be baptized, includes no mention of the liquid to be employed. We learn, from examples only, with the incidental circumstances recorded in the New Testament, that it was water. The command directs the believer's mind—not to the liquid to be used, nor to the character and qualifications of the administrator; but solely to the *act* which he, in the spirit of obedience, is to *do;* the doing of which act, and nothing else, is baptism. The force of the command, "be baptized," is directed, therefore, solely to the symbolic action which is appointed by the King of kings, to be the unchangeable token of separation to the Christian faith.

Can we ascertain what *action* this is? And is the proof sufficient to render the duty to perform that specific action, instead of any other, obligatory on the conscience of every disciple? If not, then baptism, as a positive institution of Christianity, is lost. If we cannot ascertain what baptism is, we have no right to substitute something else in its room; for this was the sin of Nadab, and Abihu, who "offered strange fire before the Lord, which he commanded them not." If we cannot ascertain what we are required to *do*, as baptism, we are absolved from all obedience to the command; if we can, then we are held accountable for the doing of it, literally. Baptism is as essential to salvation as any other duty which we can as easily understand and perform, and which is enjoined with equal solemnity and distinctness.

That the action required, as baptism, is the immersion of the body of the believer, is evident from the following, among many other reasons.

1. The Greek word, *baptizo*, which is always used to designate the rite, signifies *immerse.* It was uniformly employed in that sense, in classic and scientific writings hundreds of years before the New Testament was written. The lexicons all define the word, "to dip, to plunge, to immerse." "All lexicographers, and critics, of any note," says Prof. Stuart, "are agreed in this." Says Dr. Campbell, "It is always construed suitably to this meaning." Stourdza, a native Greek, says, "*Baptizo* has but one signification. It signifies, literally, and invariably, *to plunge.*" Bretschneider, who is considered the most critical lexicographer of the New Testament, says: "An entire immersion belongs to the nature of baptism." "This is the meaning of the word." Here is the testimony of four eminent, and impartial critics; a Greek, a German, a Scotchman, and an American; not one of whom is by profession a Baptist; and hundreds of the same kind might be added.

That the word was used in this sense by the classical writers, is fully shown by Stuart, Carson, Ripley, and others, and is not disputed.

In the Septuagint, a Greek version of the Old Testament, and in the Apocrypha, it is used in the same sense.

No instance has been proved of the use of this word in the sacred and classical writings, in all its literal and figurative applications, where it is not properly construed in accordance with the primary meaning of immersion.

It would be easy to fill a volume with quotations from eminent writers, who are not Baptists, of the same import as this specimen from Calvin: "The very word *baptize* signifies immerse, and it is certain that immersion was the practice of the ancient church."

2. The circumstances incidentally mentioned in connection with the instances of baptism, clearly imply immersion. The places selected, whenever mentioned, are in all cases adapted to immersion. John baptized "in Jordan," Matt. 3 : 6 ; "in the river of Jordan," Mark 1 : 5. The reason assigned why "John was baptizing in Enon, near to Salim," is, "*because* there was much water there." As if to prevent the possibility of misunderstanding, we are told for what purpose the water was used; "they came and were baptized." John 3 : 23.

In the case of the Ethiopian, the circumstantial minuteness of the account admits of no reasonable doubt that he was immersed. "They came to a certain water." This is the occasion of his request to be baptized. "And they *went down both into the water*, both Philip and the Eunuch, and he baptized him." Then, they "came *up out of the water*." If the meaning of the word *baptizo* were doubtful, such an example as this should settle it in the minds of candid men. No instance is mentioned of baptism in the synagogue, or on a mountain; no mention is made of water being *brought* to the place of administration for the purpose of baptism.

3. The uniform practice of the Christian world, for several centuries, and of large portions to the present day, shows in what sense the command was understood. On this point, the testimony of ecclesiastical historians, of the first order, as Mosheim, Neander, and Gieseler, is unanimous, and overwhelming, that immersion was the practice.

Among the Greeks, in whose language the New Testament was written, it is well known that immersion is uniformly practised to the present day; whether infants or adults are the subjects.

Says Prof. Stuart,* after exhibiting numerous proofs that the early churches, after the times of the Apostles, practised immer-

* Bib Rep., vol. iii, p. 59.

sion, "But enough. 'It is,' says Augusti, 'a thing made out,' viz., the ancient practice of immersion. So indeed all the writers who have thoroughly investigated this subject, conclude. I know of no one usage of ancient times, which seems to be more clearly and certainly made out. I cannot see how it is possible for any candid man, who examines the subject, to deny this."

SECT. 4. *Duty of a Church in regard to Baptism.*

It is certain, then, that the Saviour commanded believers, and no others, to be baptized—a word which then conveyed a definite meaning, about which there was no dispute—and that he required the performance of a well-known, significant action. It is highly improper to suppose that the Saviour would employ a word of doubtful, or equivocal import, in circumstances so solemn. The practice of the Apostles, and early Christians, leaves no doubt in what sense they understood the command. No doctrine of the Scriptures admits of clearer proof, than that immersion is the baptism commanded, and exemplified, by our Saviour; not a practice of the early churches, can be more fully made out. Indeed, so full is the proof, that the immersion of a believer, in the name of Father, Son, and Holy Ghost, is undoubted baptism, that this point is universally conceded, even by those who do not practise it.

What, then, is the duty of a church respecting it? In the proper place it has been shown that each church ought to take the Scriptures for its guide, and in the exercise of its collected wisdom, humbly imploring the Spirit's teaching, to interpret and apply their doctrines and precepts to all its members, and to all who seek to become so. Thus, personal piety, or regeneration, is the essential, invariable prerequisite to church-membership. This is the point to be ascertained in the case of every candidate. 'Has this person been born again? Is the evidence which he has given to this church, sufficient to warrant his reception to our fellowship?' This question the church must, in each case, decide. In order to discharge this great trust, she must understand clearly the meaning of her Lord, "except a man be born again, he cannot see the kingdom of God."

The duty of each church to decide for itself, what are the essential doctrines and duties of Christianity, has also been shown. These doctrines, the members of the church, individually and collectively, agree to maintain and promote among themselves, in their families, and in the world. In like manner each church is bound to declare for itself, what are the ordinances of the Gospel, and how they are to be administered. They must declare what they conceive to be the meaning of the command respecting baptism, and require obedience to it, as a condition of fellowship. There is "one faith," and "one baptism," as well as "one Lord." Therefore, in accordance with the principle already established, that each church is the only authoritative interpreter of the laws of Christ for its own members, the church is required to decide what that "one baptism" is, to govern all its practices accordingly, and to make it the unalterable condition of membership. The obligation of each church to maintain the law of baptism, in its integrity, is peculiarly sacred, because that law can be so easily understood and applied, and because departure from the true practice has been the source of immense evil to the cause of Christianity.

Sect. 5. *The Lord's Supper.*

I. Its nature. This ordinance was instituted by the Lord Jesus, in person, when the event which it was to commemorate was yet future. Like baptism, its significancy was, for a time, prospective and prophetic. The following are all the passages which give an account of its origin. Matt. 26 : 26–29; Mark 14 : 22–25; Luke 22 : 19, 20; 1 Cor. 11 : 23–26. From these we learn, 1. That the broken bread is the emblem of the Saviour's body, broken on the cross, for sinners; and the wine the emblem of his shed blood. 2. That the eating of one, and the drinking of the other, are essential to this ordinance. 3. That this is a representation of the death of Christ for his people. 4. That the partaking is an expression of faith in Christ as the Saviour, who, by his blood, has made atonement for sinners. 5. That it is a token of assent to the new covenant. 6. That all Christians are under obligation to observe it. 7. That it is a standing, perpetual ordinance, till the end of the world.

Like baptism, it teaches by expressive symbols. The communicant declares his entire reliance for salvation on the atonement of Christ, and his sole dependence on him for the support of spiritual life, as natural life is sustained by food and drink. It is a spiritual feast, at which the Saviour is present, as the head of his spiritual family. Through it, he assures each member of his condescending love. The sincere communicant honors the Saviour's cross, and testifies that the blood which he spilt thereon is the only source of his peace, hope, and joy; the Saviour assures him of pardon, and eternal life, through the efficacy of his sacrifice.

II. Purposes. These appear to be twofold. First, the ordinance has public and general bearings, of the highest importance to the continuance of the Christian religion in the world. It is a standing, public, unimpeachable witness of the genuineness of the New Testament writings, and of the truth of Christianity. It is impossible to explain the existence and origin of this ordinance, but by admitting that it has come down from the Apostles, and was instituted by "the Lord Jesus, the same night in which he was betrayed." It thus stands before the world, from age to age, an infallible witness of the expiatory death of Christ, and the truth of the story of his sufferings.

In the public and general bearings of this ordinance, then, it is, 1. Commemorative. "This do in *remembrance* of me." It calls to remembrance the *person* of Christ, the fact that he came in the flesh, that he walked the earth as a man. It calls to remembrance his *teachings.* It commemorates his sufferings and death. The memory of all these things is strengthened, renewed, and perpetuated, every time this ordinance is observed. 2. It proclaims, and publishes these truths: "As often as ye eat this bread, and drink this cup, ye do *show* [i. e., publish and proclaim] the Lord's death." This important purpose of the Lord's Supper, should never be forgotten, or disparaged. The remembrance of the death of Christ should not only be refreshed in the minds of Christians, but some memorial of it should ever be kept before the world. 3. It is a solemn avowal, and united expression of love for Christ, by each individual believer, and by the church as a visible body. It is His *love* which is commemorated and proclaimed. These considerations are sufficient to show its importance. The continuance of the Christian religion is identified with this ordinance. This leads us to consider,

III. Its Obligation and Perpetuity. Its public bearings and importance render the obligation to observe it peculiarly sacred. It is the visible showing forth of Christ crucified for the sins of men. It connects us, by an unbroken chain of witnesses, with the disciples around the last paschal table, and with the weeping spectators at the cross. By it, we have more than recorded proof that the nails were driven, that Jesus was lifted up, that the spear was thrust into his side. We have a standing sign, whose origin cannot be disputed; a living symbol, transmitting the same facts from witness to witness, from the Apostles to us. The death of Christ is the most momentous event in the world's history, and its expiatory nature the most important doctrine to be substantiated. The Lord's Supper testifies to the one, and teaches the other. Wherever it is set aside, Christianity becomes extinct.

This view, rather than the hope of personal benefit, should induce every Christian faithfully to observe and sustain this ordinance, in its original simplicity and integrity. Besides, the Saviour's words are explicit. "This *do* in remembrance of me." That this command was intended for all Christians, and so understood, is evident. Acts 2 : 42; 20 : 7. That it is to be

8

continued till the end of time, is plain from 1 Cor. 11 : 25. "Ye do show the Lord's death *till he come.*"

IV. Benefits. In addition to the public bearings of this ordinance, it is the medium of conveying personal blessings to the communicant. "This cup is the new testament in my blood," Luke 22 : 19; i. e., 'This wine is the sign of the new covenant, founded in my blood.' Compare Heb. 11 : 19–22; Ex. 12 : 13; 24 : 8. The ordinance, then, is the token and pledge of the benefits of Christ's death, to the believer. "This is my body, which is given for you." The flesh of Christ is eaten, and his blood is drank, in the same sense that sin is washed away in baptism—the sign, rightly used, involves the thing signified. On the contrary, "He that eateth and drinketh unworthily, eateth and drinketh damnation to himself, not discerning the Lord's body." The enlightened Christian receives great spiritual blessings in this sacred ordinance. The Saviour meets him at his table, to nourish his faith, his hope, his love and zeal, to impart comfort, and satisfy every holy desire.

The beneficial purposes of this ordinance toward individual Christians, are, 1. It is a direct *exercise* of love to Christ. It thus strengthens the first gracious affection of the renewed soul. 2. A token of the believer's permanent union with Christ. 3. A medium, or instrument of spiritual communion with him. 4. And of the communication of the benefits of his obedience and death to us. This ordinance, therefore, can never be a means of grace to the unconverted; but its effects on them, if they presume to partake of it in their spiritual blindness, must be to increase that blindness, and add to the greatness of their condemnation. 1 Cor. 11 : 29.

V. Qualifications of Communicants. The Lord's Supper is a *church* ordinance. From its nature it requires associated observance. The command of the Saviour is, "Drink *ye* all of it." Who are included in the word *ye?* The true answer to this question settles the qualifications of communicants. First, then, evidently, the disciples then present at the table. Second, all who shall become such, "till he come." Those present were, beyond question, all baptized believers; John 4 : 1; therefore the precept extends to such only. Here another question arises: In whom is the power vested, to decide who are qualified to partake? In the same hands, evidently and necessarily, as is the duty to decide who are entitled to the previous ordinance, baptism; which prerogative, as is elsewhere shown, is committed by the Saviour, to each church.—Those whom the church admits to the table, it declares to be disciples, and endorses them, as such, before the world.

Participation in the Lord's Supper is, then, an expression of fellowship, not between the individual members, but of the church as a body, to each member. Therefore, the supposed unworthy character of some who may be permitted by the church to come to the table, is not a reason why a member should stay away. He should go, not to give scope to private opinions and personal feelings, but to commemorate the Saviour's dying love, to hold spiritual communion with him, and to show forth the Lord's death. If unworthy communicants are present, the responsibility does not rest on him, if he has done what he should to induce the church to perform its duty. It is a poor resort, to turn his back on the Saviour because an unworthy person has intruded to his table, and the church has not yet driven him away.

The correctness of these views might be shown from a variety of considerations. That communicants must be baptized believers, is evident:

1. Because the Scriptures enjoin baptism as the first duty of believers. This has been already proved.

2. None but baptized believers are mentioned in the New Testament, as admitted to this ordinance. In Acts 2, those who are said, verse 41, to have been baptized, are mentioned in verse 42, as "continuing steadfastly in the Apostles' doctrine and fellowship, and in *breaking of bread*." In 1 Cor. 10 : 16–20; 11 : 20–34, the members of the church at Corinth are addressed as

communicants; and we have elsewhere proved that none but baptized believers were members of the churches; therefore no others are scripturally qualified to partake of the Lord's Supper.

3. The nature of baptism, and of the Supper, shows that baptism should precede. In baptism, the believer declares that having become dead to sin, he is buried in water, as in a grave, from which he rises to a new spiritual life, emblematical of the Saviour's death, burial, and resurrection. The Lord's Supper is a spiritual feast, in which nourishment for the renewed soul is represented. The instructive significancy of both would be lost by reversing the order. In the first, the believer avows himself a disciple of Christ, and enters his visible family. The second is a family feast, provided for the members of that visible family.

VI. Invitations to the Lord's Table. The Lord's Supper being intended for Christians, in their church family capacity, all the members, not under censure, or any disciplinary proceedings, are entitled to participate. As they only are amenable to the discipline of the church, they are the only ones who may *claim* admission as a personal right. If others beside the members are admitted, it is by invitation. Consistency requires that invitations be given only to members of churches of the same faith and practice. No person has any cause of complaint, if a church gives no invitations. Every church has an undoubted right to omit them at all times, if, in its judgment, the purity or peace of the church will be best promoted by so doing; and every church should do so, whenever its invitations may become a cause of contention, or of jealousy. It is customary, in some churches, to invite any members of other churches who may be present and wish to participate to exhibit their testimonials to the pastor and deacons for their approval, previous to the service; in others, a general invitation to "all members of sister churches," is given.

VII. Time, place, and other circumstances. The proper administrator is an ordained minister. Respecting the frequency, no rule is laid down in the New Testament. It ought to be observed so often as best to accomplish the purposes of its institution. Once a month is a good arrangement.

The Lord's day is the most convenient and proper time. The hour is not essential. The word translated *supper*, may signify any repast. In the New Testament it is used to denote the principal meal, which was taken in the afternoon. That is the time commonly chosen by our churches.

The posture is not important. The most convenient method is to sit in the customary seats, and receive the emblems from the deacons.

The proper place, is the house in which the church meets for worship. The Lord's Supper is a public, social ordinance, and should never be administered privately, to an individual in a sick chamber. Being a church ordinance, it can be properly administered only by the authority and in the presence of a church.

SECT. 6. *Public Worship.*

Without entering upon the inquiry whether the duty of external worship can be discovered by the light of natural religion alone, it is certain that the duty of public worship is taught in the Scriptures, as a part of revealed religion. It was first enjoined in connection with the Passover. Ex. 12 : 16. It was also commanded as a part of all the Jewish festivals. Lev. 23 : 2, 4, 8, 21, 24, 27 ; Num. 28 : 25, 26 ; Ex. 23 : 14–17. Public worship on the Sabbath is enjoined as a universal and perpetual duty. Lev. 23 : 3. The same duty is taught by precept, by encouragement, by allusion, and by example, in all parts of the Scriptures. 1 Chron. 29 : 20 ; 2 Chron. 29 : 28, 19 ; Ez. 3 : 11 ; 6 : 22 ; Neh. 8 : 6, 18 ; 9 : 3, 6 ; Ps. 9 : 14 ; 2 : 25 ; 26 : 12 ; 40 : 9 ; 50 : 23 ; 65 : 1 ; 68 : 26 ; 89 : 7 ; 111 : 1 ; 149.

The duty of public worship on the Sabbath has also the sanction of the Saviour's example. Luke 6 : 6 ; 13 : 10 ; and that of the Apostles. Acts 13 : 14, 42 ; 16 : 13 ; 18 : 4. These passages, as well as the nature of the institution, show that the duty of public worship on the Sabbath, is not affected by the change of the day. Compare Acts 20 : 7 ; 1 Cor. 16 : 1, 2 The neglect of public worship is also forbidden. Heb. 10 : 25.

It is evident, from these and other passages, that audible prayer, including confession of sin, petition, intercession, and thanksgiving ; praise, expressed by singing, chanting, responses, and reverential postures of the body, formed a part of public worship.

The duty of public worship is, therefore, universal, and in its tendency beneficial to all men. Every church is required to sustain it regularly, and to provide all the necessary means to render it attractive, and in the highest degree efficacious.

The order of public worship in Baptist churches, on the Lord's day, is usually the following :

Morning. 1. Singing. 2. Reading the Scriptures. 3. Prayer. 4. Singing. 5. Sermon. 6. Prayer. 7. Benediction.

Afternoon. 1. Singing. 2. Reading the Scriptures. 3. Prayer. 4. Singing. 5. Sermon. 6. Prayer. 7. Singing. 8. Benediction.

If members are to be admitted, for the first time, to the Lord's Table, it is customary for the pastor to give them the right hand of fellowship in the presence of the whole congregation, between the afternoon sermon and the last prayer. The hymns sung, are given out and read from the pulpit. In some churches, it is customary to commence the morning services with a short prayer, called Invocation, and also to sing a hymn at the *close* of the sermon.

Sect. 7. *Preaching.*

The Scriptures inform us that although the practice of discoursing publicly on religious subjects, has existed under all the forms and dispensations of revealed religion, yet preaching was first made a positive institution by the Lord Jesus Christ. A comparison of the passages which bear most directly on the subject, establishes the following points.

1. That from the earliest times, even before the flood, and through the patriarchal dispensation, when men associated for worship, preaching was sometimes practised. Compare Gen. 5 : 24, and Heb. 11 : 5, with Jude 14, 15. See 2 Peter 2 : 5; 1 Peter 3 : 19, 20; Gen. 35 : 2, 3.

2. It was sanctioned by the example of Moses and of Joshua, and of the kings and prophets of ancient Israel, though preaching was not, under the Mosaic Dispensation, appropriated to any order of men, nor to any particular times or places. Ex. 4 : 30; Deut. 1 : 1–46; 4 : 1–49; 5 : 1; 6 : 1; 8 : 1; 9 : 1; 31 : 1; 32 : 1, 44; Joshua 24 : 1–25. Preaching was not made the special duty of the priest, and most of the preachers belonged to other tribes than that of Levi. Amos 7 : 14, 15. Preaching was one means of restoring the true worship after the return of the Jews from the Babylonish captivity. Neh. 8 : 1–18.

3. By the command of the Lord Jesus Christ, illustrated by his example, preaching became a positive institution of Christianity. Mark 16 : 15; Matt. 28 : 19; Luke 24 : 47; John 20 : 21; Matt. 4 : 17, 23; 10 : 7; 13 : 2; Mark 1 : 39; Luke 4 : 44; 6 : 20; 12 : 1; 20 : 1; 21 : 37. The example of the Apostles shows how they understood this command. Acts 2 : 14–47; 3 : 12–26; 8 : 5, 35; 10 : 34–48; 11 : 19; 13 : 5, 16, 46; 16 : 13; 17 : 2, 22; 20 : 9; Rom. 10 : 14.

4. The Scriptures teach us that preaching is the special instrumentality, appointed by God for converting men, and that it naturally precedes baptism, church-fellowship, and the Lord's Supper. Matt. 28 : 19; Mark 16 : 15, 16; Acts 2 : 41, 42; 8 : 12, 35, 36, 37, 38; 10 : 47; Rom. 10 : 17; 1 Cor. 1 : 18, 21, 23, 24; 3 : 5; 9 : 16; 2 Cor. 2 : 15; 5 : 19, 20; Tit. 1 : 3. These passages show that after converts to Christ had been made by means of preaching, they were baptized, admitted to the fellowship of the faithful, and to the table of the Lord.

5. The great theme of the Apostles' preaching, was Jesus

Christ—his example, his sufferings, death, and resurrection, his ascension and exaltation, his atonement and intercession, his supreme dignity, and his right to all the love, trust, and obedience of his people forever. Acts 2 : 36; 3 : 16, 26; 4 : 33; 5 : 31; 8 : 35; 9 : 22; 10 : 42; 13 : 38; 26 : 23; Rom. 1 : 16; 3 : 22–26; 10 : 9; 14 : 10; 1 Cor. 1 : 23; 2 : 2; 15 : 3, 4; 2 Cor. 4 : 5; 5 : 14, 21; Gal. 1 : 3–9, 11, 12; 6 : 14.

6. Preaching formed a part of the exercises of public worship on the Christian and Jewish Sabbaths, as well as on other occasions, when the disciples and others were assembled. Acts 13 : 14, 44; 16 : 13; 17 : 2; 18 : 4; 20 : 7; 2 : 1.

7. Finally, we are taught that the preaching of the Gospel, is an institution designed to continue to the end of the world. Matt. 28 : 20. It is a positive institution of perpetual obligation, because the necessity and benefits of it are, in their nature, perpetual.

Sect. 8. *Civil Government.*

Every particular form of civil government is a human institution, but the duty of yielding obedience to that under which we live, is enforced by the positive precepts of Christianity, 1 Peter 2 : 13–17, and by the example of the Saviour and his Apostles. Matt. 17 : 24–27; 22 : 21; Acts 16 : 37. We are taught that civil government is an ordinance of God, that resistance to it is resisting "the ordinance of God, and they that resist, shall receive to themselves damnation." Rom. 13 : 1–7. The duty of contributing for the support of government is also taught, verses 6, 7, and of prayer "for kings, and for all that are in authority." 1 Tim. 2 : 1, 2. Ministers are commanded to inculcate obedience to rulers and to magistrates. Titus 3 : 1. At the same time, obedience to civil rulers, is not a duty when that obedience is contrary to the commands of God. Acts 4 : 19, 20.

It is not the form of government, then, but the fact of its existence that renders obedience a duty. Every Christian should be a peaceable and quiet citizen. If he lives under a government in which he has a voice in the choice of civil rulers, he is bound to give it in favor of just men, who will rule in the fear of God. A Christian is at liberty to hold office in the State, provided its duties are not inconsistent with morality and piety.

From these passages, and from all the teachings of Scripture on the subject, it is evident that the just rights and powers of civil government are all confined to temporal matters. Civil government has no right to interfere, in the least, with religion, either with doctrines, forms of worship, the administration of ordinances, or the appointment or control of ministers. These are things which God has seen fit to leave to the free action of the human mind and the human conscience. If men under the pretence of religious zeal infringe on the rights of other citizens, they may be restrained or punished as for any other crime against the peace and order of society; but for their religious opinions and practices they are accountable to God alone.

PART III.

CHURCH GOVERNMENT.

Experience has shown that human beings cannot live together in a social capacity without government. All history proves, that a just, watchful, and vigorous civil government is always necessary, to protect the quiet from the tyranny of the ambitious, and the weak from the rapacity of the strong. Pecuniary forfeitures, and penal inflictions, are the only efficient sanctions by which such a government can be maintained.

Christian churches, being composed of persons who are professedly renewed in spiritual knowledge and in love, must also have government adapted to their circumstances and wants. Their members are enlightened and sanctified but in part; they are exposed to the example of a selfish and wicked world; they, therefore, need laws,* by which to regulate their individual conduct, to preserve order, to restrain the unruly, to define and protect the equal rights of all, so that the church may be the home of peace, the pattern of propriety, the house of God, and the gate of heaven. Besides, churches are always liable to receive unsanctified persons among their number, on whom

* "Of law there can be no less acknowledged, than that her seat is the bosom of God, her voice the harmony of the world: all things in heaven and earth do her homage, the very least as feeling her care, and the greatest as not exempted from her power; both angels and men, and creatures of what condition soever, though each in a different sort and manner, yet all, with uniform consent, admiring her as the mother of their peace and joy."—*Richard Hooker.*

affectionate Christian admonition is spent in vain. But as their government and laws are founded in persuasion and love, they can, in the execution of their severest penalty, only return the transgressor to the world, from whence he came.

As the principles on which churches should be constituted* have been exhibited, with the doctrines† which they are required to believe and to teach; the remaining point of inquiry, in order to a complete view of the whole subject, is, what form of government, or course of church order, policy, and action, grows out of these principles of church constitution, and this system of doctrine, united? For it must be obvious to every attentive reader of the New Testament, that it contains no code of enactments, specific statutes, or canons, for the exact ordering of Christian churches, like those given to the Jewish commonwealth. It makes no definite form of church government essential to the salvation of its members. Personal salvation is connected with personal holiness, and there can be no surer mark of an apostate and corrupt church, than the setting up of exclusive high church claims to efficacious grace only in connection with its own ecclesiastical arrangements, and the performances of its own ministry. That form of church government which most effectually guards purity of life, Christian liberty, private judgment, sound doctrine, and peace among the brethren and among the churches; which best promotes holy zeal, activity, self-denial, and love, while it is closely and scrupulously conformed to the precepts and examples recorded in the Scriptures, and perpetuates the ordinances inviolate, as they were originally given, is undoubtedly the best.

Yet the truth cannot be too deeply engraven on the mind and the heart of every Christian, that the least deviation from the principles or precepts of the Scriptures, respecting church polity and government, is always attended with some degree of danger to the soul, and with certain, positive injury, to the cause of the Redeemer on the earth. The common distinction

* Part I. † Part II.

between essentials and non-essentials in religion, is entirely unauthorized by Scripture, and is profane and irreligious in spirit. Our Lord declared respecting the precepts, even of the Old Testament, "Whosoever shall break one of these least commandments, and shall teach men so, he shall be called the least in the kingdom of heaven; but whosoever shall do and teach them, the same shall be called great in the kingdom of heaven." Matt. 5 : 19. Compare 1 Samuel 15 : 21, 23 ; 2 : 30. The Bible contains no non-essential, unimportant, or trifling precept, principle, doctrine, or ordinance; nor any one which men can neglect or remain in ignorance of, without peril and loss.

It is of the highest importance that church government, in its principles and rules, be thoroughly understood, not only by ministers, but by all Christians. There is no priesthood appointed by Christ to govern his people, but he has made them all to be "kings and priests unto God," to administer his laws; and he holds them accountable to himself, at last, for this most solemn and important part of their earthly stewardship. They are bound, therefore, to study diligently their duties as "fellow-citizens with the saints, and of the household of God." Those church-members who take no pains to qualify themselves for the duties of church government, that they may perform their part in sustaining the discipline, the order, and the dignity of the church, are mere drones in the hive—dead weights for others to carry. The Apostle, in reproving the Corinthian church for their ignorance on this subject, says to them, "Brethren, be not children in understanding: howbeit in malice be ye children, but in understanding be men." This precept should be engraven on the heart of every church-member.

CHAPTER I.

CHURCH-MEMBERS.

A CHURCH is made up of members, and of course its character is the aggregate of theirs. We have already seen what manner of persons they ought to be.* The members of a church, collectively, ministry and private members, compose the church. They are the repository of its doctrines, and the instruments of its efficiency. The word of God, the grace of Christ, and the power of the Spirit, dwelling together in their hearts, form the principle of its perpetuity. The doctrines, ordinances, government, officers, and discipline of the church, are designed for their special benefit. The first point, therefore, in unfolding the plan of church government, is to ascertain the individual characters, rights, and duties of its members, and their relations to the church and to each other.

The proper members of a church, are such persons only as are regenerated, or "born of the Spirit." This is the fundamental principle in the formation of true churches. It implies a change, an ascertainable change, and an authorized judge of the fact.

This change† of moral character, feeling, and action, implies the belief of the Christian system as a creed, and conformity of the inward and outward life to its teachings. It is produced by the Spirit of God working in the soul, promoting right feelings towards God, and right views of truth and duty; and constituting the subject of it a disciple of Christ, and a proper subject of Christian ordinances and of church-fellowship.

This change, which every man must experience in order to be saved, is usually accompanied and succeeded by exercises of mind, of which he is conscious, and can give some account; so that those who have passed through it may be distinguished

* Part I. Chap. 1, Sect. 3. † See Part II. Chap. 3, Sect. 4.

from others, not with unerring certainty, for that is the province of Him who judgeth the heart, but with sufficient certainty to make this the dividing line between the church of Christ and the world. It is perfectly reasonable, to believe that persons who have passed through this great spiritual change, can form a reasonable judgment whether others have done so. It is easier to detect pretenders in religion than in science, though impostors of both classes frequently escape detection for a time. No one can describe those new discoveries of religious truth, and the emotions which accompany Christian experience, who has not made and felt them, except by imitation and pretence; and there are few subjects on which detection is so easy.

All who do not give satisfactory evidence of this change, ought to be regarded and treated as sinners, living without hope and without God in the world, and in the way to ruin; as not belonging to the household of faith, or proper persons to be admitted to baptism, or to the communion of the churches. All claim to church-membership is founded, therefore, on the evidence of this spiritual change, of which the assembled church is the authorized judge. This, and not the form of administering an ordinance, is the principle which lies at the foundation of all true churches, and on which all claims to their church-fellowship and principles proceed: viz., the personal satisfaction which each member has given to all the rest, that he is born of the Spirit, and is a child of God. If the assembled church is not the judge of the characters and claims of all applicants for its membership and privileges, there is no earthly judge, there can be no church-fellowship, no Scriptural discipline, no distinct, visible church.

This view is in exact accordance with the Saviour's commission to his ministers. They were commanded, First, to *make disciples;* Second, to *baptize* them, by which they become professing Christians, or church-members; and Third, to *teach** them all the doctrines and duties of religion.

* This is a very different word in the original, from the word translated "teach" in the preceding verse.

The claim of the young convert to church-membership, is founded on *the evidence of his conversion to Christ*, and not on the amount of his knowledge of doctrine.

Sect. 1. *Design of a Church.*

The purposes for which the Saviour requires his people to form churches, so far as they can be ascertained from the Scriptures, and the nature of the case, are, 1. To promote their own piety and happiness. 2. The spread of Christianity.

1. Their piety is increased by watching over, and praying for each other; by mutual exhortation; by frequent meetings for worship, hearing the word of God preached, and for partaking of the Lord's Supper; by the use of Scriptural measures to reclaim such as neglect duty, or fall into sin; and by putting away from their fellowship the disorderly and the unholy. Their happiness is promoted by their fellowship in the truth, by the exercise of brotherly love, by sympathy in each other's trials, by counsel and aid, and by the purifying, elevating influence of that social principle, which unites in sacred friendship those of similar feelings, aims, hopes, and trials.

2. As a means for the spread of Christianity. A pure, zealous, intelligent church is in itself attractive, and influential as an illustration of the truth and excellence of religion. It is a specimen of the Saviour's workmanship. It is an organized body for sustaining the ministry of the Gospel. It is a permanent missionary society to the world. In the church, Christian influence is combined, purified, and concentrated, that it may operate with the utmost power in promoting religion in its own members, and in all other men.

Such is manifestly the Saviour's design in the formation of churches. "A church, as such, has no proper connection with any measures except those which aim at the salvation of the soul. There are many projects for the melioration of human woe, in which individual Christians may properly coöperate, but the church is an institution exclusively religious, and should confine its associated action to religious objects."*

Sect. 2. *Church Fellowship.*

When Christians unite together in a church, they come into that peculiar relation to each other, which is called church-fellowship. This term, when applied to churches formed on apostolic principles, is full of meaning. "Fellowship" in the first church, Acts 2 : 42; immediately followed conversion and baptism, and formed a tie stronger than worldly interests, and stronger than the love of life.

A looseness in language, consequent on a general departure from the primitive church order, has encumbered this subject with obscurities and difficulties. An important distinction exists between church-fellowship and general Christian fellowship, as the latter term is commonly used. The former includes the latter, but the latter does not necessarily include the former. By the latter we approve all the good we see in another, so far as it goes; by the former, we testify our confidence that those to whom it is extended have conformed to the laws of the Saviour's visible kingdom. Church-fellowship extends to those only who are united in covenant in one church; Christian fellowship extends as far as we can trace any marks of piety. The former is never given unless requested, the latter whether requested or not; the former involves special duties, the latter general ones; in the former we act as the appoinied administrators of our Saviour's laws, in the latter we simply express our personal feelings; in the former the honor and welfare of the church are concerned, in the latter, of individuals only.

It has elsewhere been shown, that church-fellowship is founded on the admitted principle, that each church has, like every other associated body, the right to judge and decide upon the admission of every one who asks to be admitted to its member-

* Knowles' Manuscript.

ship. The religious experience, character, and belief of the candidate, must be freely examined, and the church must decide upon the duty of extending to him their fellowship. If they cannot find evidence that he is a convert, or if he rejects any of the prominent doctrines or ordinances of the Gospel, they must withhold from him their fellowship till he is convinced of his error, and reclaimed.

Church-fellowship is by no means confined to the Lord's table. That is only one exercise of it, though a very delightful one. The reception of converts, their baptism, the meetings, the worship, the prayers and praises of the church, the care of its poor members, the collections for the necessary expenses of the church, and for spreading abroad the knowledge of Jesus Christ, are all occasions for the exercise of church-fellowship. It is a fruit of sincere obedience enjoyed by dwelling in Him. "If we walk in the light, as he is in the light, we have *fellowship* one with another, and the blood of Jesus Christ his son cleanseth us from all sin." It is to "bear one another's burdens, and so fulfil the law of Christ."

Mutual love for any object is a basis of fellowship. A strong love of literature, of the arts, or of natural scenery, existing in many different bosoms, promotes fellowship. How much stronger, then, must be a fellowship growing out of a vital knowledge of Christ—the knowledge of him whose nature is love, whose favorite injunction to those who love him is, "that ye love one another." What a basis of fellowship, what a bond of union is here! "My beloved is mine and I am his," says the heart of every member. The Lord Jesus responds, "see that ye love one another with a pure heart fervently."

A church, too, is a community of similar hopes and fears, joys and sorrows, trials and prospects, honors and reproaches, so that "whether one member suffer, all the members suffer with it, or one member be honored, all the members rejoice with it." No other society on earth possesses such a bond of union. How strongly was this truth exhibited by the first converts, when they "continued daily with one accord in the temple," and when Peter was in danger, "prayer was made *without ceasing*, of the church, unto God for him." When subjected to public reproach, as soon as they were "let go, they went to their own company, and reported all," and the whole church lifted up its united voice to God in prayer. No friendships and attachments are so strong as those which are formed in scenes of suffering and common danger. What attachments, then, can be so strong as those of "strangers and pilgrims on the earth," who have "no continuing city nor abiding place," but are seeking "a better country, that is an heavenly?"

Church-fellowship is a privilege enjoyed in a church composed of believers only, who "first gave themselves to the Lord, and then to one another by the will of God;" and not of such persons as chance to be born within certain geographical limits, or who descended from pious ancestors. Confidence in each other's sincerity and piety, such as the relation of religious experience begets, is the basis of fellowship, and this forms the visible bond of union among the disciples of Jesus. "Without being combined in a visible union, its splendor would be only as the dim and scattered light which was diffused over the chaos in the twilight of creation, while the fellowship of the saints is the same light gathered up and embodied in the solar orb."*

Thus church-fellowship becomes the brightest, purest, and happiest exercise of the social nature of man. Love to Christ and to each other, is the ruling principle which cements the whole in one spiritual building. Each church is a little family, with the Saviour for its head, a pattern and a type of heaven. "Diversities of gifts" disturb not the harmony, since there is "the same spirit."

Church-fellowship is not, therefore, intended to be the test of salvation. Each church may, for good cause, withdraw its fellowship from any of its own members, but from no others.

* Rev. J. A. James.

for it extends to no others. No church is called upon to decide whether any other persons are worthy of its fellowship except its own members, or those who have asked to become so.

SECT. 3. *Obligations arising from Church Membership.*

The duties of church-members, as such, arise from the obligations assumed on entering into that relation. What these obligations are, must be learned from the nature of the transaction, and the engagements, either expressed or implied, in becoming a member of the visible church of Christ. These are threefold. To become a church-member, is,

I. To confirm and ratify a personal, everlasting covenant with God.

II. A public profession of the religion of Christ.

III. To enter into a specific and sacred covenant with the members of one visible church.

I. God has, in all ages of the world, allowed and invited men to enter into covenant with him, the terms of which are all fixed by himself; and peculiar blessings are promised on condition of compliance. The covenants with Noah, as the father of all mankind, and with Abraham, as the father of a great and peculiar nation, and as the head and representative of the faithful, are instances of covenants between God and men. It does not belong to this part of the subject to inquire how far men may be guilty for neglecting to enter into covenant with God, when he invites them to do so; but it is certain that great guilt is incurred by neglecting or violating a covenant once formed. To "break," or "transgress" the covenant with God, is often mentioned in the Scriptures as a sin of no common magnitude. "Thy vows are upon me, O God," was expressive of the deepest sense of religious obligation. It is "better that thou shouldest not vow, than that thou shouldest vow and not pay."

To become a church-member, is to take up a most solemn

covenant with God, of which the prescribed symbol of ratification is baptism. There is no other way under the Gospel dispensation of entering into covenant with God. Every church-member should feel, therefore, that he stands in a new and peculiar relation to God, and that this is by far the most important view of church-membership. "I have lifted up my hand unto the Lord;" "I have vowed unto the mighty God of Jacob," should be the most deeply interesting reflections of every church-member. He has deliberately and solemnly promised God, in the presence of angels and of men, that he will obey His commandments, and exhibit before others the beauty, the symmetry, and the loveliness of Christian character. He has also promised to love God supremely, to walk with God in secret and in public, to make God the object of his complacency and delight, and his service the business of his life.

II. To become a church-member is to make a public profession of faith in Christ. To confess him before men, is made by our Lord the condition of salvation, Matt. 10 : 32; Luke 12 : 8; and the language of the true convert's heart is, "Come and hear, all ye that fear God, and I will declare what he hath done for my soul." To become a church-member is to leave the ranks of Satan, and join the friends of Christ; it is to give to the public a pledge to live as a Christian and an heir of heaven ought to live; it is to say to the rest of mankind, "We know that *we* are of God, and that the whole world lieth in wickedness." It is to say to unrenewed men, "Be as you are, and be heirs of hell; be as I am, and be heirs of God, and joint heirs with Christ." "Ye are the light of the world, ye are the salt of the earth," says Christ to his disciples. This is the relation in which they stand to mankind at large. No one can become a disciple, without incurring these solemn obligations to other men, nor continue so, without discharging them. The honor of religion is pledged before the world, every time an individual becomes a member of the church.

III. Every church-member enters into a sacred and special

covenant with all the members of the church to which he unites himself. He adopts its creed, assents to its practices, submits himself to its watch and discipline, and pledges his time, his talents, his influence, and his property, to sustain its interests in every Scriptural way. No obligations can be more sacred than those of church-members to one another, and to the church of their choice. The church has stood up and pledged itself before the world, to maintain the public worship of God. This is attended with pecuniary burdens. The veracity, the honor, and the honesty, of every member, is committed to redeem this pledge: if any one refuses to bear his just proportion of the burden, he is guilty of covenant-breaking and dishonesty.

The obligations of Christians to their own churches, are ever in danger of being merged, and lost sight of, in the general claims of religious benevolence. This is a great, and very pernicious error. It is like leaving our families to suffer and perish for the sake of relieving the destitute at large. God has made it our duty to do good to all, as we have opportunity, especially to them who are of the household of faith; but yet has declared, "He that provideth not for his *own*, and especially for those of his *own house*, hath denied the faith, and is worse than an infidel." The same principle applies to the members of a church. Their first and most sacred duties to Christ, and his people, and to a perishing world, are to and through the church of which they are members. Let this obligation be felt as it ought to be, and the interests of every church and of Christian benevolence at large, will be provided for.*

The obligations and consequent duties of church-members are, therefore, a threefold cord, binding them, in a peculiar sense,

* "That which inwardly each man should be, the church outwardly ought to testify. And therefore the duties of our religion which are seen, must be such as that affection which is unseen ought to be. Signs must resemble the things they signify. If religion bear the greatest sway in our hearts, our outward religious duties must show it, as far as the church hath outward ability."—*Richard Hooker.*

to God, to duty, and to each other. A failure to discharge them in one of these respects, is a failure in all: fidelity in one, implies fidelity in all. In this light let us view them more particularly.

In addition to the universal duty of love to all men, as the creatures of God, as brethren of the human race, as capable of immense happiness, and as exposed to great danger; and in addition to the love which we are to bear to all professed Christians, as far as we see in them the image and the Spirit of Christ, we are bound to love the members of the same church with peculiar complacency, and tender, affectionate regard. Of them we have received satisfactory assurance that they are the children of God; as such we welcome them to the baptismal waters; with them we have cast in our lot, and stand up before the world as the disciples of our common Lord. We love them, not only on principles of consanguinity, or friendship, or general esteem, not as reputed Christians, merely, but as those whom we most sincerely and intelligently believe to be such; and we therefore love them for Christ's sake. The love and holy confidence between members of the same church, bears the nearest resemblance to the love of heaven, for every church is intended to be a type of heaven. There, love will be based on certain knowledge; here, on the highest earthly assurance of each other's piety.

Love between church-members should be expressed by sympathy. "Rejoice with them that do rejoice, and weep with them that weep." Our Saviour was eminent for sympathy. Witness his conduct at the grave of Lazarus, and his conversation with the weeping sisters. Oh, how precious is Christian sympathy! How it blesses every heart through which it flows! It is as "the dew of Hermon, that descended upon the mountains of Zion."

To pray one for another, in secret, is the duty of church-members. How often does the Apostle Paul mention this duty, and assure his brethren that he daily bowed his knees before

God, burdened with desire that Christ might dwell in their hearts by faith, and that they might know the love of Christ, which passeth knowledge. Genuine prayer will beget sympathy, which will be expressed by visiting the brethren in their afflictions, bearing each other's burdens, and distributing to their necessities. All these are expressions of love, which produce more love. And if members pray for one another, they will watch over each other with earnest solicitude. A decline of piety in a brother, will fill them with deep concern; a relapse into sin, with inexpressible grief.

"Forbearing one another in love," is another sacred duty of church-members. They will see in each other many imperfections, and much that is disagreeable. They must not speak or think harshly of weak brethren, or even of vulgar brethren, if such there are, but with all gentleness seek to make them better. The Saviour did not seek out the amiable and the refined, and make them his sole companions. Christians differ, too, in their views of some points of doctrine, or, which is oftener the case, in the manner of expressing their views, and here is room for forbearance.

Church-members are under the deepest obligations to keep the unity of the spirit in the bond of peace. For this purpose, while valiant for the truth, they should be tender of each other's feelings. They must not be self-willed, not tenacious of their own way. They must watch against the spirit that "loveth the preëminence." They must not think nor say too much about *equal* rights. "I am as good as you," should never be uttered, or thought, by a church-member, but "You are as good as I," should be their language; or, rather, "In lowliness of mind, let each esteem other *better* than themselves." Subordination, modesty, a delicate regard to the distinctions of sex and age, should characterize church-members. "Ye younger, submit yourselves to the elder, yea, all of you, be subject one to another, and be clothed with humility."

Church-members are bound to attend all the meetings of the

church when in their power, to feel a deep interest in its welfare, to seek its peace and prosperity by devoting their abilities of every kind to its service. This they virtually pledged themselves to do, in becoming members. They have no right to scatter their attendance on different meetings, to the neglect of those of the church. They should readily engage as Sabbath-school teachers, or pupils, be ready to exhort or pray in social meetings, act on committees, or give counsel, if needed, and in every proper way seek to promote the temporal and spiritual prosperity of the body.

Sect. 4. *The Rights of Church Members. Private Judgment.*

The rights of church-members may be considered under two general divisions: First, those which they acquire in becoming members; and Second, those which are inalienable, and which the church cannot control or abridge.

1. Church-members acquire the right to all the privileges of the church. They are entitled to an equal voice in the election of its officers, and the transaction of all its business. In the admission and exclusion of members, they are entitled to act in concurrence with the church, according to the precepts and principles of the Gospel. They have a claim to the instructions, the oversight, and intercessions of the pastor. This is a privilege which those who are not members may enjoy, as every pastor should feel it to be a duty to bestow them on all within his power; but they may be justly claimed and expected, by members of the church.

The privilege of participating at the Lord's Table, is also one of the rights of church-members, whenever that ordinance is celebrated by the church. The members of each church, and no others, are entitled to this privilege as a *right.*

2. The previously existing natural and political rights of men are not increased, or abridged, by becoming church-members, or church officers. Their rights to property, and to citizenship,

remain unchanged. The rights of parents to control their children, the duty of children to obey their parents, and of the wife to be in subjection to her husband, and to be loved as Christ loved the church, are only rendered more sacred by their all becoming members of the church.

The right of private judgment in religion, belongs to every church-member.* This right is to be considered, in opposition to the claims, not only of lords temporal and lords spiritual, but also of numbers. Not only the authoritative recommendations of conclaves and councils, of synods and conferences, but the resolutions of conventions, of associations, and the votes of church majorities may infringe upon it.

There is constant danger that the free action of churches will be crippled by large religious assemblies, and the rights and responsibilities of individual Christians be abridged by the combined power of the church. This danger should be guarded against by a proper understanding, and firm adherence to the right of private judgment. A deep and wide-spread feeling of personal responsibility is the palladium of our freedom, our safety, and our strength. This feeling should not be awed nor restrained, but encouraged. In the same ratio that the proper sphere of private judgment is narrowed, will the feeling of personal responsibility be destroyed.

It may not be easy to define the exact limits of private judgment. As has already be shown, the nature of the church relation and covenant does not require exact uniformity of opinion, but specific elements of character, obedience to plain commands, and an intelligent assent to those fundamental doctrines which are clearly revealed in the Scriptures. The question arises, What doctrines must be believed as essential to church-membership, and what may be safely left to private judgment? Without attempting to settle this point in detail, a remark or two may throw some light upon it. And first, the leading doctrines of religion are subjects of *experience*, quite as much as of *investi-*

* See Fuller's Works, vol. iii. p. 447.

gation; they are often, if not usually, implanted in the *heart*, before they assume a form in the *head*. The justice and holiness of God, the sinfulness of man, the certainty of future judgment and eternal retribution, the atonement and divinity of Christ, and the doctrine of the Spirit's influence, spring up spontaneously in the renewed heart. They are all the branches of one plant—faith—the seed of which is love planted by the Spirit of God, and this is the germ of all true religious doctrine, and prepares the way for the reception of all needful truth. Second, the belief of positive error is more dangerous than a deficiency of belief of even important truth. Third, in drawing the line between errors which must lead to shipwreck of faith, and those which are less dangerous, it should be remembered, that although as a general rule, a man's belief shapes his character and his life, yet experience proves that particular forms of error are much less dangerous to some persons than to others.

No reason can be given why exact conformity in doctrine should be required in all the members of a church, any more than uniformity of health, stature, intellectual ability, or of attainments in piety. We are sometimes asked by those who seem to think that heaven and earth should pass away sooner than that one jot or tittle of their creed should fail to be believed, "can two walk together except they be agreed?" Certainly not; if that want of agreement necessarily includes hating each other. But we ask, in the name of Christian charity, must a want of similarity in opinion be attended with hatred? And if we are to admit none to our fellowship but such as agree with us in opinion, where is the place for charity, that crowning grace in the church of Christ? Is it the part of charity to make every difference of opinion an evidence of a corrupt heart?

So we may allow among brethren differences of opinion, arising from early prejudice or peculiarity of character. We may even allow private brethren to entertain opinions which we should be unwilling to have them teach. If a brother persists in attempts to spread abroad a doctrine which is grievous to the church, he should be called to account, with the distinct understanding that it is not for holding, but for *propagating* errors, which, though comparatively harmless to him, may be injurious to others, and destructive to the peace of the church. A schismatic spirit is far more reprehensible and dangerous than a quiet belief of error.

Let it never be said of Baptist principles, that they restrain religious inquiry. They admit the freest range over the wide field of truth, assured that fruits rich and fair remain yet to be gathered; only forbidding those who enjoy this privilege to bring home bitter and poisonous berries. Making the widest and most equal distribution of power, they give the many every needed protection against the few, while by defining and limiting the power of majorities, they protect the rights of the humblest individual. May these principles be preserved inviolate, and transmitted untrammelled to posterity.

CHAPTER II.

CHURCH OFFICERS.

Although the term *officer*, is applied to those who are chosen to places of labor and trust in the churches, and although office implies authority, yet every church officer is the servant of Christ, to obey his will implicitly, and of the church, to labor for its welfare. The officers have no right to rule the church, nor the church the officers; but both are to rule and to serve together, with pure conscience under Christ. Church officers are chosen to their places because they are believed to be those whom Christ has chosen; as such they should be honored and obeyed. As the servants of Christ, they are bound to obey him in all things; as the servants of the church, they are bound to labor for its good. Church-members are individually bound by the law of Christ to set an example of obedience and submission to their officers as his servants, to esteem them very highly in love, to guard their reputation, and promote their influence and usefulness by every proper means in their power. The reputation of a faithful minister is the Lord's property; to tarnish and weaken it is robbing God.

The duty of a church officer is to discharge the duties of his station in the church according to the will of Christ. His power is purely spiritual. He possesses no mysterious power. His outstretched hand is the conductor of no sanctity; his uplifted hand has no special power to bless. The Gospel has no priesthood to act as the almoners of the Divine favor. We have one only Mediator and High Priest, even "Christ, who through the eternal Spirit, offered himself without spot to God," and Christians are all "a holy priesthood," having the same means of access "to the holiest of all." The prayers of a minister have no special influence or saving efficacy by reason of his office, nor give any nearer access to the mercy-seat than those of any other Christian of equal piety. The authority of his preaching does not consist in any sacredness about his person, but in the fact that it is a message from God.

The obligation of every church to have officers and to seek a minister who has been divinely called to the work is plain, from the examples recorded in the New Testament, and from experience. Although a church may exist, yet it cannot prosper nor fulfil its trust without officers. In selecting them, personal feelings, preferences, and prejudices, should be laid aside; and regard to the will of Christ should be supreme. All party feeling and party measures should be carefully avoided. Churches should remember that their business is very different from that of a political caucus, or town meeting. Everything should be done in the spirit of prayer, and of humble dependence on God.

When officers are chosen, churches should beware of the too common error of considering them as responsible for the spiritual condition and the prosperity of the church. That responsibility is shared by all the members in common, and the officers are responsible only for the discharge of their duties. When church-members depend on their officers to stir them up, the church is in a sad state. It is the duty of every private member to be wholly devoted to God. Yet inasmuch as all are not so, the men who are chosen to these offices, should be men "full of faith and of the Holy Ghost."

SECT. 1. *Choice and Ordination of a Pastor.*

In the early churches it appears that teachers, pastors, and deacons, were usually selected from their own number. Such as were endowed with talents for public speaking, joined with knowledge of the Gospel, strong faith, zeal, and love, united to prudence and sound sense, were chosen, in obedience to the directions of the Apostle. 1 Tim. 3 : 1–13; Tit. 1 : 6–9. The same principles are to be observed and the same qualifications required still. But as churches have increased in intelligence and wealth, higher intellectual qualifications are demanded, and adequate support is given, so that ministers are more frequently trained up in schools of learning. One consequence of this change is, that churches oftener choose a pastor with whom they have had little or no previous acquaintance. This should be done with great caution, deliberation, and prayer.

Let it be understood that the candidate is one who has been baptized into the fellowship of some regular church of Christ, on giving to them satisfactory evidence of true piety, that he believes himself called by God to the ministry, that he has commenced a course of preparation by the approval of the church, has completed it, has preached and otherwise conducted so far to the satisfaction of the church to which he belongs, that he has been approved and licensed by them to preach the Gospel. Yet to the church who contemplate electing him to be their pastor, he is comparatively a stranger. He should be with them several months at least, before any decisive steps are taken, that all may be able to form a deliberate judgment. Should it appear that there is not a good degree of unanimity, it is better not to proceed to a vote.

When sufficient time has elapsed for both the candidate and the church to form a prayerful, deliberate judgment, if there is a prospect of a vote nearly unanimous, the church may proceed to a choice. The call is communicated to the pastor elect by a joint committee. If he accepts, a council is called, and a day is fixed upon for a public ordination. The Scriptural authority for ordination, and the principles involved in it, have been before given. All that remains is, to point out the most approved practice which has grown out of those principles.

For this purpose, a council of pastors and delegates is assembled by letters missive to the neighboring churches, with a deputation from the church itself, before whom are laid the proceedings of the church in calling the candidate, with his answer, his original license to preach, and the vote of the church admitting him as a member. The candidate then gives an account of his religious experience, states the evidence of his call to the ministry, and presents his views of Christian doctrine and church order. All the members of the council are at liberty to question him freely. The council, if satisfied, declare by vote that they find all the proceedings in accordance with approved usages of the churches, and proceed to recognize him publicly as a minister of the Gospel, and as the pastor of that church.

It is always to be borne in mind, however, that the duties of the council are not limited to the mere preservation of regularity in the forms of proceeding. They have come together to discharge a solemn duty to the church that convenes them, to the churches at large, and to the Saviour. It is their duty to inquire very carefully into the moral character, the piety, the doctrinal views, and the literary qualifications of the candidate; to ascertain whether he possesses theological knowledge, practical talents, and good sense, adequate to the arduous and responsible work of the ministry. They should also attend to any objections which may be made from any quarter, previous to, or during their deliberations. By consenting to this ordination, they attest before God and men their confidence in him as a minister of Christ. If everything is satisfactory, the council vote to proceed to the public services of ordination.

The proceedings of the council are first read by the clerk, then follow invocation, the reading of the Scriptures, prayer, a sermon, ordaining prayer, charge, hand of fellowship, address to the church, concluding prayer, and benediction; interspersed by singing. The parts are usually assigned by vote of the council, though the wishes of the church, and of the candidate, are consulted. While the ordaining prayer is offered, the officiating minister, and as many others as conveniently can, lay their hands on the head of the candidate, in conformity with Apostolic practice,* and as an appropriate and solemn token of approbation and love, but not as indicative of any spiritual influence or blessing which the presbytery can bestow.

The sermon is usually delivered by one previously selected by the church and the candidate, the council concurring, the charge by some minister of confirmed piety and experience, the hand of fellowship by one of similar age and circumstances with the candidate, and the ordaining prayer is usually assigned to an aged minister, of long standing in the vicinity.

The charge is a solemn message, in the name of Christ and of the churches in whose name the council was called, to the pastor elect, consisting of advice, warning, and encouragement, suited to the nature of the ministerial work. 1 Tim. 4 : 11–16; 5 : 21–25; 6 : 13–21; 2 Tim. 4 : 1–8. In regard to the right hand of fellowship, we have already considered the grounds on which the duty rests of consulting neighboring churches and their pastors in regard to the settlement of a minister. The giving of the hand of fellowship by a member of the ordaining council in the name of the churches and their pastors present and represented, is designed to express publicly their concur-

* Acts 6 : 6; 13 : 3; 1 Tim. 4 : 14; 5 : 22; 2 Tim. 1 : 6.

rence and approval, and their hearty Christian welcome of the new pastor to their brotherhood and coöperation.

If the council are not satisfied of the propriety of ordaining the candidate, they ought to decline to do so, even if the congregation were assembled to attend the services. The council should meet some time previously to the day appointed for the public ordination services, and the examination should always be public.

When a candidate is to be ordained to the work of an evangelist or missionary, a council is invited by the church to which he belongs, and the services are similar to those in the ordination of a pastor, with such modifications as the nature of his work, or his particular designation may require. In this case he is not chosen nor ordained to any office in any church, but is simply recognized as an accredited minister of Christ.

Sect. 2. *Election and Duties of Deacons.*

There are many important services needed in the church which the pastor cannot perform, requiring a different order of talent and of habits from those of a pastor. Every church should, therefore, elect one or more men to the office of deacon.

The general duties of deacons may be inferred from the circumstances in which the office probably originated, Acts 6 : 1–6; and the duties assigned to the individuals then chosen. The special object in the choice of those men at that time was, to relieve the Apostles from the labor and embarrassment of managing the funds contributed for the sustenance of the poor. There is no evidence that Stephen and his six associates were deacons, but circumstances in the church at Jerusalem had shown the necessity for another office—the superintendence of the charitable distributions. To this office they were elected. The permanent office of deacon undoubtedly grew out of the same necessity, and was probably suggested by this precedent. The phrase "to serve tables," means to manage pecuniary affairs. Such affairs the ancient church, and even the Saviour's company had, and so must every church. On them devolves the duty of being almoners of the church to the poor. They are expected to take charge of the communion service, and distribute the bread and wine from the hands of the pastor, make proper arrangements for, and assist at baptisms, assist the pastor in visiting the sick, and in conducting meetings for prayer and conference. The word *deacon* means *waiting servant*, a term significant of a highly important and responsible office in the church.*

The qualifications prescribed by the Apostle show that he so regarded it. "Likewise must the deacons be grave, not double-tongued, not given to much wine, not greedy of filthy lucre, holding the mystery of faith in a pure conscience. And let these also first be proved; then let them use the office of deacon, being found blameless. Even so must their wives be grave; not slanderous, sober, faithful in all things. Let the deacons be the husbands of one wife, ruling their children and their own houses well. For they that have used the office of a deacon well, purchase to themselves a good degree, and great boldness in the faith, which is in Christ Jesus."

Although no age is prescribed, it is evident that a very young man could not possess all the qualifications. They must be "grave," must "first be proved," or tried men, by being members of the church sufficient time to ascertain their fitness for the office, and if "found blameless" they may be chosen. Nor could a very aged man possess the requisite strength and activity. If mature in wisdom and piety, it is desirable that they be young in years, as well as in bodily and mental vigor.

The Scriptures give no rule respecting the number of deacons. A church, therefore, may elect as many as it deems necessary. For a small church two or three are usually thought sufficient—in a large church six or seven are needed.

* The laws of Massachusetts (Revised Statutes, Part I. tit. 8, chap. 20, sect. 39) declare the deacons of churches to be "bodies corporate," and trustees of all the property of the church.

No rule is given in the Scriptures to determine the duration of individual continuance in the office. In the early churches it is probable that all officers were elected without any specification of time. That custom still prevails in respect to deacons, although the pastoral office has become very changeful. It is desirable that both offices be as permanent as possible, particularly that of pastor. As the office of deacon is not an exclusive calling, and as it can be changed without a violation of duty, or personal inconvenience, there are some reasons for limiting the term of office to a shorter period than during life. It is impossible to foresee how well a man will fill any office till he is placed in it; then his health, his mental faculties, and even his piety may decline, or God may raise up better men in the church. If he becomes unfitted through age, or mental feebleness, or spiritual deadness, he is usually the last to find out the fact. If the church undertake to dismiss him by vote, an unpleasant excitement may be raised; if his brethren endeavor privately to persuade him to resign, jealousies may be aroused; if he, with the best of motives, resign voluntarily, false and injurious inferences may be drawn; all of which would be avoided, if his term of office regularly expired by its own limitation. Besides, the church would have frequent opportunities to place her most active and pious men in this office. Yet the *annual* election of all the deacons would be very undesirable. A rule by which each should be elected for a term of five, six, or seven years, with a provision that the office of one or more should expire each year, or each alternate year, might be found most convenient.

The deacons are all equal in official authority, which does not extend beyond the church to which they belong. If a deacon is dismissed to another church, his office ceases. The office of deaconess, which anciently existed in some of the churches in Asia, on account of the peculiarities of Eastern manners, has become unnecessary as a permanent office. When a deacon is to be chosen, some time should be taken for reflection and prayer, and the pastor should instruct the church respecting the proper qualifications for the office. If diversity of preference is known to exist, the church should resort to prayer, and the choice should be delayed. If, when the ballot is taken there should be a large minority against the choice, it is better in ordinary cases for the candidate to decline, and in all cases the deacons elect should take suitable time to give the subject a prayerful consideration, previous to deciding the question of acceptance.

A clerk and treasurer are also needed in every church, chosen either from the deacons, or from the body. Large churches especially in large cities have their Standing Committees, annually elected to inquire into the characters of applicants for membership, to report cases of delinquency, and to assist the pastor by mutual counsel. Some churches are divided into classes or sections of convenient numbers, at the head of each of which a leader, or visitor is placed to look after each of the members, and promote mutual acquaintance and active piety. These arrangements are very useful and proper.

Sect. 3. *The Duties and Rights of a Pastor.*

The first duty of the pastor is to preach the Gospel. He must make this the great business of his life. He must "study to show himself approved unto God, a workman that needeth not to be ashamed, rightly dividing the word of truth." He must not be confined in his preaching to one topic or set of topics, nor to one round of arguments, or illustrations, or form of words, but with all variety, fertility, and freshness, hold forth the word of life in a form adapted to all shades of character and circumstances. He must not shun to declare all the counsel of God. He must never be warped, nor intimidated by men. If any cardinal truth, or doctrine, is opposed, or overlooked, he must advocate it with more study, caution, and earnestness. He must study the best methods of preaching, with the earnest application of the Painter, and the vigilant circumspection of the General. He must improve his powers of persuasion to the utmost, and devote them all to the work of winning souls. He must always bear in mind that his business is to *preach*,—not politics, not morality, not philanthropy, not outward, or special reform, not science—but the pure Gospel which saves the soul. He is sent to invite guests to the marriage-supper. He is the servant of Christ, who has work enough for him to do.

The pastor must not only teach publicly, but, as far as time and strength permit, from house to house. He must visit the sick and the mourners, inculcate the duty of family religion, and of secret prayer. He must see that the children are instructed in the precepts of religion, and encourage parents and Sabbath-school teachers in the work. He must "warn every man, and teach every man, in all wisdom, that he may present every man perfect in Christ Jesus."

As an overseer, or pastor, he is the representative of the "Chief Shepherd," whose disinterested, watchful, affectionate example he must follow. He must expound the Saviour's laws to the church, and urge them to a prompt, faithful execution. He is to administer the ordinances of the church, express its fellowship, pronounce its censures, and its excommunications. He must instruct the church in the exercise of discipline, and use all proper means to see it vigorously maintained. He must remember that the church may become lukewarm, inactive, lax, corrupt, and even apostate, through his neglect or cowardice. He is the messenger through whom the Lord speaks to the church. He should watch against the entrance of incipient errors and irregularities. He should labor to have a pure, active, and a holy church, rather than a numerous one.

Although a pastor is bound to do what he can for the general interests of religion, yet his first duties are to his own flock, and to the families of his charge. He is not at liberty to neglect them, for the promotion of other objects, however important.

In the fulfilment of these duties, he has a right to the constant and candid attention of his people on his instructions. He has a right to expect them to coöperate with him in his efforts, and yield to him deference, as the ambassador of God. It is his right to preach to them the doctrines of the Bible, as he understands them, in all faithfulness and plainness.

As the pastor and religious teacher of the church, he has the right to decide whom he will admit to the pulpit, and while he has no right to force an unwelcome preacher on the church, they have no right to invite a preacher to the pulpit contrary to his wishes.

The pastor has a right to a pecuniary remuneration for his services, equal to the talent and diligence with which they are performed, whether it amount to more or less than a bare support. An Apostle has told us that "the laborer is worthy of his hire;" which is in amount precisely what he earns. The Scriptures give no countenance to the common notion that ministers are to be *comfortably supported*, like gentlemanly paupers, not that their services are to be estimated by a different rule from those of any other classes of men. They are to be *justly remunerated;* whether it amount to more or less than a comfortable support. Nor do the Scriptures teach that property in their hands is more likely to be injurious than in the hands of private Christians. The true principle is, that the minister is entitled to precisely that pecuniary remuneration which his labors would command in any of the common vocations of life. If he choose to relinquish a part of his just claim for the sake of serving his Master, he can do so.

As a man and a citizen, he has the same political and social rights as others. He neither gains nor loses in these respects by becoming a minister. He may find it expedient, and may feel it his duty, to waive the exercise of them, in some respects, for the sake of his work, but they cannot be justly taken away.

SECT. 4. *Duties of the Church to the Pastor.*

The duties of individual church-members and of the church as a whole, to the pastor, should be reckoned among their most sacred duties to the Saviour, who said to his ministers, "He that despiseth you despiseth me, and he that despiseth me despiseth him that sent me." The relation of a pastor to the people of his charge is peculiarly sacred. He is sent of God *to them.* In this belief they have chosen *him* as their spiritual teacher and shepherd. To neglect, oppose, despise, or traduce him, is a sin of no common dye. The duties which they owe to him are not for his sake merely, not on account of any supposed sanctity about his person, but they are duties through him to the Saviour, to God, to themselves, and to a perishing world. Woe to the people who prove faithless to such a relation.

The first duty of people to their pastor, is to attend diligently upon his instructions. He is *their* spiritual teacher and guide, they should not, therefore, leave his ministrations to attend on those of another. No slight excuse should be sufficient to detain them from public worship. His discourses may be so connected and related that the loss of one may cause the misunderstanding of another. Every absence discourages the pastor, and is a bad example to others.

Prayer for, and coöperation with, the pastor, is a sacred duty on the part of the church. The one, in all ordinary cases, implies the other. When people pray sincerely, "Give us this day our daily bread;" they put forth efforts to obtain it, and if they sincerely pray for their pastor's happiness and usefulness, they will join faith and works together. Even an Apostle needed the prayers of his brethern that he might have utterance, that he might open his mouth boldly, aud that he might be delivered from danger, and he even ascribes his deliverance to their "helping together by prayer for us." Their liberal offerings were precious to him as a pledge of their sincere, fervent prayer. Let the spirit of prayer for the pastor be acted out in faithful coöperation, and the pastor's hands are held up, his heart is cheered, his usefulness is increased, and the church is prosperous. Church-members may assist and cheer the pastor by frequently reporting themselves to him, by looking after each other, by a readiness to labor in the Sabbath-school, and in conference-meetings, by giving him information of any facts which may be useful to him, by conversing with inquirers and with the impenitent, and by bringing as many as possible to attend on his ministry. No church can truly prosper without a zealous, vigilant, faithful coöperation on the part of all its members with the pastor.

The church should promote and exemplify correct views of the pastor's authority. This is a point of great importance, and far too much overlooked. Could a teacher profit a school in which his just authority was not respected? Deprive a parent of his just parental authority, and however wise, faithful, and affectionate, he could not discharge his duties with advantage to his family. So when a pastor is deprived of his proper authority, it is a great calamity to the church. The Scriptures* speak of pastors as rulers, and enjoin submission and obedience to them as Christian duties. On them rest great responsibilities; they are chosen to their office as being wise and good men; they are bound to understand many subjects better than the members of the church, and if they are not fit to bear rule, in the Scriptural sense, they are not fit to be pastors at all. Does any one ask how far this authority extends? How far does the authority of a father extend over his grown up children? or of the husband over the wife? Can the limits in these cases be marked? Or can the exact specifications be given? In all these cases it is the authority of love, directed by good sense, courtesy, and dignity. The pastor's authority, like that of a parent, should be exerted, not for his personal good, but for that of the church.

A few distinctions may help to make this subject still more

* 1 Cor. 15 : 16; 1 Tim. 5 : 17; Heb. 13 : 7, 17.

plain. The pastor is not to rule the church, but to rule in the church, in connection with the brethren. His authority, which is limited to spiritual matters, is over the members as individuals, rather than over a church as a collective body. He owes obedience to the whole church, yet individual members owe a certain degree of obedience to him. No member has a right to set up a persevering opposition to the measures of the pastor, nor to join a faction for this purpose. Nothing can justify opposition but a reasonable, deliberate, prayerful conviction, that the course of the pastor is contrary to the Scriptures. But when he comes into the presence of the assembled church, gathered together in the name, authority, and presence of Christ, the pastor's authority is at once merged in that of the church, and every member has a right to express his views freely, and to vote on every question as his own judgment and conscience dictate, whether in accordance with the pastor's wishes or not.

A church should carefully guard the pastor's influence. The pastor's reputation, unsullied, is a tower of strength; and is among the choicest treasures of the church. Satan and wicked men know this, and they usually attack religion in the persons of its professors, but especially of its ministers. If their characters and influence can be broken down, the devil triumphs. A church should seek a pastor of unblemished reputation, and then carefully preserve it. They should speak of his faults to no one but himself. If parents who are members of a church, speak lightly of their pastor, how sad must be the effect on their unconverted children! Instead of this, they should guard him from the breath of slander and suspicion. His reputation is dearer to him than life, because his usefulness depends so much upon it.

Finally, it is the duty of every church to render to the pastor an adequate pecuniary compensation. On this point the Scriptures are very plain. "Let him that is taught in the word, communicate unto him that teacheth in all good things." "If we have sown unto you spiritual things, is it a great thing if we shall reap your carnal things?" "Even so hath the Lord ordained, that they who preach the gospel, should live of the gospel." "Let the elders that rule well, be counted worthy of double honor, (i. e., as the connection implies, *compensation*,) especially they who labor in the word and doctrine: for the Scripture saith, Thou shalt not muzzle the ox that treadeth out the corn: and the laborer is worthy of his reward."* The principle here brought to view, is that of reciprocity in the support of the pastor, not the duty of charity. It is RIGHT, that every person who enjoys the ministrations of the Gospel, as every one ought to, should pay something to support them. A minister has an undoubted right, as far as man is concerned, to preach for nothing, if he pleases, or to be supported by one class of persons, while he labors for another, but the true principle of *justice* in the case is, that those who receive the benefit of his labors, should pay for them.

But inasmuch as the principle is of difficult application, as ministers are loth to speak of their pecuniary claims or wants, as many feel it to be their duty to preach the Gospel whether they are compensated or not, and as many churches are unable to insure an adequate pecuniary reward to their pastors, on their settlement, the members should remember this part of their duty, and individually communicate to the pastor's wants. They should, if possible, furnish him with the pecuniary means of devoting his *whole* time and strength to the work of the ministry. They should be in the habit of presenting him, frequently, with substantial marks of their kindness and esteem. Thus his heart will be cheered, his love for them increased by the tokens of their love to him, and his labors will be more efficient.

SECT. 5. *Removal of a Pastor.*

It is desirable that the pastoral relation be as permanent as possible. A good man acquires influence by being known. This is the Lord's property, which it is wrong to sacrifice light-

* Gal. 6 : 6; 1 Cor. 9 : 11, 14; 1 Tim. 5 : 17.

ly. In accepting the charge of a church, a pastor should consider it his duty to remain till death, unless God shall clearly indicate his duty to remove. The relation between a church and pastor should, in all ordinary cases, be formed in this expectation.

Yet it may be a pastor's duty to remove. His health may require it. A state of feeling may exist among his people, which may render his continuance, in his view, undesirable.

If the pastor has come to the decision that it is his duty to remove, he should communicate his wishes in writing to the church, with the reasons for them, and ask their consent to the termination of his pastoral engagement. The church, after prayerful deliberation, should proceed to vote on the question. If they accede, the relation is terminated, if not, they will send to him a communication, endeavoring to dissuade him from his purpose.

The question is sometimes asked, Is it orderly and right in itself, for one church to invite the pastor of another church to be its minister? If one church *wants* the pastor of another church, that is not a sufficient reason why he should be invited. The church where he now is wants him also, and in this respect they stand on equal ground. But the latter church has regularly obtained him, hence their right is paramount. Nor is the prospect of a larger salary a sufficient reason. But if a church can sincerely offer such reasons for desiring to obtain the pastor of another church, as they believe the Saviour will approve, they may properly invite him. But no pastor should leave the service of a church when he is useful and happy, without their concurrence in his views of duty, or that of a disinterested council.

CHAPTER III.

CHURCH MEETINGS.

A CHURCH, assembled with its pastor and deacons to transact business, should be regarded as the most solemn, dignified, and important meeting ever convened on earth. Questions of infinite moment, and eternal in their consequences, are there considered and decided. The young convert with trembling hope relates his spiritual exercises, seeks admission to her bosom, and takes the everlasting covenant of God upon his lips; the unfaithful member is tried, found guilty, and is sorrowfully put away from the fellowship of the saints on earth and from the hope of heaven till repentance prepares him to resume his place among them; while Christ, whose eyes are like a flame of fire, is walking among them, noting all their doings, with approval or displeasure.

The church is to ascertain and execute his will. It must judge by the Scriptures whether those who seek its ordinances and fellowship are true and obedient disciples, and whether an accused member is guilty of an offence, which is deserving of excommunication.

Each church, too, being a missionary body to the world, is to devise ways and means and measures to discharge this high trust. Its united piety, zeal, wisdom, and pecuniary liberality, are all to be brought into requisition. Questions more weighty, objects more magnificent, and projects more sublime, than ever occupied the cabinets of earthly monarchs, are to be considered and matured.

This business is the common concern of all the members, by their equality as brethren, their mutual covenant, and their common obligation to Christ. It requires much mutual consultation. All the members of the church should, therefore, attend the meetings, and unite in imploring the blessing of God upon their labors. No church business can be well done when but a part of the members are present, and it is a gross neglect of the Saviour to stay away.

SECT. 1. *Order of Business.*

Every efficient, well-regulated church has frequent meetings for business. The frequency must depend on the amount of business to be done, and other circumstances. It is desirable that considerable time in each meeting be spent in devotional exercises.

The pastor is usually the moderator of the church meetings; if he be absent the clerk, or senior deacon calls the church to a choice of a moderator. Every meeting should be commenced by reading the Scriptures and prayer.

A record should be kept of all the proceedings, by the clerk, and at the opening of every meeting the record of the preceding meeting should be read, corrected if necessary, and approved.

The reception of candidates for admission, if there are any, is first attended to, during which any well-disposed and serious persons, not members of the church, who desire it, are permitted to be present; but all who are not members should be requested to withdraw previous to the transaction of church business.

Applications for dismission and reports of committees are next acted on, and then new business may be introduced.

A church should be governed in all its deliberations by the common parliamentary rules, applied and submitted to in the exercise of courtesy and Christian love.

In all the church meetings every brother has an equal right to speak on any subject before the church, but he must confine his remarks to the question, must not speak too long, nor too often, and he must be kind and courteous.

All matters of business are decided by a vote of the majority of the brethren, to which it is the duty of the minority cheerfully to submit, though a bare majority should never press any question, especially if important.

SECT. 2. *Voting.*

As all questions on which a diversity of opinion is likely to exist in a church must be decided by the will of the majority, every member is bound, by his covenant with his brethren, to submit to that will, when fairly expressed. A difference of opinion among brethren should never produce alienation of affection. The cool, deliberate, dispassionate, prayerful decision of a majority, should, in all ordinary cases, be submitted to, as the will of Christ. There should be no exciting, argumentative debates in church meetings, no offensive personalities, no attacking of each other's arguments, nor impugning of motives. Those who speak, should communicate whatever information they may possess, which bears on the question, and express their opinions modestly, with the reasons for them, and then leave all to the decision of the body. If a question is likely to produce much division, it should be withdrawn, or postponed, unless one of vital importance, and requiring prompt action.

Voting is done by raising the hand, or by rising, except in the choice of a pastor or deacon, when the ballot is used. The method of voting by ayes and noes is not suited to the dignity and sacredness of a church meeting; and it is highly undesirable that they should ever be entered on the church records. This method should be resorted to unless a vital principle is at stake, on which the members wish their votes to stand recorded.

All the members of a church have equal rights, and are equally entitled to vote. A church is a spiritual society, formed for spiritual purposes, all the members of which hold to it a spiritual relation. "There is neither Jew nor Greek, there is neither bond nor free, there is neither male nor female: for ye are all one in Christ Jesus." Christians, united to Christ, and heirs alike of an eternal inheritance, have equal rights and privileges, though the duties and responsibilities differ with their circumstances. Their connection and equality in the church do not affect their previous lawful and proper relations in their families and in society, nor impair any previously existing obligations.

This principle may aid in determining whether *females* and *minors* have a right to vote in church meetings. Viewed simply as members, their rights are the same as those of other members. But their rights are modified and limited by previously existing relations. A father and his son, yet a minor, are members of the same church, and as such, they have equal rights; but the son owes a filial respect to his father, and is legally and morally bound to obey him. All would acknowledge the impropriety of a young son or daughter voting, in church meeting, in opposition to the wishes of a father. Church principles would, in that case, become the authors of confusion, and not of peace, in families. The same is true respecting a master and his apprentice, when both are members of the same church. There is no scriptural precept which annuls the previously existing obligation, which, therefore, remains in full force. It would be obviously improper for a wife to vote in opposition to her husband, to whom she is required to be obedient in all things, Eph. 5 : 22–24, and clearly inconsistent with the general subordination of the female sex, which God has himself established, that they should set themselves in opposition to the male members. 1 Cor. 14 : 34, 35; 1 Tim. 2 : 11–15. If they are not at liberty to vote freely, they are manifestly not in a suitable condition to vote at all.

It does not follow, however, that because females are not allowed to vote in the church, they have no rights. The law allows them no political suffrage, yet it guards their rights, fully. It is sometimes objected, that if females may not vote in the church, their rights are taken away; whereas their rights in the church are just as extensive, and of the same general character, as in the family or in the civil State. The church takes no right away, it only conforms its usages to the established principles of civil law, the teachings of nature, and the direct precepts of the Scriptures. The Scriptures command, "Wives, submit yourselves to your own husbands, as unto the Lord:" yet the Bible is the best guardian of female rights. The husband must exercise his authority with a due regard to the happiness of the wife, and the male members of a church, though they have the general superiority in governing, are bound to consult the wishes of the female members. The females have a deep interest in the concerns of the church, are usually the most numerous, often the most devoted, and, in many questions, they are, perhaps, equally well qualified to form an opinion. It would be manifestly as unjust, as it would be impolitic, for a few male members to settle or dismiss a pastor, in opposition to the wishes of many females.

There is some diversity of practice on this subject among our churches, in their efforts to give equal rights to all. When great questions are to be decided affecting directly the spiritual interests of the whole church, such as the election or dismissal of a pastor or the choice of a deacon, it is the practice of some churches, first, to ascertain the wishes of all the members, by an informal ballot, and afterwards the male members, in view of all the facts, come to the final decision. Common matters of business, such as the choice of committees, raising money, building a house for worship, &c., are decided by the male members of twenty-one years of age, and upwards. The reception of candidates to fellowship is not voting, as will be shown in the next section.

SECT. 3. *Admission of Members.*

When the candidates come before the church, they severally relate the manner in which they were brought to believe on Christ, with the evidences of their present hope, and their views, as far as they have formed any, of Christian doctrine, duty, and ordinances. Questions are freely proposed by the pastor, or by any of the members of the church. The candidates then retire, and the question of reception is taken on each case, separately.

Any member has the right to object, for good cause, to any of the candidates, or to communicate any information touching their moral and religious characters which he may possess. If sufficient cause appears, or if any member is not satisfied in respect to the Christian experience of any one of the candidates, the case should be postponed.* If no objection is made, the question of reception is put to the church, and all the members, old and young, male and female, should express their fellowship by rising. Members are not *voted* into the church. In this case the decision is not made by a mere majority. There should be unanimity. If any member object to the reception of a candidate with whom the church generally are satisfied, he is bound to give the grounds of his objection; and if it arise from prejudice, or ill-will, the objector subjects himself to censure. In this respect the church is entirely different from a mere voluntary society, into which members are voted at the will of a majority. It is, or should be a hearty unanimous welcome to the fellowship, the watch-care, the privileges, and the toils of the church.

This method of receiving members has many important benefits. It is the best earthly means of ascertaining the true character of professed converts. The language and the feelings of a real convert cannot easily be so counterfeited as to impose on a whole church, and an impostor would not often encounter such an ordeal. Every genuine relation of a religious experience meets a response in the bosom of every Christian, kindles afresh his first love, increases and diffuses knowledge of God's dealings with his children, awakens gratitude and joy, and furnishes encouragement to labor and pray for the conversion of sinners. The candidate and the church become at once closely united in fellowship and mutual interest.

* When Saul of Tarsus first offered himself to the fellowship of the church at Jerusalem, he was not admitted at once, on account of an objection against him by the *disciples*, nor until that objection was removed. Acts 9 : 26, 27. And Peter did not admit Cornelius and his family to baptism, till he had inquired if any of the *brethren* present had any objection. Acts 10 : 47.

To make the pastor and a few brethren judges of the fitness of each candidate, would throw too much labor and responsibility on them if they were faithful; if they were unfaithful, a dangerous avenue to corruption would be opened.

The foundation of church-fellowship, with all the advantages attending the communion of saints in that important relation, as well as of all efficient church discipline, is laid in this Divinely appointed method of receiving members. Each member has thus given to all the rest his reasons for the hope that is in him, so that a bond of union, of confidence, and of love, of the strongest kind is formed, at the very threshold of the church. Nothing so quickly and so strongly unites the disciples of Christ, as the relation of their spiritual exercises.

It is to be earnestly hoped, therefore, that this custom will always be carefully maintained in the churches. Should they ever relinquish it, their decline and ultimate ruin is certain. In cases of extreme diffidence, the church may be under the necessity of relying chiefly on the evidence obtained in private conversation, and reported by other individuals, but such cases are rare.

When members are received by letter from other Baptist churches, it is proper to require them to relate their religious experience. This is the uniform practice in many, if not in most of our churches. This course does not impair the credit of the letter, nor in any sense impugn the character of the church from whence it came. As each church is independent, it may require such evidence as it deems satisfactory, without giving reasonable cause of offence to any other church, and as each is separately accountable for the characters of those whom it receives as members, it has the right, and is in duty bound to examine for itself. Letters are often presented from distant unknown churches, sometimes of old date, so as to render a personal examination proper in the view of all; and as it is inconvenient, and often embarrassing to make such cases exceptions, it is better to have a uniform rule. And if there were no other reason, the fact that the custom has all the advantages referred to in the case of new members, should induce every church to adhere to it.

Sect. 4. *Absent Members.*

When a member expects to be absent from the church for a limited time, he should take from the pastor, or clerk, a letter* of recommendation to the watch and fellowship of some sister church. This is sometimes called a "letter of occasional communion," and it should be expressly limited to one year, or less from its date. This letter should be presented immediately, and the bearer should attend regularly on the worship and communion of that sister church. At the end of the year, if unforeseen circumstances prevent his return, he should communicate to his own church an account of his situation, his religious views and feelings, and whether he is enjoying the privileges of the Gospel. He is still under the care and subject to the discipline of the church, and if he does not take such a letter, or does not make a proper and seasonable report, the church should inquire respecting him, and call him to account.

If a member removes to a place where there is no sister church, he should attend on the best religious instruction in his power, and make an annual or semi-annual communication to the church. Such cases, however, will be rare, when religious improvement and usefulness are the leading objects in choosing a residence.

If a member removes to a distance with or without such a letter and makes no report of himself to the church for a year or more, the circumstance should be inquired into, and if his place of residence cannot be ascertained, his name, after suitable inquiry, should be erased from the list of members. If he afterwards give satisfaction to the church by confession or explanation, he should be restored. No church should suffer its records to be encumbered with a list of the names of unknown members.

* For an example of such a letter or certificate, see Acts 18 : 27 ; Rom. 16 : 1, 2. Compare 2 Cor. 3 : 1 ; Col. 4 : 10.

Sect. 5. *Dismission of Members.*

If a member desires, for good cause, to be dismissed to a sister church, he makes application to the church of which he is a member for a letter of dismission and recommendation to a church which he specifies, and if no reason appears why his request should not be granted, the church vote to grant it, and he receives a certificate signed by the clerk, or pastor. He is still a member of the church which grants such letter until received by the other, as much subject to its watch and discipline as before, and the language of the letter should always distinctly express or recognize the fact.

The dismission of members is merely a transfer of membership from one visible church, or congregation of believers, to another. To this transfer there are three parties; the member desiring a dismissory letter, the church *from* which, and the church *to* which he proposes to be dismissed. Each of the parties is entitled to an independent voice in the measure, and each should be reasonably satisfied of its propriety.

If some improper motive be apparent in a member asking to be dismissed, the church should refuse his request, and endeavor to reclaim him to a proper state of feeling. Or if his brethren think a member ought not to leave them, he should distrust his own judgment, and not terminate a relation formed by solemn covenant, without serious, prayerful consideration. A member might be very important to the welfare, or even to the existence of a church, and he ought not lightly to withdraw. In ordinary cases, however, the member is the best judge of his duty, and the church should dismiss him at his request.

No member can properly be dismissed to another church who is not in good standing. To dismiss a member under censure, or liable to it, to another church, is deception and imposition. The church that does not act with good faith in this matter, will be cursed and blighted. Let no church so far forget its duty as to dismiss a member to get rid of him, and escape the labor of discipline. Such a course is wicked in the extreme. The church must not allow a member to obtain a dismission to escape an act of discipline.

No authority is found in the Scriptures, for dismissing a member from the church to the world. The fact that a member is dissatisfied with the doctrines or the doings of the church, or deems himself unfit for church-fellowship, is not a ground of dismission. A husband might be convinced that he is unfit for that relation, or become tired of his wife, yet that furnishes no ground for a divorce. Every one should understand, when he enters a church, that there is no private egress; the relation then formed can be terminated only by a transfer to a sister church, by excommunication, or by death.

Sect. 6. *Admissions to Occasional Communion.*

When such a letter as is described in Section 4, is presented to the church, the fact, together with the date of the letter, should be entered on the records, and the individual presenting it should be admitted by vote to the privilege of occasional communion. Persons thus admitted are allowed to attend church meetings but not to vote. With this exception, they have the same privileges as the members of the church.

It is the duty of the church to watch over such persons, and if they deserve to be subjected to discipline, the church should withdraw from them the privilege of communion, and give prompt notice thereof to the church to which they belong.

In all cases of this kind it should be understood that the object of such letters is temporary. Whenever the residence of such persons becomes permanent, they should become members in full of some church.

It is the custom of some churches to admit no strangers to the Lord's Table, who do not present written certificates of church-membership and good standing.

CHAPTER IV.

CHURCH DISCIPLINE.

Discipline in a church is the regular, vigorous application of the principles, doctrines and rules of divine revelation, in promoting the purity, knowledge, order, peace, and useful efficiency of each of the members and of the entire body. It is, therefore, an extensive subject. A church must have laws sufficient to preserve its integrity, and the rights of members, with power and obligation properly vested, to secure their prompt execution, for its *own* sake. This is one part of discipline. But it has, also, a further and a higher aim. Scriptural church discipline is designed, and adapted to increase, concentrate, and direct the agency of Christians in the conversion of the world.

It has become customary to speak of discipline in a church as having sole reference to the treatment of disorders and offences. This is a very contracted view of the subject. A church is the *Family of Christ*, in which subordination, regularity, instruction, order, watchful kindness, reproof, and love, are daily blended in family discipline. The church is a *School of Christ*, every member of which is in a process of education, and is bound to make the utmost improvement in manners, knowledge, and holiness. They have "one master, [teacher,] even Christ," all whose rules they are bound to observe. The church is an *Army of Christ*, every soldier being a volunteer. But what would become of an army, whose whole discipline consisted in trying delinquents, and drumming rogues out of the camp? A well-disciplined church is like a well-disciplined army, in which every officer and soldier is at his post, with arms and armor bright, each faithfully coöperating with all the rest in the common cause. Discipline in such a body is an all-pervading influence; extending to every member, at all times.

A church which neglects discipline, is like a garden without walls, or a city without magistrates and laws. However excellent its creed, it will soon sink into confusion and wretchedness. The first tendencies therefore to laxity in discipline should be met and checked. The daily watchword of the church should be, "The Lord Jesus expects every member to do his duty." Let this higher purpose of discipline be always kept in view, and the occasions for church censures and excommunication would be seldom.

SECT. 1. *Nature and Design of Discipline.*

The leading element in church discipline is love to the Saviour. The church is his body; and what can be so dear to every member's heart, as the health, the vigor, the beauty, and the attractiveness of "the body of Christ?" To preserve or promote it, he should be willing to sacrifice a right hand, or a right eye. Social and relative attachments should all be subordinate to this high principle, in every act of discipline.

Profound reverence for the word of God, is essential to the proper exercise of church discipline. We are not to consult public opinion, nor the views or practices of other religious communities, nor our own feelings, nor our judgment of what is expedient; but always to bear in mind that SCRIPTURE, given by inspiration of God, is profitable for doctrine, for correction, for reproof, and for *discipline;* as the only infallible guide.

Tenderness and love towards all the brethren, united with a humbling conviction of our own weakness and unworthiness, should characterize our church discipline. Although the church is appointed to "judge those that are within," yet it is only in accordance with its Master's will, who would not break the bruised reed, whose command is, to "lift up the hands which hang down, and the feeble knees, and make straight paths for your feet, lest that which is lame be turned out of the way; but let it rather be healed." To be guarded against severe and unfeeling treatment of an erring brother, we are to "consider ourselves, lest we also be tempted."

The nature of church discipline may be further seen in the fact that it is intended for pious persons, who are regenerated by the Spirit of God, and walk in a new life. Were they perfect in holiness, they might still need some system of discipline to keep them so, yet as they are still imperfect, and "going on to perfection," they need discipline adapted to their condition. As the power of an army is increased by discipline, so that a small body of well-drilled and thoroughly disciplined troops is able to conquer a much larger body of undisciplined men of equal courage and strength, so it is with the church of God.

Its nature is further illustrated by the fact that the disciplinary powers and duties of each church extend to all its own members, and no farther. "Each church being competent in itself for all the purposes of government and discipline"—its covenant extending to its own members only, admitting no others to take any part in the administration of its government, having power to cite them and no others to appear and answer to charges—must of course confine its church censures and all its disciplinary proceedings to its own members. Were the case otherwise, any member might find himself subjected to the discipline of churches without number, from some of which he is, in form, excluded, in others under censure, in others in full fellowship. But by the simple apostolic principle, that a church-member can hold church-fellowship in one church only, at the same time, and of course be subject to the discipline of that body only, all is plain. The watch-care of each disciple is provided for among those who know him best, while the rights of each church, and of each individual member, are secured inviolate. It is a violation of all order and propriety, for one church to put forth its disciplinary censures against the members of other churches. They may be classed in the same denomination, they may deserve to be called to account, but it is the duty of the particular church of which they are members to do it, and their neglect does not warrant another church in going beyond the limits of its duty. Our neighbor's children may deserve correction, which rightly administered might do them good, as well as produce a salutary effect on all the children in the neighborhood, but it does not follow that it is our duty, or that of our family, to go around and administer it gratuitously. "What have I to do," says the Apostle, "to judge them that are *without?* do not *ye* judge them that are *within?* [i. e., your own members.] But them that are without God judgeth. Therefore put away from *among yourselves* that wicked person."

The duty of maintaining church discipline belongs to the *members* of the church, individually and collectively, and if faithfully and affectionately performed by them, in obedience to the rules of the Gospel, it is a salutary exercise of their Christian graces. It is a sinful shrinking from duty to be absent from the meetings of the church because cases of discipline, even though painful, are to be attended to. This is deserting the post of duty in the hour of danger.

The higher objects to be accomplished in church discipline are,

1. The increase of piety. When a church is in a state of vigorous and wholesome discipline, "the whole body fitly joined together, and compacted by that which every joint supplieth, according to the effectual working in the measure of every part, maketh increase of the body, to the edifying of itself in love." The influence of elevated piety and exemplary Christian faithfulness, in church-members, is reciprocal. "Iron sharpeneth iron, so a man sharpeneth the countenance of his friend." One of the plainest duties involved in church-fellowship is, the increase of the piety and holiness of the church. Hence the members are commanded, "Confess your faults one to another, and pray one for another, that ye may be healed." The "faults" here referred to, are not, of course, such offences as require corrective proceedings, but such as retard the growth of piety. To accomplish this high purpose of Christian discipline, the Apostle exhorts the members of the Philippian church to "stand fast in one spirit, with one mind striving together for the faith of the

gospel." The increase of piety in a church is the true preventive of offences and apostasy.

2. To increase brotherly love. "God hath tempered the body together, . . . that the members should have the same care one for another. And whether one member suffer, all the members suffer with it: or one member be honored, all the members rejoice with it." "Be ye all of one mind, having compassion one of another: love as brethren, be pitiful, be courteous." 1 Cor. 12 : 24–26. 1 Peter 3 : 8. The increase of brotherly love is the best preventive of strifes and divisions, against which Christians are frequently and solemnly warned.

3. To illustrate the excellence of religion before the world. "Ye are the light of the world. A city that is set on a hill cannot be hid." "If the light that is in you be darkness, how great is that darkness." "I am with you in the spirit, joying and beholding your order." "I thank my God through Jesus Christ for you all, that your faith is spoken of throughout the whole world." Matt. 5 : 14; Col. 2 : 5; Rom. 1 : 8. When the Christian graces of the church at Jerusalem shone brightest, they are described as "praising God, and having favor with all the people." So when the Corinthian church had manifested their abhorrence of sin, and their tender, earnest regard to the commands of Christ, the Apostle says to them, "Ye are our epistle, written in our hearts, known and read of all men: forasmuch as ye are manifestly declared to be the epistle of Christ ministered by us, written not with ink, but with the Spirit of the living God; not in tables of stone, but in fleshly tables of the heart."

4. To increase the efficiency of the church by calling into useful activity every member, in the sphere best adapted to his powers. "For as we have many members in one body, and all members have not the same office; so we, being many, are one body in Christ, and every one members one of another. Having then gifts differing according to the grace that is given to us, whether prophecy, let us prophesy according to the pro-

portion of faith; or ministry, let us wait on our ministering; or he that teacheth on teaching; or he that exhorteth on exhortation." Rom. 12 : 4–8.

Thus far the influence of church discipline is preventive. If delinquencies call for corrective discipline, the objects are,

1. To reclaim those who fall into sin. "Brethren, if a man be overtaken in a fault, ye who are spiritual restore such an one." "Brethren, if any of you do err from the truth, and one convert him, let him know, that he who converteth the sinner from the error of his way shall save a soul from death; and shall hide a multitude of sins." Gal 6 : 1; James 5 : 19, 20. Such is also the spirit and purpose of the Saviour's command in regard to an offending brothre.

2. The purity, honor, and consequent usefulness of the church. "But I have a few things against thee, because thou hast them that hold the doctrine of Balaam." "Know ye not that a little leaven leaveneth the whole lump? Purge out therefore, the old leaven, that ye may be a new lump." Rev. 2 : 14; 1 Cor. 5 : 6, 7.

3. To prevent sin in others. "Them that sin rebuke before all, that others also may fear." "If any man obey not our word by this epistle, note that man, and have no company with him, that he may be ashamed." 1 Tim. 5 : 20; 2 Thess. 3 : 14.

Sect. 2. *Church Covenant and Watch.*

One important means of maintaining a high state of discipline in the church, and preventing sin in the members, is, their vigilant watch over each other. Gross sins in church-members are preceded by smaller ones, and these by smaller still, and by neglects of duty which a timely admonition might have prevented. This mutual watch is not only the soul of church discipline, but affords the best exercise of the piety of its members.

When believers join the church, they not only make a public profession of their faith, but enter into a special covenant, either expressed or implied, with that particular body of Christians; and it is this covenant which unites the baptized believer in church-fellowship to the members of that church, and engages him to perform certain duties to them, in virtue of the relation and obligations assumed in the church covenant. It is customary in some churches to have written or printed articles of covenant expressive of the obligations thus assumed, which every candidate for membership is expected to sign, in token of cordial assent to the same.

The adoption of this covenant creates no new obligation to God or man; but simply expresses the intention of the professed convert to perform specific duties. Jacob entered into a special covenant with God, attested by the erection of a stone; Gen. 28 : 16–22; and David adopted a written covenant for the guide of his conduct; Psalm 101. A church covenant is of the same nature, though being extended in its application to a company of believers, its practical value is still more obvious. The following forms having been extensively adopted by the churches, may be considered as fair specimens of the

CHURCH COVENANT.

"Having been, as we trust, brought by Divine grace to embrace the Lord Jesus Christ, and to give up ourselves wholly to Him; we do now solemnly and joyfully covenant with each other, TO WALK TOGETHER IN HIM WITH BROTHERLY LOVE, to His glory as our common Lord. We do, therefore, in His strength engage,

"That we will exercise a mutual care, as members one of another, to promote the growth of the whole body in Christian knowledge, holiness, and comfort; to the end that we may stand perfect and complete in all the will of God.

"That, to promote and secure this object, we will uphold the public worship of God and the ordinances of His house; and hold constant communion with each other therein; that we will cheerfully contribute of our property for the support of the poor, and for the maintenance of a faithful ministry of the gospel among us.

"That we will not omit closet and family religion at home; nor allow ourselves in the too common neglect of the great duty of religiously training up our children, and those under our care with a view to the service of Christ, and the enjoyment of heaven.

"That we will walk circumspectly in the world, that we may win their souls; remembering that God hath not given us the spirit of fear but of power, and of love, and of a sound mind; that we are the light of the world and the salt of the earth, and that a city set on a hill cannot be hid.

"That we will frequently exhort, and, if occasion shall require, admonish one another, according to Matthew 18th, in the spirit of meekness, considering ourselves lest we also be tempted; and that as in baptism we have been buried with Christ, and raised again, so there is on us a special obligation thenceforth to walk in newness of life.

"And may the God of peace, who brought again from the dead our Lord Jesus, that great Shepherd of the sheep, through the blood of the everlasting covenant, make us perfect in every good work to do His will; working in us that which is well pleasing in his sight, through Jesus Christ: to whom be glory, forever and ever. Amen."

ANOTHER.

"As we trust we have been brought by Divine grace to embrace the Lord Jesus Christ, and by the influence of his Spirit to give ourselves up to Him, so we do now solemnly covenant with each other, as God shall enable us, that we will walk together in brotherly love; that we will exercise a Christian care and watchfulness over each other, and faithfully warn, rebuke, and admonish one another, as the case shall require; that we will not forsake the assembling of ourselves together, nor omit the great duty of prayer, both for ourselves and for others; that we will participate in each other's joys; and endeavor with tenderness and sympathy to bear each other's burdens and sorrows; that we will seek Divine aid to enable us to walk circumspectly and watchfully in the world, denying ungodliness and every worldly lust; that we will strive together for the support of a faithful evangelical ministry among us; and, through life, amidst evil report and good report, seek to live to the glory of Him who hath called us out of darkness into his marvellous light."

By such a covenant church-members agree to notice each other's errors and dangers with affectionate concern, and to give or receive such timely warning and reproof as occasion may require. Any member who knows of anything in another inconsistent with his profession or his hopes, be it an error in doctrine, a neglect of duty, or an impropriety of conduct, or of language, is bound to give him friendly caution, with a view to his amendment. "Thou shalt in any wise rebuke thy neighbor, and not suffer sin upon him."

Besides actual faults, we may see a brother exposed to temptation, unconscious of his danger. How many, through some peculiar weakness, or easily besetting sin, are exposed to fall, who might be saved by timely warning; and how precious, in such a case, is a clear-sighted, true-hearted brother, to raise the voice of affectionate solicitude! It is cruel and wrong to wait till he actually falls. In such a case, how sacred is the duty of "looking diligently lest any man *fail* of the grace of God." And if we see our brethren growing cold, and declining in religious feeling we should remember the duty of our covenant and watch, to "stir up their pure minds by way of remembrance."

There is far more hope of saving an erring brother before his sin is aggravated and notorious, than afterwards. The private labors and affectionate solicitude of individual brethren are more winning than the open public proceedings of the church; his conscience is more tender; he is not chafed by suspicions and reports. Prevention is better than cure. But alas! how often is the pledge of members to watch over each other neglected till a cure is impossible; expulsion is the only resort, the church is disgraced, and a soul is ruined, it may through its neglect.

This mutual, affectionate watch, is one of the chief benefits of our church union. "Faithful are the wounds of a friend, but the kisses of an enemy are deceitful." A brother who will in kindness admonish and reprove us, is above all price. "Let the righteous smite me; it shall be a kindness; let him reprove me; it shall be an excellent oil." Why should it be deemed so unpleasant, and be so much neglected, when, like charity, it "is twice blessed; it blesseth him that gives, and him that takes?" That the faithful discharge of this duty is peculiarly acceptable to the Saviour, is manifest. "Now we exhort you, brethren, warn them that are unruly, comfort the feeble-minded, support the weak, be patient toward all men." 1 Thess. 5 : 14.

The utmost kindness and wisdom are requisite in performing this duty. A distrustful, meddlesome, fault-finding spirit must be carefully guarded against. In giving admonition, regard should be had to the age and station of both parties. "Rebuke not an elder, but entreat him as a father; and the younger men as brethren; the elder women as mothers; the younger as sisters, with all purity." 1 Tim. 5 : 1, 2. The time, the place, the circumstances, as well as the manner and spirit of giving reproof, are all important. If we are not in a temper to receive reproof meekly and thankfully, we are not prepared to give it. The duty is mutual and correlative. "Confess your faults one to another, and pray one for another, that ye may be healed."

And finally, to reject or resent a reproof, kindly given by a Christian brother, is a great wrong to him, and a violation of a solemn covenant. "He that hateth reproof is brutish." Such an evidence of faithfulness and affection should greatly increase our love to him who bears it. The duty of giving reproof implies the duty of receiving it kindly, and of endeavoring to profit by it.

SECT. 3. *Offenses requiring Church Action.*

As "it is impossible but that offenses will come," even into the purest and best regulated church, it is of great importance that every member clearly understand, and faithfully carry into practice, the Scriptural rules for treating them.

As this part of church discipline consists in the right application of the law of Christ to offending members, it is necessary to inquire what offenses require church action. Natural imperfections of character are not to be classed as offenses. A church-member may be constitutionally bold or timid, too forward or too backward, loquacious or taciturn; but these traits of character are not "offenses," which furnish occasion for church action. An *offense* is a wrong *act*, purposely done, either privately, against the rights of an individual, or publicly against morality or religion; but not against any one individual more than another. Offenses may be classed under two heads: private or personal, and public offenses. The ground of this distinction, is in the circumstances of the case, and the different treatment required; and not in any supposed difference in the degrees of sinfulness involved. A private offense is a wrong act of one church-member to the injury of another. A public offense is any wicked conduct of a church-member: any neglect of duty, or manifestation of unholy temper, which, if persevered in, would prove him destitute of the Christian spirit. The distinction is similar to that between "civil" and "criminal" actions, in judicial proceedings. The ground of the distinction, in both cases, consists in the fact that different proceedings are adopted to secure the ends of justice and mercy. Let us consider these two classes of offenses, and the treatment proper to each.

I. *Private Offenses.* A church-member may know, or believe, that another member has done or said something to his injury personally. If he has not *certain knowledge* that it is so, he is bound either to seek a private explanation, or to dismiss all suspicions from his mind. If he has *certain knowledge* that his brother has trespassed against him, but not *proof*, sustained by the testimony of "two or three witnesses," it is a private, personal offense, for the treatment of which the Scriptures furnish clear and specific rules. "If thy brother shall trespass against thee, go and tell him his fault, *between thee and him alone.*" The first duty is private, affectionate expostulation between the aggrieved and offending brother only. No third person should be informed of it. If the aggrieved brother tells the secret to any other person, he disobeys the command of Christ. The Saviour's precept has made his duty plain.

One of three results will follow this proceeding. Either, 1. The offending brother may admit the charge, confess his fault, and make full satisfaction. In this case "thou hast *gained* thy brother." And what a gain it is! "He that converteth the sinner from the error of his way, shall save a soul from death, and shall hide a multitude of sins." It is an occasion of devout thanksgiving to God, and it must never be mentioned again. "If thy brother trespass against thee, rebuke him; and if he repent, forgive him;" and there the affair ends. Or, 2. He may deny the act charged, while the injured brother has certain knowledge that he is guilty, though no witnesses by which to prove it. In this case, he adds the sin of lying to his first offense. What must be done?

It is obvious that the injured brother cannot proceed to take the second step enjoined in Matt 18: for he has no "witnesses" to take. Suppose he should take with him one or two brethren, and repeat the charge in their presence. The charge is again denied, and they ask for proof; but there are no witnesses. They must, of course, decide that the charge is not sustained. But now suppose that the real offender brings against the other of defamation. These brethren are witnesses to the fact that he has charged him with an offense which he could not prove. And if required by the church to confess the crime of falsehood or suffer expulsion, he could not confess without telling actual falsehood. An innocent member might thus be excluded from the church through his own indiscretion, in departing from the law of evidence laid down in the Scriptures.

What, then, is the law of evidence? It is this: "One witness shall not rise up against a man for any iniquity, or for any sin, in any sin that he sinneth: at the mouth of two witnesses, or at the mouth of three witnesses, shall the matter be established. If a false witness rise up against any man, to testify against him that which is wrong, then both the men between whom the controversy is, shall stand before the Lord, before the priest and the judges which shall be in those days. And the judges shall make diligent inquisition; and, behold, if the witness be a false witness, and hath testified falsely against his brother, then shall ye do unto him as he had thought to do unto his brother; so shalt thou put away evil from among you. And those which remain shall hear, and fear, and shall henceforth commit no more any such evil among you." Deut. 19 : 15–20. A false witness is one who makes false charges, or charges which, however true, he cannot prove by "two or three witnesses." To this law our Saviour's directions in Matt. 18, conform. "In the mouth of *two or three witnesses* shall every word be established." See also 2 Cor. 13 : 1; 1 Tim. 5 : 19; Heb. 10 : 28.

But it is asked, what must the aggrieved brother do? He is required to forgive the offender "if he repent," but not otherwise. He does not repent, but adds lying to his other sin. Must he feel towards him, and treat him, as a brother in full fellowship? No, he cannot do that. He may rebuke him in secret, tell him that he is not forgiven, that he is regarded as an unjust man and a hypocrite, and there he must leave it, with the offender's conscience and his God. He must not turn his back on the Lord's table; if he does so, he makes himself a transgressor; for he should go there to commune with the Saviour and with the church. The settlement of difficulties between individual members has nothing to do with communion at the Lord's table. A difficulty of this kind is one for which the only remedy is prayer and patience; and if he will lay the case before God, and wait with the patience enjoined in the 37th Psalm, he will, in due time, see the offender brought to repentance, or his guilt made manifest to all.

If any are not satisfied with this course, they must take the consequences of pursuing a different one. If they imagine that God will sustain them in exposing sin, while they disregard his revealed law of evidence, let them listen to the salutary cautions which wisdom gives, as to the probable consequences. "Go not forth *hastily* to strive, lest thou know not what to do in the end thereof, when thy neighbor hath put thee to shame. Debate thy cause with *thy neighbor himself;* and discover not a *secret to another;* lest he that heareth it put thee to shame, and thine infamy turn not away." Prov. 25 : 8–10. The church is bound, by the commandment of her Lord, to act only on the testimony of witnesses, and when she so acts and decides, common sense approves her decisions.

Or, 3. As another result of this private interview, the offender may admit the *act* charged, yet justify himself in it, and refuse to give satisfaction. He is willing that others should know what he has done. In this case, the way is open for calling in "one or two more," who may, if necessary, act as witnesses; because, in addition to the aggrieved brother's own *certain knowledge* of the act which he considers an offense, he will have proof derived from the offender's own admission; and the case must be treated precisely as if there had been original witnesses of the fact.

This brings us to consider the case of a private or personal offense, of which the injured party not only has *certain knowledge*, but *proof* by witnesses, or by the admission of the offender. The first duty of the aggrieved member, in this case, also, is thus enjoined by the Saviour. "If thy brother shall trespass AGAINST THEE, go and tell *him* his fault, *between thee and him alone*." Here are four things to be noticed. 1. It is a case of *personal* injury, known to the injured party. 2. It is the *injured party* who is commanded to move in the matter. 3. *He* is to tell his grievance to his *offending brother*. 4. And to *him alone*. Beware, O church-member, lest thou say, in thy wicked heart, 'I have *proof* against him, which will exclude him from the church, when known; let him come to me and confess.' Your Master has told you to *go to him*. He enacted this rule, not to excuse, or extenuate his guilt, but because he will not come to you—his sin has hardened his heart, and if you do not go to him, he may be lost forever. Before you go, pray that much of the mind that was in Christ Jesus, who, "while we were yet enemies, died for us," may be in you. Here let it be borne in mind, that, although the injured brother has witnesses of his wrong, his first duty is a *private* one. He is not to begin by telling his complaints in church meetings, nor to the pastor, or deacons. If he does so, he should be met with a prompt reproof. His *first* duty in the case is strictly a *private* one, between him and his offending brother *only*. The reasons for this course are numerous. The injury may not be so great as he supposed, or he may find that a part of the blame belongs to himself. "He that is first in his own cause seemeth just, but his neighbor cometh and searcheth him." The offender may even now be sorry for it, and when he sees that one whom he has injured is tender of his reputation, and solicitous for his welfare, he may be so softened that reconciliation and love may be restored at once.

The object in going must not be to dispute, to criminate, nor to threaten, but to "*gain*" thy brother. You go to him in the spirit of love, state plainly and fully the wrong which you believe him to have done you, and then labor to convince him of his fault. It may appear to you much smaller when you hear his explanation. It may be that his conscience is already tender, and that a kind, faithful word from you would prepare the way for reconciliation. If the brother be ignorant, or disagreeable, it is still your duty to go to him. "Take heed," says the Saviour, "that ye despise not one of these little ones." Recollect he stooped much lower to save you. And he appeals to you, "If a man have an hundred sheep, and one of them be gone astray, doth he not leave the ninety and nine, and go into the mountains, and seek that which is gone astray? And if he find it, verily I say unto you he rejoiceth more of that sheep, than of the ninety and nine which went not astray. Even so it is not the will of your Father in heaven, that one of these little ones should perish." If you have not the spirit of Christ in this thing, you are none of his.

Go then to your brother in private, not in a reproving, fault-finding manner. Think of your own infirmities and sins. Address him kindly and humbly. Do not perform this duty as a mere preparatory step in a course of discipline. Remember that the probabilities of your saving an erring brother are much greater here than in any subsequent stage of proceedings. Labor with him as you would to save your own child from impending death. Let all be done in private, making no mention of it further than is strictly necessary for inquiry or advice. If he shall hear thee, confess his fault, and ask forgiveness, what a blessed triumph of Christian love! Let your reconciliation be perfect, and let the subject never be mentioned to his reproach again.

"If he will not hear thee, then take with thee one or two more, that in the mouth of two or three witnesses, every word may be established."

This is the second step, which is to be taken only in case of the failure of the first. There is less hope of saving the offender, yet there is ground for hope that mutual friends may effect what the aggrieved brother failed to do. The case is now becoming a serious one, it is assuming a judicial form, so that witnesses may be needed. It is necessary, therefore, that everything be done with strict accuracy. And, 1. Make out a *written statement* of the injury done you. Be careful you do not overstate it. 2. Find out what proof you can bring, and see that your charges are not greater than the proof. 3. If the offense which can be proved is not such as would require the excommunication of the offender, should he refuse to retract, you must stop where you are. 4. Let the brethren selected be persons of acknowledged piety, candor, and sound judgment, who are not reasonably objectionable to the offending brother.

The part which these brethren are to perform is, 1. That of mediators. The accuser and the accused are brethren—their brethren. Their first object is to win the erring back to duty. In the first place they are to ascertain whether an offense has been committed sufficient to require church action. If so, they expostulate calmly with the offender, point out the sinfulness of his act, the increased sinfulness of adhering to it, and the consequences which must follow. If they find the accuser also in fault, or if he has magnified little things into great grievances, they advise him to make concessions also, so that harmony may be restored. 2. They go as witnesses. They may or may not have been witnesses of the original act of offense, and there may be others who were witnesses of it, but they become witnesses of the offender's wrong temper, and of his refusal to give satisfaction, or be reconciled to his brother. It will be seen, then, that although the first step in this disciplinary process makes no provision for a *trial*, this second step does. It is in fact a preliminary trial, and is preparatory to the final trial, from which there is no appeal. 3. They go to give advice; first to the offender, but "if he neglect to hear them," they advise the aggrieved brother to "tell it to the church," if they deem it a case requiring church action, and how to do it.

As the first object is to effect a reconciliation, the inquiry is sometimes made, When may an offense be regarded as removed? The reply is, when mutual love is restored, and not till then. No false delicacy, or desire to avoid trouble, should prevent frankness and plain dealing. Mere surface healing is useless. And when an offense is confessed and forgiven, it should be, as in the case of the Divine forgiveness, "remembered no more," "cast behind the back," "removed as far as the east is from the west."

If a church-member is asked to go as a mediator, a witness, and counsellor, to assist in removing an offense, he should not refuse but for very weighty reasons. "Blessed are the peacemakers." In that character they should go. A brother feels aggrieved. Another brother is charged with wrong. Go, and if possible prevent the breach from becoming wider; produce reconciliation; save the church from agitation and dishonor. And who knows but a word now fitly spoken will "save a soul from death?"

If the offender still refuses to give satisfaction, preparation must be made for the third step in the process. The complaint, in writing, should be submitted to judicious brethren, who might be able to point out any mistake or deficiency, and the witnesses should affix their names, to certify the correctness of the charges. The aggrieved member should then notify the offender of the time when he shall present the case in church meeting.

"If he shall neglect to hear them, tell it unto the church."

This is the third and the last step which the aggrieved brother is to take in the matter. When he has laid the facts and testimony before the church, he has done his duty, and the church must now take the case in hand.

At the proper stage of the meeting, the aggrieved brother, or some one in his behalf, (which in many cases would be the preferable course,) arises, and, addressing the Moderator, asks leave to introduce a case of private grievance. No name should be called, no attempt made to tell what it is. The Moderator should allow nothing more to be said till the church are certified that the first and second steps enjoined by the Saviour, have been taken, that the witnesses are present, and that the alleged offender has been notified of the proceedings. If the complainant has not done all this, his movement should be adjudged out of order; nor should he, or any other member, be allowed to bring the case, in any shape, before the church, till all this has been done.

If it appears that all the steps required have been taken, the complaint is read, and the testimony of the witnesses is called for. The original charge is proved, and, also, the refusal of the accused to give satisfaction when urged to do so.

The offender is now called upon to "hear the church." If the offense charged against him is fully proved, he should be required to give satisfaction. The whole authority of the church,—the body of Christ, and his visible representative on earth,—is now brought to vindicate an injured member, and bring an offender to repentance. The brethren, one after another, address him, labor to convince him of his unjust and unholy temper, and the dangers to which it is exposing him. He *may*, even now, relent. But if all appeals are in vain, the fourth and last step in this painful process must be taken.

"If he neglect to hear the church, let him be to thee as a heathen man and a publican: verily, I say unto you, whatsoever ye shall bind on earth, shall be bound in heaven; and whatsoever ye shall loose on earth, shall be loosed in heaven."

To treat one "as a heathen man and a publican," is, to withdraw from him fellowship, and the communion of saints. It is highly desirable that a vote of exclusion be unanimous, though not necessary to its validity; but in all cases the vote, with the reasons for it, should be correctly entered on the records of the church.

If the accused insists that justice will not be done him on account of alleged prejudices against him, or if a serious division is known to exist, it may be well, before final action, to call in the aid of the pastors and elders of neighboring churches as counsellors; but in no case should a council be called to adjudicate between a church and one of its members, or one who has been excluded from it.

If the offending member refuses to come before the church he of course "neglects to hear the church," who may proceed to hear evidence and judge as though he were present; and this contempt of its authority is an additional offense.

It should not be forgotten that in all cases of private offense the duty of reparation really devolves, first, on the offending brother. "If thou bring thy gift to the altar, and there rememberest that *thy brother hath aught against thee*, leave there thy gift before the altar, and go thy way; first be reconciled to thy brother, and then come and offer thy gift."

If the offending brother neglects to do this, the duty of the aggrieved brother to proceed according to these rules, is sacred. He has no right to put up in silence with a real injury, under the plea that it is the offender's duty to come to him, or from a desire to avoid the unpleasantness of the process. For the sake of one who, by wrong doing, is involved in a far greater calamity than himself, for the sake of Christ and his church, for his own sake, that he may not incur the guilt of suffering sin upon his brother unreproved, nor be robbed of spiritual peace, he should faithfully and promptly perform this duty.

A private offense must be treated in the same manner as a public offense after the first two steps have proved unavailing, and the case has been regularly presented to the church. It then becomes an offense against public virtue, morality, and religion. And, on the other hand, a personal offense, though committed publicly, should be treated according to the rule given in Matt. 18, for the removal of private offenses.

As to the *nature* of private offenses, they are real injuries committed by one member against the person, character, or property of another. Assaults on the person rarely occur as matters of church discipline. Slanderous attacks on character are more frequent, and, as there must be witnesses, are more easily proved. An *habitual* slanderer is termed in the Scriptures a "*railer*;" and he is classed as a *public offender*, with the fornicator, the drunkard, and the idolater; with whom the Christians are commanded "not to keep company, ... no, not to eat." But slander, as a private or personal offense, consists in originating or circulating reports injurious to the reputation of another, whether known to be malicious falsehoods or taken up and circulated without evidence of their truth. The good man "backbiteth not with his tongue, nor doeth evil to his neighbor, nor *taketh up a reproach* against his neighbor." He who does either of these, commits a "trespass" against his brother, who, if he regards it as requiring correction or redress of any kind, is bound to pursue the course enjoined by the Saviour for private offenses.

As to *pecuniary* difficulties between members of the same church, some special rules for their adjustment are given in 1 Cor. 6 : 1–11. Although the circumstances of that church were very different, in some important respects, from those of churches in Christian lands living under free governments at the present day, yet the leading principle of that passage is applicable to all churches, at all times. The principle established in the passage is, that *church-members should refer all their differences about pecuniary matters to their brethren for adjustment; and in no case, while they continue to be members of the church, should they go to law with each other in the civil courts.* Sooner than do this, they are commanded to "take wrong," and "suffer themselves to be defrauded."

Difficulties and misunderstandings between Christians respecting pecuniary affairs should be referred to wise brethren, who are able to judge in such matters. If either party is unreasonable, and unjust, there will be witnesses of his conduct, if it should be necessary to bring it before the church. If he will not submit to the judgment of brethren, nor hear the church, but persists in manifest injustice, he should be excluded; and, if necessary, may be prosecuted, as any other person, in the civil courts.

II. *Public Offenses.* These are offenses against morality, or religion, or against the church; such as intemperance, profaneness, Sabbath-breaking, frequenting improper places of amusement, disseminating false doctrines, sowing discord, or neglecting covenant obligations. These cannot be brought before the church in the same manner as private offenses, because, not having been committed against any individual in particular, no one can make them personal matters. They may be classed as follows:

1. Immoralities. "But now I have written unto you not to keep company, if any man that is called a brother be a fornicator, or covetous, or an idolater, or a railer, or a drunkard, or an extortioner; with such a one, no, not to eat. For what have I to do to judge them also that are without? Do not ye judge them that are within? But them that are without God judgeth. Therefore put away from among yourselves that wicked person." 1 Cor. 5 : 11, 12, 13. See also 6 : 9, 10; Jude 4–13; Heb. 12 : 15, 16.

2. Denial of the essential truths of the Gospel, or the belief of errors subversive of them. "If there come any unto you, and bring not this doctrine, receive him not into your house,

neither bid him God speed." "Though we, or an angel from heaven, preach any other Gospel unto you than that which we have preached unto you, let him be accursed. As we said before, so say I now again, If any man preach any other Gospel unto you than that ye have received, let him be accursed." Gal. 1 : 8, 9 ; 2 John v. 10. See also Gal. 5 : 12 ; 2 Thess. 3 : 14 ; Rev. 2 : 2, 14, 15, 20. It is the duty of the church to reject those who reject the Gospel. This is obvious from the nature of the case, as well as from these passages. The only question is, what truths must a man reject, or what errors must he imbibe, to render him worthy of exclusion? Great allowances should be made for weakness of mind, and for defective or erroneous early education. "Him that is weak in the faith receive ye." All reasonable liberty should be allowed for independent, private judgment. Yet errors in regard to fundamental doctrines should not be allowed in church-members.

3. Making divisions and disturbances in the church. "A man that is an heretic, after the first and second admonition, reject." "Mark those who cause divisions and offenses, contrary to the doctrine which ye have learned, and avoid them." Tit. 3 : 10 ; Rom. 16 : 17, 18.

4. Covetousness manifested by a neglect to provide for one's family, or in a refusal to bear a reasonable part in the pecuniary support of the Gospel. "If any provide not for his own, and specially for those of his own house, he hath denied the faith, and is worse than an infidel." "Let him that is taught in the word, communicate unto him that teacheth, in all good things." "If any man that is called a brother, be a fornicator, or *covetous*, ... with such an one, no not to eat." "For this ye know, that no whoremonger, nor unclean person, nor *covetous man, who is an idolater*, hath any inheritance in the kingdom of Christ and of God." 1 Tim. 5 : 8 ; Gal. 6 : 6 ; 1 Cor. 5 : 11 ; Eph. 5 : 5. If "the laborer is worthy of his reward," it is dishonesty to keep it back ; if "the Lord hath ordained that those who preach the Gospel should live of the Gospel," it is open

disobedience to him; and if done under the influence of that "covetousness which is idolatry," it is worthy of censure and reprobation.

5. An indolent, useless, disorderly life. "We hear that there are some who walk among you disorderly, working not at all." "Withdraw yourselves from every brother that walketh disorderly." 2 Thess. 3 : 6–12; 1 Tim. 5 : 13.

6. Refusal to be reconciled to a brother, as before shown, is a proof of the want of the spirit of the Gospel, and is a sin against the fellowship, authority, and welfare of the church. "First be reconciled to thy brother, and then come and offer thy gift." "If he refuse to hear the church, let him be unto thee as a heathen man and a publican." Matt. 5 : 24; 18 : 17.

7. A protracted and unnecessary neglect of the meetings and ordinances of the church. The soundness of this rule is evident from the nature of the church covenant, in which all engage "not to forsake the assembling of themselves together," and from the sacredness of the command in reference to the Lord's Table—"This do in remembrance of me."*

* The inquiry may arise, how far these Scriptural rules in reference to offenses requiring church action are observed by Baptist churches. The Kehukee (N. C.) Association, in 1783 considered this question: "What shall a church do with a member who shall absent himself from the communion of the Lord's Supper?" They returned answer: "It is the duty of the church to inquire into the reason of his thus absenting himself from the communion, and if he does not render a satisfactory reason, the church should deal with him." In the Minutes of the Georgia Association for 1835, occur four queries and answers on the same subject. 1. "Is it the duty of church-members to partake of the Lord's Supper, when regularly administered in the church? *Ans.* Yes. 2. Are members excusable who take their seats in order, but refuse to partake of the elements? *Ans.* No. 3. Is it the duty of the church or not, when members take their seats and do not commune, to inquire into the reason thereof? *Ans.* Yes. 4. When members take their seats at communion, and fail to partake on account of a want of fellowship with some brother or brethren, and yet do not lay charges against those for whose sake they refuse to commune, ought the church to deal with

Sect. 4. *Mode and Spirit of Proceeding.*

How are public offenses to be brought before the church? What preliminary measures are required? We have already seen how private offenses must be introduced, if introduced at all, to the notice of the church. If it does not appear that the steps required in the Saviour's rule have been taken, the complaint should be at once dismissed. If they have been taken in vain, the offense becomes a public one, and should be treated as such.

If a member happens to be the only witness to an act in a fellow-member, glaringly inconsistent with the Christian profession, the same course, essentially, should be pursued, at first, as in a private offense. Although no personal wrong is done him, yet a brother's soul is in peril, and he should seek to reclaim him to repentance and to duty. No unnecessary publicity should be given to the fact; the sole object should be to bring the offender to repentance, and to such an acknowledgment and reparation as the case requires. If he denies or extenuates the fault, or evinces no contrition, any brother who has proof of the facts, is bound to bring them to the notice of the church. This is the duty of every church-member; and any one who neglects or refuses to pursue this course, becomes accessary to the sin of his brother, and violates his covenant.

them who thus act? *Ans.* Yes, *after Gospel steps have been taken.*" In 1798, the same Association gave as their opinion, in reference to "those professors who do not hold worship in their families," that the churches "first admonish, exhort, and reprove them, but if they will not be reclaimed, then deal with them as neglecters of known duty." In the Minutes for 1808, this query and answer occur. "Should a brother be continued in fellowship, who, though able, will not assist in supporting the Gospel? *Ans.* We are of opinion, where the ability is *obvious* on the one hand, and the unwillingness positive on the other, and the brother cannot be brought to his duty by proper means, he ought to be excluded."—Hist. Ga. Ass., p. 130, as quoted in the *Baptist Expositor* for Oct. 1842.

If a gross offense is charged against a member by common report, it is the duty of any brother to inquire into the facts, and, if reasonably convinced of its truth, to bring the subject before the church; though it is better, in most cases, that a deacon, or a brother of experience, should do it. A committee may then be appointed to investigate the facts, and report. In cases of gross immorality, such as fornication, the offender should be excluded at once, whether penitent or not, as soon as proof of his guilt is obtained. The honor of religion, and a regard to the best good of the offender, require this course. While the incestuous man at Corinth was retained in the church, he repented not, but when cast out, he was filled with penitential grief and was restored.

It is highly important that all cases of delinquency requiring church action, be attended to promptly. The conscience of the offender will be stupefied by communing with guilt, the proof will be more difficult, and the honor of the church will suffer by delay. And every case, once taken up, should be faithfully and firmly carried through, till it results either in the reformation or the excision of the offender.

It is never proper for a church to pass a vote *suspending* a member from church privileges, but when a church commences any disciplinary proceedings with a member, such member is, by that act, suspended from all the privileges of membership, till such proceedings are stayed.

The course of the church should always be uniform and consistent in its treatment of offenses. Some churches, like the Pharisees of old, "strain at a gnat, and swallow a camel." They notice some offenses, and pass by others; sometimes they are very strict, at other times exceedingly lax. Such vacillation is very injurious to religion.

What offenses should be brought to the notice of the church?* Such only as, if persisted in, would require the offender to be

* On the legal right of church-members to institute charges, see Judge Mills' charge in Law Reporter for Sept. 1847, p. 220.

excluded from the church. These are, First, those which, if persisted in, would exclude the offender from heaven. Second, such eccentricities of opinion or of conduct as are subversive of the doctrines, and destructive to the peace, of the church. Third, a voluntary departure from the covenant and fellowship of the church.

Though every case is to be decided by vote of the brethren, yet the pastor should instruct the church in regard to the Scriptural rules which apply to it; and he must administer the censure, or pronounce the vote of excommunication, which should be done with great solemnity. It is sometimes pronounced in the most public manner, from the pulpit, but this is not necessary as a general rule.

And it should be remembered that, in all cases, the church is to form its judgment solely *on evidence*, not on prejudice, or hearsay reports. The church is appointed by Christ to judge of the law and the evidence; that is, to decide whether, and in what way, the law of Christ applies to the offense charged, and whether the charge is *proved* by the evidence, if it be not confessed. "In the mouth of two or three witnesses shall every word be established." Members should be very careful not to have their minds made up, nor in any degree biased, beforehand.

The spirit of obedience and love to the Saviour should be supreme in all these proceedings. No class of duties requires a higher exercise of all the Christian graces than these; and the faithfulness with which they are performed is the surest test of a pure, faithful, and useful church. "Ye are my friends, if ye do whatsoever I command you," says our Lord; and he commends or rebukes the seven churches in Asia, according to their faithfulness or remissness in this duty. When the Apostle taught the Corinthian church to forgive and restore the guilty man whom he had in his first epistle required them to exclude, he declared that one object was, to prove *them*. "Though I wrote to you, I did it not [solely] for his cause that had done the wrong, nor for his cause [only] that had suffered the wrong;"

...... "for to this end, also, did I write, that I might know the *proof of you*, whether ye be *obedient in all things*."

To cherish the right feeling toward an erring brother is sometimes a difficult, but always an important duty. The first object should be, "to *restore* such an one in the spirit of meekness," with all the tenderness and watchful care of a surgeon in setting a broken bone. When this is effected, all is gained. Before commencing with him we should seek to be divested of the Pharisaic spirit. We must not approach him in an assuming, censorious, or dictatorial manner. We must make him feel that he is treated like a brother, though an erring one, and that our earnest desire is to do him good.

SECT. 5. *Treatment of Excluded Persons.*

Exclusion, or excommunication, is the most solemn exercise of that judicial executive power vested by the Saviour in the churches. It is not the power to shut any one out of heaven by a church vote, nor the power to change a man's moral character, nor to determine the final judgment of God. It implies no imprecations, no anathemas, does not affect his civil relations, releases him from no natural or social obligations, does not release others from the duties of kindness or of benevolence toward him.

It should be remembered that there are different degrees of censure implied in exclusion, according to the nature and aggravation of the offense. A grossly immoral man, or manifestly base impostor, is expelled by the most solemn reprobation of his crime; while he who falls under the influence of erroneous opinions, should be treated with more tenderness. From some all Christian fellowship is withdrawn, and all social intercourse. "But now I have written unto you not to keep company, if any man that is called a brother be a fornicator, or covetous, or an idolater, or a railer, or a drunkard, or an extortioner, with such an one, *no, not to eat*." The passage indicates that some excluded persons should be treated with more marked disapprobation and reserve, even, than other sinners of the same grade. This course is to be pursued towards the worst offenders against Christian morality; but towards another class a different course is to be pursued. "If any man obey not our word by this epistle, note that man, and have no company with him, that he may be ashamed: yet count him not as an enemy, but admonish him as a brother."

The first object in the treatment of the excommunicate is, to vindicate the honor of religion; the second, to bring them to repentance. They are in a wrong and unhappy state. If not Christians at all, they need the prayers and labors of the church; if real, but fallen disciples, they should be reclaimed and restored, if possible. The church of which they once were members is under special obligations to look after them.

The first duty is, to abstain from intimacy with them. "Let him be to thee as a heathen man and a publican,"—persons with whom the hearers of Christ held no intercourse. Such, in addition to the passage already quoted, are the repeated injunctions of the Apostle. "Now I beseech you, brethren, mark them which cause divisions and offenses, contrary to the doctrine which ye have learned, *and avoid them.*" Familiar intercourse with an excluded person is rendering null in action the censure we have expressed by vote. It would expose a Christian to danger of being infected by the same sins or errors, would imply that the offender's fault was not seriously disapproved, and lessen the efficacy of his exclusion as a means of reformation. All our deportment toward him should sustain, and be consistent with, the object of the censure.

The second duty requires that they should be treated with kindness, mingled with a tender concern for their spiritual welfare. His former brethren, while they show a disapproval of his conduct, should also show that they still love him, and desire his restoration. They should pray for him, be ready to impart counsel or affectionate admonition, and encourage him to hope for forgiveness on sincere repentance.

Should he forsake his sins, or renounce his errors, satisfy the church by a proper confession, and again exhibit the Christian character, he may, after sufficient time, be restored to fellowship. He should be encouraged to apply for readmission, when the church is satisfied of his repentance and thorough reformation. The interests and honor of religion, and his own happiness and growth in piety require, that when the act of exclusion has accomplished its intended effect, he should resume his place in the household of faith. His discipline, though painful, was merciful. If he is a true penitent, he will bless the Saviour and the church for it. The Scriptures now require his restoration. "Sufficient to such a man is his punishment, which was inflicted of many. So that, contrariwise, ye ought rather to forgive him and comfort him ; lest, perhaps, such a one should be swallowed up with overmuch sorrow. Wherefore I beseech you that you would confirm your love toward him."

An excluded member may apply for admission to another church. Every church has, of course, a right to receive any one whom it judges qualified for membership. Yet each should render due respect to all others, and sustain their proper authority. Each should presume that another has done right in excluding a member, and not take his story as evidence to the contrary. If he has been wronged, the wrong should be rectified where it was committed.

If, however, a case should occur in which, manifestly, a member was improperly and unjustly excluded, and the church should persist in refusing to restore him, he ought to have a remedy. Another church being fully convinced that he is entitled to membership, should, after suitable delay and a careful investigation of the case,—the other church having been duly notified of their intention,—receive him. Such a case, however, seldom occurs, and this course is justifiable only in extreme cases.

SECT. 6. *Treatment of a Delinquent Pastor.*

The pastor, as a member of the church, is subject to its watch and discipline, like any other member, in everything which relates to morals and Christian character. His station entitles him to respect, and to caution in receiving charges against him, as will soon be shown; but not to exemption from needful discipline. Even the Apostle Peter, when called to account by the brethren of the church in Jerusalem, (Acts 11,) of which church he was a member, claims no official privilege of exemption; but pleads his case before them by an array of facts and arguments. And the church at Ephesus was praised for having "tried them who say they are Apostles, and are not." Of the same nature is the direction of Paul to the churches in Galatia to proceed at once to the excommunication of their false teachers, who were leading them astray. "I would they were even cut off which trouble you;" 5 : 12. And this they were to do in the exercise of their Christian liberty; ver. 13.

If the pastor is guilty of a scandalous sin, the church have power to investigate the facts, and exclude him from fellowship. But this is not all that the case requires. For although it is plain that if he is unfit to be a church-member he is unworthy to be a minister, yet, as the agency of the presbytery was called in to invest him with the ministerial office, it is equally necessary in order to divest him of it. One church may not undo that which properly required the consent and agency of many churches to do; and if a presbytery, or council, composed of the pastors and elders of other churches, is in any sense necessary to ordain a man to the ministerial office, it is necessary in the same sense, and to the same extent, in order to depose him from it. Other churches, also, and their pastors, have a deep interest in the removal from office of one who has sustained so important a relation to them all, as a public teacher of religion. A fundamental law respecting the conferring of office is, that the same power which makes may unmake.

A council should therefore be first called, to investigate charges of delinquency against a minister. It is right that every man should be tried by his peers, when charges are brought against him relating to his official character. This sound general principle is peculiarly applicable to the minister of the Gospel. And if he deserves to be deposed from the ministry, and expelled from the church, the former step should be first taken; and after he is divested of his official character, the church can proceed without embarrassment, to his expulsion from fellowship. This course should always be taken, unless a pastor is guilty of scandalous sins, of which there is full proof; in which case the church may expel him without delay, call a council to depose him from the ministry, and thus the melancholy affair is ended. But such an exception to the general rule rarely oçcurs, if ever.

Some persons, who object to this view, contend that the church to which a minister belongs is the only body by which he can properly be tried and deposed, or in any way punished, if found guilty. This they suppose is necessary to the preservation of church independence. But this is clearly an error; for by the same argument they may prove, with equal conclusiveness, that each church must ordain its ministers without the agency or coöperation of other churches, or abandon its independence. The truth is, the calling of a council, or presbytery, to investigate charges against a minister, has nothing to do with the church's independence, nor with its right of discipline over all its members, the pastor included; because the jurisdiction of the council in such cases extends only to the minister's *office*, not to his church-membership. A council may depose him from the ministry, but have no right to exclude him from the church.

Much injury to religion might be prevented by strictly adhering to this rule, the propriety of which is so obvious. Whatever charges are made against a minister, they lie, first, against his ministerial character. The first question, therefore, is, whether he has forfeited that character. The proper authority to settle this question, is the same that invested him with the office.

If the church proceeds first to exclude him from fellowship, he is still a regularly authorized public teacher of religion. This office was given to him not by one church, but by many churches; therefore one church cannot deprive him of it. This office he holds, not in virtue of being a church-member, but in addition to it. As he may be a church-member yet not fit to be a minister, so he may be deposed from the ministry though not unfit to be a church-member. If the charges against him relate to official improprieties, or irregularities, or to doctrinal errors, the necessity of a council to investigate them, composed in part of ministers, would be obvious to all. If accused of immoralities, it must be remembered that the charge is to be *proved* before he is condemned. Does not every one see that the investigation of such a charge could be performed with greater accuracy and thoroughness, and with less injury to the cause of morality and religion, by a council of ministers and elders selected from the churches, than by a single church? Is it any surrendry or infringement of church independence to delay church disciplinary action till such investigation is had? And is it not unwarrantable haste for any church to expel a minister from membership before the judgment of such a council has been obtained?

The investigation before such a council should be thorough, and a full record of all the facts proved should be entered on its minutes, with the names of witnesses; and a copy should be transmitted to the church, who may proceed to an original investigation if not satisfied with that of the council. If the offense is such as to require his exclusion from church-fellowship, they can now proceed without embarrassment, in the same way as with any other member.

In receiving charges against a minister, great caution should be used. "Against an elder receive not an accusation but before two or three witnesses," is a Scriptural rule. As a minister is presumed to have stronger motives and greater advantages for maintaining purity of character than other Christians, it is reasonable that stronger evidence of misconduct should be required.

His office, too, exposes him peculiarly to malice and calumny, and the prosperity of religion depends so much on the reputation of its ministers, that the church ought to guard their characters with scrupulous care, and receive charges against them with caution.

Ought a minister who has been silenced and expelled, to preach again, if restored to the church? It is probable that the interests of religion would be best promoted by his remaining in a private station. At least, in regard to one crime, the rule should be invariable and inflexible. A minister convicted of fornication, while holding the sacred office, should never be allowed, in any circumstances, to assume the functions of the ministry again. If a church is strongly of opinion that one who has been silenced and expelled for any offense of a milder cast, and again restored to fellowship, on repentance, ought to preach, it has the power to license him; and a council, properly convened, may, if it sees fit, ordain him. He is a private member, and without such license and ordination he certainly ought not to preach. A council called for this purpose ought to be large, and should be composed of men of wisdom and experience.

SECT. 7. *Treatment of a Delinquent Minister at Large.*

A minister who is not the pastor of any church may become corrupt in morals, or in doctrine, or disorderly in practice. Should such a case occur, what course is to be adopted?

He is accountable to the church of which he is the member, as well as to the ministry and to the churches generally, because they have the same power to disown him if he proves himself unworthy, as they had to introduce him to the sacred office when they believed him worthy of it. It is, therefore, the duty of the church of which he is a member, to call him to account. Or, if a minister at large becomes disorderly, and his influence manifestly injurious to religion, it is the duty of any church, knowing the fact, to send due notice thereof to the church to which he belongs. If they neglect or refuse to call him to account, any church may proceed to call a council to investigate the case, giving due notice to the accused; and if, in the opinion of the council, he ought to be silenced and expelled from the ministry, they should so decide, and publish the result of their doings to the world.

It is highly desirable that such a council be sufficiently numerous; that it be composed of men whose integrity, discretion, and weight of character, will cause their decision to be respected. The duty of the pastors and elders to guard the flocks of which the Holy Ghost hath made them overseers, against grievous wolves in sheep's clothing, is of the most sacred character.

The duty of respecting the decision of such a council, unless there is the clearest proof of injustice in their proceedings, is obvious. A minister so silenced should not be employed, nor countenanced, in preaching, or sowing the seeds of error and division. The Scriptures are very explicit on this point. "Beware," says our Saviour, "of false prophets, [teachers,] who come to you in sheep's clothing, but inwardly they are ravening wolves." Paul had much to do to counteract the influence of false teachers among the Corinthian and Galatian churches, as is evident from his epistles to them. To the latter he says, "I would they were even cut off which trouble you." To the Philippians, on the same subject, he says, "Beware of dogs." Peter speaks of "false teachers," who "bring in damnable heresies," who, "through covetousness, with feigned words, make merchandise" of believers; and he calls them "wells without water, clouds that are carried with a tempest, to whom the mist of darkness is reserved forever."

With such precedents before them, it is clearly a sacred duty of the watchmen in Zion to put down false teachers, and of Christians generally to assist them in so doing.

CHAPTER V.

VARIOUS USAGES.

THE system of church government taught in the New Testament and exemplifiied, substantially, in the practice of Baptist churches, inasmuch as it makes each church its own and its only authoritative interpreter of Christ's laws, readily admits some variety in ecclesiastical practice. Thus far, those points have been presented on which there is a general agreement; but there are, also, various usages, which have prevailed to a greater or less extent, in the churches in various parts of the world.

It is well known that the practices of these churches differ on some minor points, according to the state of society, form of government, and other circumstances. This is not inconsistent with the unity enjoined in the Scriptures; nor is it to be regretted, except as an unavoidable part of human imperfection, so long as the essential principles of church order, doctrine, and government are held inviolate, and the ordinances of Christ are faithfully observed. Each church which holds fast the form of sound words, and the Scriptural example, may manifest its love to Christ, and to a perishing world, in its own way.

Christian churches have no more reason to expect a direct positive precept for every duty, than individual Christians. He would be a poor Christian, who should perform no duty for which he could find no specific command in the Bible. Where, for instance, could an individual, or a church, find a Scriptural command to sustain the Sabbath-school, erect a house for worship, or even to make preaching, praying, and singing, to constitute the worship of the Lord's day? And what pious, consistent Christian would desire it?

Does any one ask, What usages, or practices, not enjoined in the Scriptures, may be safely and profitably adopted by churches? The answer is, First, They must not be contrary to Scriptural precept or precedent. Second, They must be in accordance with the spirit of Christianity, and the design of churches.

Sect. 1. *Relations of the Church to the Society.*

It is usually the case, that persons who are not members of the church desire to attend public worship, and to contribute for its support. In connection with such male members of the church as choose to do so, they frequently form a society for sustaining the public institutions of religion.

In some cases, the society is composed of the pew-holders, more or less of whom, perhaps a majority, are members of the church, in others, all who subscribe a certain amount for the pastor's salary are members of the society; in others, still, those who in any way assist in sustaining the expenses, either by submitting to be taxed, or by contribution, and yet are not members of the church, constitute the society.

When a house for worship is to be erected, a common mode of proceeding is, after the object and plan are sufficiently understood, to form a joint stock company, on specified conditions, by opening a subscription for shares, the holders of which organize, choose a building committee, and authorize them, under certain regulations, to build the house. When it is completed, it is, of course, the undivided property of the stockholders, as a body, who are responsible for whatever debt, authorized by them, may remain unpaid. The pews are then appraised at a rate sufficient to cover the expenses of the building, and an annual sum is assessed on each pew, to be paid quarterly, sufficient to meet the probable expenses of maintaining worship. A plan of the house is now made out, exhibiting the situation of each pew, with its appraised value, and the annual tax; and then the choice of the pews is disposed of to the highest bidder among the stockholders, who thus transfer their joint ownership of an undivided house, to a special ownership of a pew or pews, by each; the ownership of a pew being simp'- the right to occupy it for the purposes of worship. A deed of the house and land is given to the deacons of the church, *ex officio*, to hold the property in trust for the uses of the church and society, the latter, in cases of this kind, being composed entirely of the pew-holders.

In some parts of the country the practice has prevailed of erecting houses for worship by donations, the house being secured, by a deed of trust, to the church, through its deacons, as before, the seats being free. This way may be preferable in places where a very few persons are willing to assist, but it is attended with inconvenience and evils.

The methods of raising the salaries of pastors are various. In some churches it is done by an assessment on the pews, as above described; in others, by an equal assessment on property; in others, by voluntary subscription, year by year; in some instances, by a weekly contribution from the congregation, or by voluntary contributions of provisions, fuel, &c. Churches are at liberty to take that method for raising the expenses of worship which they judge best adapted to their circumstances. But they should, in all cases, see that his salary be sufficient, and that it be promptly paid at the end of each quarter, or at the time agreed upon.

SECT. 2. *Licensing Candidates for the Ministry.*

When a member of a church thinks it his duty to become a preacher of the Gospel, he makes known his feelings to his pastor, or to such brethren as he deems qualified to give advice in so important a matter. Or, if the pastor and brethren perceive evidences of ministerial gifts in any one of their number, they converse with him, and encourage him to improve his powers, and opportunities, with a view to the work. No one should be thus encouraged, who is known to be heterodox in doctrine, worldly in spirit, deficient in piety, eccentric in manners, or wanting in prudence, sound common sense, and practical judgment.

When a license is properly applied for, the church appoint a time for the candidate to address them from a passage of Scripture, and if, after having heard him several times, they are satisfied that the Saviour is designing him for the work, they give him a license to preach as he may have opportunity. If the candidate be a young man, deficient in knowledge of the Scriptures, yet possessing promising talents, it is his duty to *prepare* to preach, rather than to enter at once on the work. It is usual, in such cases, for the church to give him a testimonial, expressing its conviction that the Saviour designs him for the ministry, and recommending him to prosecute a course of preparatory studies. It is soon enough to give him full license, when he is prepared to teach profitably. While in his novitiate, he may be useful as a Sabbath-school teacher, in conference and prayer-meetings, conversing, and distributing tracts; and, if he continues to grow in piety and knowledge, he may be licensed with more safety. There is no need of haste in this matter, for it is safer that five suitable candidates be delayed, than that one improper person be licensed; and until a young man has nearly completed his preparatory studies, he may be quite as useful without a license to preach.

The exercise of the right of licensing to preach, devolves on the churches a high responsibility. They should, in all cases, require a candidate to speak before them several times, and never give a license, till fully satisfied of the propriety of so doing. If a licentiate manifests unfitness for the work of the ministry, the church may, and ought, to revoke his license.

Sect. 3. *Installation.*

When an ordained minister is to be publicly introduced to the pastoral care of a church, a council is called, and the same proceedings take place as in the case of ordination, except that there is no laying on of hands, and an *installing*, instead of an *ordaining* prayer is offered. The object is, not to introduce a candidate into the ministry, but to publicly recognize him as the pastor of *that church.* It is suitable that some public religious services should be held on so important and solemn an occasion. Neighboring churches and their pastors have a deep interest in the event; they should feel a proper confidence in the pastor elect, and it is highly desirable that they should give him some public pledge of their approval, fellowship, and coöperation. To enable them to do this, they must be satisfied respecting his ministerial character and doctrines, by an examination, which is done most conveniently by a council.

The advantages of installation services are, to promote a good understanding and harmony between churches and ministers, to check the career of improper men who have intruded into the pastoral office, to deepen the public estimation of the importance and solemnity of that office, and thus to contribute to render the pastoral relation more permanent. A relation lightly assumed is apt to be lightly dissolved; and the permanence of that pastoral relation which is formed without special, solemn, public prayer, may well be doubted. The occasion is a suitable one to impress on pastor and people a deep sense of their mutual duties.

If it be said that a church has a *right* to call and settle a pastor without the aid and sympathies of other churches, no Baptist will dispute the point. But it must be recollected, on the other hand, that every pastor has a *right*, also, to know what sort of a man he is to invite to his pulpit, and to coöperate with, and so has every church. Rights and duties are always coëqual and coëxtensive. If any objection be made to the term *installation*, the word *recognition*, if preferred, may be substituted.

Sect. 4. *Councils.*

Councils are called to aid in organizing churches, in ordaining, installing, or dismissing pastors, to assist in adjusting difficulties betwen churches, and to depose and silence unworthy ministers. They are founded on the general principle already explained,* that there is an endeared relation between Christian churches, and that there ought to be mutual, kind, respectful recognition and intercommunion. The general principles which apply to them, are these:

Individuals may, of course, meet for consultation, at any time; but a council is a body composed of pastors and of delegates, appointed by several churches. Councils derive all their authority from the churches who have delegated their members to act, in a given case, as representatives of their views, each church being regarded as present in the presence of its delegates. Councils have, therefore, no inherent power. They have no authority over any church, no right to interfere with church discipline. They have the power to examine and decide the question which is committed to them, and nothing more.

A council called to ordain, install, or depose a minister, should be composed of ministers and brethren; in other cases, the presence of ministers is not indispensable.

When a council is called to ordain a candidate to the ministry, the question whether he ought to be ordained is submitted to them; they have the right to decide on his fitness or unfitness for the work; and their decision should be respected and adhered to. This being the only question submitted to them, is the only one which they have the power to decide.

So, if a council is regularly called to investigate charges against a minister, they have the power to call for proof, examine witnesses, decide whether the charges are sustained, and, if so, whether he ought to be expelled from the ministry; and their decision should be respected and adhered to by all churches and ministers.

Difficulties between a pastor and some of the deacons of a church sometimes occur, of so serious and complicated a character that the church finds itself unable to adjust them. In this case, the church may invite pastors, or brethren, from sister

* Part I, Chap. 2, Sect. 8.

churches, distinguished for piety and wisdom, to aid them by their counsel, as individuals; or the parties to the difficulty may, with the consent of the church, submit certain specific questions to the decision of a council, under a mutual agreement to abide by that decision. But the church should reserve to itself all questions relative to the discipline of its members, as members.

The method of calling a council, is this: The church or churches, which agree to invite one, send letters missive to certain specified churches previously agreed upon, mentioning the object, time, and place of holding the council, and requesting the attendance of the pastor, with one or two brethren from each. Each of the letters missive should also mention what churches are to be invited to form the council. If the churches see fit to comply, they so decide by vote, and choose delegates accordingly. The delegates meet at the time and place appointed, elect a chairman and clerk, and, after prayer, proceed to examine the credentials of the members. Being thus organized, the council proceeds to consider the business for which it was called together, and when that is finished, the council is dissolved. If the subject be one of general interest, the council may, by vote, order its proceedings to be made public. This is usually necessary when an unworthy minister is deposed, in order to warn the churches against an artful and designing man. In most cases, it is proper that the members of the council should report to the churches to which they severally belong, at their next church meeting, the doings of the council.

Such, it is believed, are, substantially, the doctines of Baptists respecting councils. Some believe that councils should never be called, unless to assist in ordaining a minister; and it is certain that councils for other purposes are quite unfrequent among them. They all agree in maintaining that each church should perform all needful acts of discipline on its own members.

SECT. 5. *Associations, and Ministers' Meetings.*

An Association consists of pastors, and delegates from several neighboring churches, and meets annually, for purposes specified in its constitution. Each church sends with its pastor one or more delegates, with a letter giving a brief account of its condition and its history during the preceding year, and a statistical account of the members added, dismissed, deceased, and excluded, with such other information and opinions as may be thought of sufficient importance.

After an introductory sermon, by some persons appointed at the preceding meeting, the Association is organized, by choosing a moderator and clerk. The letters are then read, and topics of interest to the churches are introduced and discussed. A "circular letter" to the churches, prepared by some one previously appointed, is read before the Association, after having been examined by a committee, and, if approved, is adopted. Delegates from other Associations are usually present, and sometimes a "corresponding letter" to other Associations, containing a summary statement of the condition of the churches, is prepared and sent to corresponding bodies. Devotional exercises and preaching occupy a portion of the time. Minutes of the proceedings, with the circular letter, are printed, to be distributed among the churches.

An Association is wholly a voluntary union. No church is bound to join it. It has no authority to make laws for the churches, interfere with their discipline, nor in any manner to control them. If a church becomes disorderly, or corrupt, the Association ought, through a committee or otherwise, to endeavor to restore it to a healthful state; and, if unsuccessful, to withdraw from it the fellowship of the body. This right and obligation arise from the fact that the church in question has violated the terms of the compact; but the Association has no other power over a disorderly church than to dissolve all connection with it.

The objects of Associations are, to promote the union of the churches by a mutual report of their condition, to increase their piety and knowledge by a season of devotion and preaching, and to look especially to the state of religion within their own borders. "It should be exclusively a *religious meeting*, for the special benefit of the associated churches, leaving to the proper organizations the adoption and execution of measures for the general good of Zion.*

When a church wishes to join an Association, it sends its delegates, with a letter; and the Association, after a satisfactory inquiry into its condition, admits it by vote, and the hand of fellowship is presented by the moderator, to its pastor or one of its delegates, acting as the representative of the church. Any church may withdraw from an Association, at any time, if it sees fit, or be dismissed, by vote, to another Association, on presenting a request to that effect.

Ministers' meetings are formed by the ministers within certain limits uniting, and agreeing to meet statedly once in two or three months, for mutual improvement, and the communication of intelligence from their respective churches. Essays, doctrinal and practical, interpretations of difficult passages of Scripture, and plans of sermons, are exhibited, for mutual remark and friendly criticism. Questions of discipline are introduced and discussed, and mutual advice and encouragement imparted. In many places it is usual to have one or more sermons preached during the meeting, which sometimes occupies nearly two days.

SECT. 6. *State Conventions.*

A General Association, or State Convention, is composed of delegates from each local association within the limits of a State. Its objects are, to assist feeble churches to procure and support pastors, to maintain domestic missionaries or ministers at large within the State, to encourage the formation of new churches,

* Knowles's Manuscript.

to circulate the Scriptures, tracts and useful books, to promote ministerial education; and, in some cases, the cause of foreign missions is included among them. Unlike local Associations, they usually have some method of raising funds, and employ secretaries, agents, and missionaries. Their usual character is that of a domestic missionary society; in some cases confined to the State, in others they act as auxiliaries to the Home Missionary Society.

Each convention usually holds a meeting annually, called its "anniversary," at some place previously appointed; at which a report is presented, officers chosen, including a board of trustees, to transact the business for the ensuing year, sermons and addresses are delivered, and resolutions adopted. Like local Associations, they have no power whatever to interfere with the churches. Their objects are prescribed in a written constitution, in which there is usually a clause disclaiming any form of ecclesiastical power.

Sect. 7. *Voluntary Societies.*

The church is the only society appointed by the Saviour for the spread of religion throughout the world. It has been proved to be the best that could be devised; and as such, should be honored and trusted in. Its members are not merely persons of one theory, but of one heart. They are an "habitation of God through the Spirit," "an holy temple to the Lord." The Lord Jesus, himself, is "in the midst of them," and has promised to be "with them alway, even to the end of the world." Of no other society on earth can this be said. The church should, therefore, be honored as a society of God's own appointment. It should never be disparaged by being placed on a level with societies of merely human origin.

Yet there is a convenience in having some special associations for particular objects. A judicious division of labor is advantageous in religious enterprises, as well as in other concerns. Order and efficiency are promoted by assigning to a special organization a particular department of benevolent effort. Some Christians, and some churches, are more interested in one branch of pious activity than another, and, by a division of labor, the energies of all will be most effectually enlisted.

A number of societies have accordingly been formed; some of a general character, as the Baptist General Convention, now changed to the American Baptist Missionary Union, the Baptist Home Mission Society, the American and Foreign Bible Society, the Baptist Publication and Sunday School Society, and others more limited in their design; as the Northern Baptist Education Society, the New England and Sabbath School Union; and others still more limited and local in their objects.

These societies have no direct or necessary connection with the churches. No church-member is bound to join or assist any of them, unless he pleases; and no church has a right to prevent a member from joining, or aiding them, if he thinks proper. A church, or any of its members, may make any of these societies the channel, or instrumentality through which to expend their pious benefactions, if they judge best.

A great increase of voluntary societies for strictly religious objects, is undesirable. The churches ought to be regarded as the divinely appointed organizations for extending the kingdom of Christ on the earth, and as such they should be honored. Whatever tends to diminish the activity of the churches, must be ultimately injurious to the cause of Christianity.

APPENDIX.

In presenting a few forms of letters for the calling of councils, transmission of members, etc., the chief design is, to illustrate the main points which should be embraced in such letters, and not to fix the phraseology which should always be used, nor to intimate that many other forms of expression would not be equally appropriate. In many cases it might be proper to embrace the leading circumstances in the occasion of calling a Council; and the letters might, of course, be worded according to the taste of the writer.

I.

TO CONSTITUTE A CHURCH.

B——, ——, 18—.

To the Baptist Church of Christ in ——

In behalf of a company of brethren belonging to different Baptist churches, whom as we humbly trust, the Great Head of the church has moved by his Spirit to unite in religious worship, with a view to the establishment of a church of our faith and practice, at ——, we invite you to send your pastor and two brethren as delegates, to sit in council at the house of ——, to assist us, by your counsel and prayers, to know the will of our Lord respecting this proceeding; and, if judged proper, to assist in forming and recognizing us as a church of Christ, in fellowship with the churches of our faith. The number of brethren who unite in this request, is ——, and of sisters, ——, all of us with the knowledge and cordial approval of the churches to which we now belong, from which we have letters dismissing us to the proposed church, whenever it shall be formed. The churches invited are the following: ——, ——, ——.

Praying that we may be so guided in all our proceedings as to glorify our Lord and Master,

We subscribe ourselves,

—— ——,
—— ——, } *Committee of Arrangements.*
—— ——,

Or, if the call for such a Council comes from a church, as, in many cases, would be the preferable course, it may be as follows:—

II.

E——, ——, 18—.

The Baptist Church of Christ in E——, to the Baptist Church of Christ in S——, sendeth Christian salutation.

Beloved in the Lord,—

Whereas several members of this church, with others belonging to the church in ——, and the church in ——, have, for some time past, met for religious worship at ——, and are now desirous to be formed and recognized as a distinct church, to sustain the worship and ordinances of the house of God, we invite you to unite with us, by sending your pastor and two delegates, to sit in council at the house of ——, on the — day of ——, at ——, for the purpose of considering this request. The churches invited are the following: ——, ——.

Praying that grace, mercy, and peace, may abound unto you from God our Father, and the Lord Jesus Christ, we subscribe ourselves,

In behalf of the church,

—— ——, *Church Clerk.*

III.

FOR AN ORDAINING COUNCIL.

The Baptist Church in ——, to the Baptist Church in ——.

Beloved in the Lord,—

It is our happiness to inform you, that, having enjoyed the public ministrations of Mr. ——, for some months past, (or as the case may be,) and having earnestly sought the Divine guidance, it hath pleased our blessed Saviour to unite the hearts of this church in the choice of him to be our pastor and teacher. In this choice, the congregation worshipping with us cheerfully concur. We therefore invite you to send your pastor, with two brethren, to sit in council, at the house of ——, on ——, at ——, to examine the candidate, and, if satisfied of his fitness for this great work, to give him and us the tokens of your approval, fellowship, and coöperation in the same. The churches invited are the following: ——, ——.

Earnestly soliciting your prayers, that the proposed union may be for the glory of Christ and our advancement in holiness, we subscribe ourselves,

Your brethren in Christ,

——— ———, *Church Clerk.*

IV.

FOR A DISMISSING COUNCIL.

———, ——, 18—.

Brethren, beloved in the Lord,—

We are desirous, as a church, to know the will of our common Lord respecting the longer continuance of the labors of the Rev. Mr. ——— among us, as our pastor. (Here state the reasons which have rendered the question embarrassing to the church—as, that the pastor desires to be dismissed on account of the failure of his health, or the prospect of more usefulness in another place, or there are divisions in the church.) We therefore invite you to assist us to know the will of that Saviour whom we desire always to please, by sending your pastor, and two brethren, to sit in council, at ———, on ——, to unite with us in prayer for Divine guidance, and to give us such counsel as may seem best to them, after a full hearing of the facts. Brethren, pray for us. The churches invited are, ———, ———.

Wishing you grace, mercy, and peace, we subscribe ourselves,

Your brethren in Christ,

——— ———, *Church Clerk.*

V.

FOR THE TRIAL OF AN ACCUSED MINISTER.

Beloved in the Lord,—

We address you in deep affliction. Charges of a serious nature are made against the ministerial and Christian character of the Rev. Mr. ———, a member of this church, (or pastor, if such be the fact,) supported by such evidence that we feel constrained, by a regard for the honor of Christ, and the character of his ministry, to ask that they be investigated by an Ecclesiastical Council. For this purpose we invite you to send your pastor, with two brethren, to sit in council, at ———, on ——. The churches invited are ———, ———.

Praying that this affliction may be sanctified to the good of our beloved Zion, we subscribe ourselves,

Your brethren in Christ,

——— ———, *Church Clerk.*

VI.

MINUTES OF A COUNCIL.

———, ——, 18—.

An Ecclesiastical Council was convened at ———, on ——, by letters missive from the church in ———.

The council was organized by the choice of ——— as Moderator and ——— as Clerk. Prayer was offered by ———. The vote of the church inviting the Council was then read, as follows: (copy the vote.)

The credentials of delegates were called for, from which it appeared that the following brethren are entitled to seats in the council.

Churches. *Pastors and Delegates.*

As to the *doings of the Council,* if the business be to examine a candidate for ordination, it is sufficient to say, " The Council then heard the candidate relate his Christian experience, the evidences of his call to the ministry, his views of doctrine and of ministerial duty, which, being satisfactory, the council unanimously,

Voted, that &c. &c.

If the business be, to investigate charges against a minister, a record should be kept of all the evidence, and of the decision of the council. In every case the doings of the Council, signed by the Moderator and Clerk, should be entered on the records of the church by whose vote it was convened. A similar course would be proper in case of a council convened to assist in constituting a church.

VII.

LICENSE TO PREACH.

[The following license, written on parchment, was found in the handwriting of the late Rev. William Staughton, D.D. It shows the importance which that distinguished preacher and eminent teacher of candidates for the ministry attached to the solemn act of licensing a candidate to preach the Gospel.]

"To All whom it may Concern,—

"The Baptist Church in Sansom Street, Philadelphia, send Christian salutation.

"The bearer hereof, our beloved brother, Flavel Shurtleff, being a man of good moral character, real piety, and sound knowledge of divine things, and having been called to the exercise of his ministerial gifts, of which we have had considerable trial, both in private and public, we have judged him worthy, and do, therefore, hereby LICENSE and authorize him to preach the Gospel wherever he may have a call; not doubting but that in due time, circumstances will lead on to a more full investiture of him in the MINISTERIAL OFFICE, by ordination. In the meantime we recommend him to favor and respect, praying the Lord may be with, and abundantly bless him.

"Done at our regular meeting, Dec. 19, 1814, and signed by order and in behalf of the church.

"WILLIAM STAUGHTON, *Pastor.*"

VIII.

DISMISSING AND RECEIVING MEMBERS.

BOSTON, ——, 18—

To the —— *Baptist Church in* ——.

This certifies that —— —— is a member, in good standing, of the Baldwin Place Baptist Church, and, in compliance with —— request, is affectionately recommended and dismissed to your fellowship.

If, within one year from date, we receive the accompanying certificate, with the blanks filled, showing that —— has been received by you as a member, or a certificate equivalent thereto, we shall consider —— relation to us as discontinued; otherwise this letter shall be null and void.

In behalf of the Church,

—— ——, *Clerk.*

[The foregoing is printed on one leaf of a letter sheet, and the following on the other, to be filled, certified, and returned to the church granting the letter of dismission; and when it is done, the name of the member is discontinued from its roll.]

This certifies, that —— ——, recommended and dismissed by the Baldwin Place Baptist Church, in Boston, by a letter dated Boston, ——, 18—, was, on the —— ——, received as a member of the —— Baptist Church, in ——.

Attest: —— ——, *Clerk.*

IX.

LETTER OF OCCASIONAL COMMUNION.

———, ——, 18—.

THIS MAY CERTIFY, that the bearer, A. B., is a member of the Baptist Church in P., in good and regular standing; and, as such, is affectionately recommended to the sympathy, watch-care, and communion of the brethren and the churches.

By a standing rule of the church, this letter continues valid only one year.

——— ———, *Pastor.*

A letter of this kind requires no vote of the church, but may be given by the pastor, or clerk; but the fact should be reported to the church, and entered on its records.

X.

DISMISSION OF MEMBERS TO FORM A NEW CHURCH.

The ——— Baptist Church, in regular church meeting, ——, 18—.

The request of the following-named brethren and sisters, now in regular standing with us, to be dismissed from us, for the purpose of uniting in the formation of a new church at ———, was presented viz.: (Here give a list of the names) Whereupon it was *Voted,* That we cordially approve their proposal, and hereby give our hearty consent to the same; and when they shall be regularly constituted a church of Christ, we shall consider them as dismissed from our immediate watch-care.

VALUABLE WORKS

PUBLISHED BY

GOULD AND LINCOLN,

59 WASHINGTON STREET, BOSTON.

THE CHRISTIAN'S DAILY TREASURY.

A Religious Exercise for Every Day in the Year. By E. TEMPLE. A new and improved edition. 12mo, cloth, $1.00.

A work for every Christian. It is indeed a "Treasury" of good things.

THE SCHOOL OF CHRIST;

Or, Christianity Viewed in its Leading Aspects. By the Rev. A. L. R. FOOTE, author of "Incidents in the Life of our Saviour," etc. 16mo, cloth, 50 cents.

THE CHRISTIAN LIFE,

Social and Individual. By PETER BAYNE, M. A. 12mo, cloth, $1.25.

The demand for this extraordinary work, commencing before its publication, is still eager and constant. There is but one voice respecting it; men of all denominations agree in pronouncing it one of the most admirable works of the age.

GOD REVEALED IN THE PROCESS OF CREATION,

And by the Manifestation of Jesus Christ. Including an Examination of the Development Theory contained in the "Vestiges of the Natural History of Creation." By JAMES B. WALKER, author of "Philosophy of the Plan of Salvation." 12mo, cloth, $1.00.

PHILOSOPHY OF THE PLAN OF SALVATION.

By an AMERICAN CITIZEN. An Introductory Essay, by CALVIN E. STOWE, D. D. New improved edition, with a SUPPLEMENTARY CHAPTER. 12mo, cloth, 75 cts.

This book is generally admitted to be one of the best in the English language. The work has been translated into several different languages in Europe. A capital book to circulate among young men.

A WREATH AROUND THE CROSS;

Or, Scripture Truths Illustrated. By A. MORTON BROWN, D. D. Recommendatory Preface, by JOHN ANGELL JAMES. Beautiful Frontispiece. 16mo, cloth, 60 cents.

THE BETTER LAND;

Or, The Believer's Journey and Future Home. By REV. A. C. THOMPSON. 12mo, cloth, 85 cents.

A most charming and instructive book for all now journeying to the "Better Land," and especially for those who have friends already entered upon its never-ending joys.

THE MISSION OF THE COMFORTER.

With copious Notes. By JULIUS CHARLES HARE. With the Notes translated for the American edition. 12mo, cloth, $1.25.

DR. WAYLAND'S UNIVERSITY SERMON

Delivered in the Chapel of Brown University. 12mo, cloth, $1.00.

THE RELIGIONS OF THE WORLD.

And their Relations to Christianity. By FREDERICK DENISON MAURICE, A. M., Professor of Divinity, King's College, London. 16mo, cloth, 60 cts.

SACRED RHETORIC;

Or, Composition and Delivery of Sermons. By HENRY J. RIPLEY, Professor in Newton Theological Institution. Including Professor Ware's Hints on Extemporaneous Preaching. 12mo, 75 cts.

THE PREACHER AND THE KING;

Or, Bourdaloue in the Court of Louis XIV. An Account of that distinguished Era, Translated from the French of L. F. BUNGENER. With an Introduction by the Rev. GEORGE POTTS, D. D. New edition, with a fine Likeness, and a Sketch of the Author's Life. 12mo, cloth, $1.25.

It combines substantial history with the highest charm of romance. Its attractions are so various that it can hardly fail to find readers of almost every description. — [Puritan Recorder.

THE PRIEST AND THE HUGUENOT;

Or, Persecution in the Age of Louis XV. Translated from the French of L. F. BUNGENER. 2 vols., 12mo, cloth, $2.25.

☞ This is truly a masterly production, full of interest, and may be set down as one of the greatest Protestant works of the age.

FOOTSTEPS OF OUR FOREFATHERS.

What they Suffered and what they Sought. Describing Localities and portraying Personages and Events conspicuous in the Struggles for Religious Liberty. By JAMES G. MIALL. Thirty-six fine Illustrations. 12mo, $1.00.

An exceedingly entertaining work. The reader soon becomes so deeply entertained that he finds it difficult to lay aside the book till finished. — [Ch. Parlor Mag.

A work absorbingly interesting, and very instructive. — [Western Lit. Magazine.

MEMORIALS OF EARLY CHRISTIANITY.

Presenting, in a graphic, compact, and popular form, Memorable Events of Early Ecclesiastical History, etc. By JAMES G. MIALL. With numerous elegant Illustrations. 12mo, cloth, $1.00.

☞ This, like the "Footsteps of our Forefathers," will be found a work of uncommon interest.

WORKS BY JOHN HARRIS, D. D.

THE PRE-ADAMITE EARTH. Contributions to Theological Science. 12mo, cloth, $1.00.

MAN PRIMEVAL; or, the Constitution and Primitive Condition of the Human Being. With a fine Portrait of the Author. 12mo, cloth, $1.25.

PATRIARCHY; or, THE FAMILY. Its Constitution and Probation; being the *third* volume of "Contributions to Theological Science." $1.25.

THE GREAT TEACHER; or, Characteristics of our Lord's Ministry. With an Introductory Essay. By H. HUMPHREY, D. D. 12mo, cloth, 85 cts.

THE GREAT COMMISSION; or, the Christian Church constituted and charged to convey the Gospel to the World. Introductory Essay by W. R. WILLIAMS, D. D. 12mo, cloth, $1.00.

ZEBULON; Or, the Moral Claims of Seamen. 18mo, cloth, 25 cts.

PHILIP DODDRIDGE.

His Life and Labors. By JOHN STOUGHTON, D. D., with beautiful Illuminated Title-page and Frontispiece. 16mo, cloth, 60 cents.

THE EVIDENCES OF CHRISTIANITY,

As exhibited in the writings of its apologists, down to Augustine. By W. J. BOLTON, of Gonville and Caius College, Cambridge. 12mo, cloth, 80 cents.

VALUABLE WORKS PUBLISHED BY GOULD & LINCOLN, BOSTON

WORKS BY DR. TWEEDIE.

GLAD TIDINGS; or, The Gospel of Peace. A series of Daily Meditations for Christian Disciples. By Rev. W. K. TWEEDIE, D. D. With elegant Illustrated Title-page. 16mo, cloth, 63 cts.

THE MORN OF LIFE; or, Examples of Female Excellence. A Book for Young Ladies. 16mo, cloth. *In press.*

A LAMP TO THE PATH; or, the Bible in the Heart, the Home, and the Market Place. With an elegant Illustrated Title-page. 16mo, cloth, 63 cts.

SEED TIME AND HARVEST; or, Sow Well and Reap Well. A Book for the Young. With an elegant Illustrated Title-page. 16mo, cloth, 63 cts.

☞ The above works, by Dr. Tweedie, are of uniform size and style. They are most charming, pious, and instructive works, beautifully gotten up, and well adapted for "gift-books."

WORKS BY JOHN ANGELL JAMES.

THE CHURCH MEMBER'S GUIDE; Edited by J. O. CHOULES, D D. New edition. With an Introductory Essay by Rev. HUBBARD WINSLOW. Cloth, 33c.

CHRISTIAN PROGRESS. A Sequel to the Anxious Inquirer. 18mo, cloth, 31c.

☞ one of the best and most useful works of this popular author.

THE CHURCH IN EARNEST. Seventh thousand. 18mo, cloth, 40 cents

MOTHERS OF THE WISE AND GOOD.

By JABEZ BURNS, D. D. 16mo, cloth, 75 cents.

We wish it were in every family, and read by every mother in the land.—[Lutheran Observer.

MY MOTHER;

Or, Recollections of Maternal Influence. By a New England Clergyman. With a beautiful Frontispiece. 12mo, cloth, 75 cents.

This is one of the most charming books that have issued from the press for a long period. "It is," says a distinguished author, "one of those rare pictures painted from life with the exquisite skill of one of the 'Old Masters,' which so seldom present themselves to the amateur."

THE EXCELLENT WOMAN.

With an Introduction by Rev. W. B. SPRAGUE, D.D. Containing twenty-four splendid Illustrations. 12mo, cloth, $1.00; cloth, gilt, $1.75; extra Turkey, $2.50.

☞ This elegant volume is an appropriate and valuable "gift book" for the husband to present the wife, or the child the mother.

MEMORIES OF A GRANDMOTHER.

By a Lady of Massachusetts. 16mo, cloth, 50 cents,

THE MARRIAGE RING;

Or, How to make Home Happy. By JOHN ANGELL JAMES. Beautiful illustrated edition 16mo, cloth, gilt, 75 cents.

A beautiful volume, and a very suitable present to a newly-married couple.—[N. Y. Christian Intelligencer.

WORKS BY WILLIAM R. WILLIAMS, D. D.

RELIGIOUS PROGRESS: Discourses on the Development of the Christian Character. 12mo, cloth, 85 cts.

This work is from the pen of one of the brightest lights of the American pulpit. We scarcely know of any living writer who has a finer command of powerful thought and glowing, impres[illegible] language than he.—[DR. SPRAGUE, Alb. Atl.

LECTURES ON THE LORD'S PRAYER Third edition. 12mo, cloth, 85 cts.

Their breadth of view, strength of logic, and stirring eloquence place them among the very best homilitical efforts of the age. Every page is full of suggestions as well as eloquence.—Ch. Parlor Mag.

MISCELLANIES. New improved edition. *Price reduced.* 12mo, $1.25.

IMPORTANT WORK.

KITTO'S POPULAR CYCLOPÆDIA OF BIBLICAL LITERATURE. Condensed from the larger work. By the Author, JOHN KITTO, D. D., Author of "Pictorial Bible," "History of Palestine," "Scripture Daily Readings," &c. Assisted by JAMES TAYLOR, D. D., of Glasgow. With *over five hundred Illustrations.* One volume octavo, 812 pp., cloth, 3,00.

THE POPULAR BIBLICAL CYCLOPÆDIA OF LITERATURE is designed to furnish a DICTIONARY OF THE BIBLE, embodying the products of the best and most recent researches in biblical literature, in which the scholars of Europe and America have been engaged. The work, the result of immense labor and research, and enriched by the contributions of writers of distinguished eminence in the various departments of sacred literature, has been, by universal consent, pronounced the best work of its class extant, and the one best suited to the advanced knowledge of the present day in all the studies connected with theological science. It is not only intended for *ministers* and *theological students*, but is also particularly adapted to *parents, Sabbath school teachers, and the great body of the religious public.* The *illustrations*, amounting to *more than three hundred*, are of the very highest order.

A condensed view of the various branches of Biblical Science comprehended in the work.

1. BIBLICAL CRITICISM, — Embracing the History of the Bible Languages; Canon of Scripture; Literary History and Peculiarities of the Sacred Books; Formation and History of Scripture Texts.
2. HISTORY, — Proper Names of Persons; Biographical Sketches of prominent Characters; Detailed Accounts of important Events recorded in Scripture; Chronology and Genealogy of Scripture.
3. GEOGRAPHY, — Names of Places; Description of Scenery; Boundaries and Mutual Relations of the Countries mentioned in Scripture, so far as necessary to illustrate the Sacred Text.
4. ARCHÆOLOGY, — Manners and Customs of the Jews and other nations mentioned in Scripture; their Sacred Institutions, Military Affairs, Political Arrangements, Literary and Scientific Pursuits.
5. PHYSICAL SCIENCE, — Scripture Cosmogony and Astronomy, Zoology, Mineralogy, Botany, Meteorology.

In addition to numerous flattering notices and reviews, personal letters from *more than fifty of the most distinguished Ministers and Laymen of different religious denominations in the country* have been received, highly commending this work as admirably adapted to ministers, Sabbath school teachers, heads of families, and *all* Bible students.

The following extract of a letter is a fair specimen of individual letters received from *each* of the gentlemen whose names are given below:—

"I have examined it with special and unalloyed satisfaction. It has the rare merit of being all that it professes to be, and very few, I am sure, who may consult it will deny that, in richness and fulness of detail, it surpasses their expectation. Many ministers will find it a valuable auxiliary; but its chief excellence is, that it furnishes just the facilities which are needed by the thousands in families and Sabbath schools, who are engaged in the important business of biblical education. It is in itself a library of reliable information."

W. B. Sprague, D. D., Pastor of Second Presbyterian Church, Albany, N. Y.
J. J. Carruthers, D. D., Pastor of Second Parish Congregational Church, Portland, Me.
Joel Hawes, D. D., Pastor of First Congregational Church, Hartford, Ct.
Daniel Sharp, D. D., late Pastor of Third Baptist Church, Boston.
N. L. Frothingham, D. D., late Pastor of First Congregational Church, (Unitarian,) Boston.
Ephraim Peabody, D. D., Pastor of Stone Chapel Congregational Church, (Unitarian,) Boston.
A. L. Stone, Pastor of Park Street Congregational Church, Boston.
John S. Stone, D. D., Rector of Christ Church, (Episcopal,) Brooklyn, N. Y.
J. B. Waterbury, D. D., Pastor of Bowdoin Street Church, (Congregational,) Boston.
Baron Stow, D. D., Pastor of Rowe Street Baptist Church, Boston.
Thomas H. Skinner, D. D., Pastor of Carmine Presbyterian Church, New York.
Samuel W. Worcester, D. D., Pastor of the Tabernacle Church, (Congregational,) Salem.
Horace Bushnell, D. D., Pastor of Third Congregational Church, Hartford, Ct.
Right Reverend J. M. Wainwright, D. D., Trinity Church, (Episcopal,) New York.
Gardner Spring, D. D., Pastor of the Brick Church Chapel Presbyterian Church, New York.
W. T. Dwight, D. D., Pastor of Third Congregational Church, Portland, Me.
E. N. Kirk, Pastor of Mount Vernon Congregational Church, Boston.
Prof. George Bush, author of "Notes on the Scriptures," New York.
Howard Malcom, D. D., author of "Bible Dictionary," and Pres. of Lewisburg University.
Henry J. Ripley, D. D., author of "Notes on the Scriptures," and Prof. in Newton Theol. Ins.
N. Porter, Prof. in Yale College, New Haven, Ct.
Jared Sparks, Edward Everett, Theodore Frelinghuysen, Robert C. Winthrop, John McLean, Simon Greenleaf, Thomas S. Williams, — and a large number of others of like character and standing of the above, whose names cannot here appear.

H

DR. RIPLEY'S NOTES.

NOTES ON THE GOSPELS; Designed for Teachers in Sabbath Schools and Bible Classes, and as an Aid to Family Instruction. By HENRY J. RIPLEY, Prof. in Newton Theological Inst. With a MAP OF CANAAN. *Two volumes in one.* cloth, 1,25.

The pastors of churches in Boston and vicinity have united in the following testimony in favor of the work :—

"The undersigned, having examined Professor Ripley's Notes on the Gospels, can recommend them with confidence to all who need such helps in the study of the sacred Scriptures. Those passages which all can understand are left 'without note or comment,' and the principal labor is devoted to the explanation of such parts as need to be explained and rescued from the perversions of errorists, both the ignorant and the learned. The practical suggestions at the close of each chapter are not the least valuable portion of the work. Most cordially, for the sake of truth and righteousness, do we wish for these notes a wide circulation."

NOTES ON THE ACTS OF THE APOSTLES; with a beautiful MAP, illustrating the Travels of the APOSTLE PAUL, with a track of his voyage from Cesarea to Rome. By Prof. HENRY J. RIPLEY. 12mo, cloth, 75 cents.

The following Notices apply to both the above Works.

DR. PATTISON, *Prof. in Newton Theological Institution,* says: I know not that I have ever read so much commentary with so few occasions to dissent from the views of the author. I should sooner recommend the Notes to that class of persons for whom they were designed than any other with which I am acquainted.

DR. CHAPLIN, *late President of Waterville College,* says: He seems to have hit on the proper medium between the conciseness which leaves the mind of the reader unsatisfied, and that prolixity which exhausts his patience and loads his memory with useless lumber.

DR. CHAPIN, *late President of Columbia College,* says: His notes preserve a just medium between the diffuse and the concise. One excellence is, that he helps the reader where he *needs* help, and when he does not, he lets him go alone.

REV. J. A. WARNE, *editor of the Comprehensive Commentary,* says: It may not seem proper to institute comparison between Ripley and Barnes; and yet I will just say, that Prof. Ripley is, in my judgment, by far the safer guide; and I cannot but wish he were adopted universally, in place of Barnes, in our Sabbath schools.

The late DR. KENDRICK, *Prof. of Theology, Hamilton Literary and Theological Institution,* says: I think them superior to any exposition I have seen of this part of the Divine word.

The late PROF. KNOWLES, *in the Christian Review,* says: Prof. Ripley has given us a specimen of the right kind of Commentary; the Notes are more strictly explanatory than those of Mr. Barnes; they occupy a smaller space; the style, though less pointed and vivacious, exhibits more sobriety; the principles of interpretation are more cautiously applied, and the explanations more correct.

DR. TURNBULL, *Pastor of the First Baptist Church, Hartford,* says: The value of the Notes consists chiefly in their brevity, judiciousness, and simplicity. The difficult passages are satisfactorily discussed, while those of a plainer and more intelligible nature are passed over with brief notices.

DR. BACON, *President of Columbia College,* says: The teacher or scholar will find in this work a greater number of just such questions as he would desire to ask intelligibly and satisfactorily answered than in any other. I should be happy to see it in every family, and in the hand of every Sabbath school teacher and scholar of suitable age, in the land.

The Biblical Repository, Andover, says: There are three things in these Notes which have given us much satisfaction; first, the kind and catholic spirit every where manifest; second, the labor is bestowed upon the really *difficult* texts; third, the practical reflections are few and to the point.

We are impressed, first, by the wonderful perspicuity, simplicity, and comprehensiveness of the author's style; secondly, by the completeness and systematic arrangement of the work, in all its parts, the "remarks" on each paragraph being carefully separated from the exposition; thirdly, by the correct theology, solid instruction, and consistent explanations of difficult passages. The work cannot fail to be received with favor. A beautiful map accompanies them.— *Watchman and Reflector.*

☞ The above works by Prof. Ripley should be in the hands of every student of the Bible, especially every Sabbath school and Bible class teacher. They are prepared with special reference to this class of persons, and contain a mass of just the kind of information wanted. J

WORKS FOR SABBATH SCHOOLS.

MALCOM'S (NEW) BIBLE DICTIONARY of the most important Names, Objects, and Terms found in the Holy Scriptures; intended principally for Sabbath School Teachers and Bible Classes. By Rev. HOWARD MALCOM, D. D., President of Lewisburg College, Pa. 16mo, cloth, 60 cts.

☞ The former Dictionary, of which more than *one hundred and thirty thousand copies* have been sold, being highly commended by Conventions, Associations, Ministers, Superintendents, Papers, Reviews, etc., throughout the land, as the best Bible Dictionary extant, is made the basis of the present work; yet, so revised, enlarged, and improved, by the addition of new material, a greatly increased number of articles, new illustrations, the adoption of new and beautiful type, increased number and size of pages, etc., as to render it essentially a NEW DICTIONARY.

The advantages of *this* Dictionary over similar works consists in the following particulars: —

1. It contains greatly more *actual illustration* of the word of God. No space is consumed with rehearsals of Scripture history nor biographies which can be better read in the Bible itself, nor tedious discussions on disputed points; nor statements long since superseded by modern research.

2. It quotes more extensively *those passages which may be explained* by the article; thus making it a brief commentary on the whole Bible.

3. It gives the *modern names* of places mentioned in the Bible, in all cases where there is any certainty; thus defining and fixing the reader's conceptions.

4. Events and personages prominent in profane history are mentioned in connection with names and events in the Scripture history, so as to form a *chronological arrangement* in the mind of the reader, and assist his memory by association of ideas.

5. The name of each book in the Bible is given, followed by an article which briefly gives all that is known of *writer, date, design*, etc., thus often giving a key to the whole.

6. It contains a sufficient *geography of the Bible*, and much more convenient for Sunday Schools than a separate work on that subject can be, because, by the alphabetical arrangement, every one may find the desired information.

7. The full description of all the animals, birds, reptiles, insects, plants, minerals, etc., to which important allusions are made, furnishes an adequate *natural history* of the Bible.

8. A large part of the work *is new*, being derived from recent sources. Upwards of *four hundred articles* are not found in other Bible Dictionaries. When the article itself is not new, it has been improved, if any additional light has been thrown upon the subject by recent writers.

9. Distinct and correct impressions of what could not well be taught by words, are given by *engravings*, faithfully and elegantly drawn; and names liable to erroneous pronunciations are *accented*.

For the above reasons, the value of the book is not lessened by the possession of any *other* Bible Dictionary.

In addition to the common purposes of a *dictionary*, this may furnish not only a useful, but a very delightful Sunday exercise in the family. Let a parent read a few articles in course, while the other members of the family, each with Bible in hand, look out the references, and read them aloud. Great light would thus be cast on important subjects, and happy effects produced in fixing sacred truth upon the memory.

SABBATH SCHOOL CLASS BOOK; comprising copious Exercises on the Sacred Scriptures. By E. LINCOLN. Revised and Improved by REV. JOSEPH BANVARD, author of "Topical Question Book," etc. 18mo, 12½ cts.

United testimony of Dr. Malcom, author of "Bible Dictionary," Dr. Stow, author of the "Doctrinal Question Book," and Dr. Hague, author of "Guides to Conversations on the New Testament": —

"Having examined the Sabbath School Class Book, it gives us pleasure to express our satisfaction with its design and execution. We think the work is well adapted to the end designed, having avoided, in a great degree, the evils of extreme redundance or conciseness."

LINCOLN'S SCRIPTURE QUESTIONS; with Answers annexed, giving, in the Language of Scripture, interesting Portions of the History, and a concise View of the Doctrines, Duties, etc., exhibited in the Bible. 8⅓ cts. per copy, or 1,00 per doz.

☞ Where Bibles cannot be furnished to each scholar, this work will be found to answer an admirable purpose, as the Scripture text is furnished in connection with the questions.

THE SABBATH SCHOOL HARMONY; containing appropriate Hymns and Music for Sabbath Schools, Juvenile Singing Schools, and Family Devotion. By N. D. GOULD. 12½ cts.

K

WORKS ON MISSIONS.

It has been said, that, "to imbue men thoroughly with the missionary spirit, we must acquaint them intimately with the missionary enterprise."

The following valuable works contain just the kind of information needed for all who desire to become fully acquainted with the toils, sufferings, and successes of the heralds of salvation who have gone forth to heathen lands.

THE MISSIONARY ENTERPRISE; a collection of Discourses on Christian Missions, by American Authors. Edited by BARON STOW, D. D. Second thousand. 12mo, cloth, 85 cts.

☞ *This volume contains the greatest efforts of a number of the greatest minds, and most popular writers of the age.*

You here see the high talent of the American church. We venture the assertion, that no nation in the world has such an amount of forcible, available talent in its pulpit. The energy, directness, scope, and intellectual spirit of the American church are wonderful. These discourses are among the very highest exhibitions of logical correctness, and burning, popular fervor. — *New Englander.*

This work contains *fifteen sermons* on Missions, by Rev. Drs. Wayland, Griffin, Anderson, Williams, Beecher, Miller, Fuller, Beman, Stone, Mason, Stow, Ide, and Kirk. It is a rich treasure, which ought to be in the possession of every American Christian. — *Carolina Baptist.*

This is truly a rich collection of the best productions of the ablest friends and active promoters of Missions in this country. The volume contains a large amount of the purest and most instructive literature, which deserves, and will no doubt meet, an extensive sale. — *Watchman and Reflector.*

The friends of Missions will prize it as one of the jewels in their libraries. — *Baptist Register.*

MEMOIR OF HENRIETTA SHUCK, First Female Missionary to China. By REV. J. B. JETER, D. D. With a likeness. 18mo, cloth, 50 cts.

We have seldom taken into our hands a more beautiful book than this. The style of the author is sedate and perspicuous, such as we might expect from his known piety and learning. The book will be extensively read and eminently useful. — *Family Visiter.*

It is a precious memorial of an interesting and devoted Christian lady. — *Journal and Messenger.*

I have been much interested in reading the Memoir of Mrs. Shuck. In the preparation of this Memoir, Dr. Jeter has made a valuable contribution to the cause of Christ, and its wide circulation will be attended with the happiest results. — RYLAND, *Ch. Index.*

The volume is full of interest, and the compiler's discriminating judgment is strikingly developed in the plan and execution of his delightful task. — *Carolina Baptist.*

It brings before us the life of a simple, self-denying and devoted woman, who, before she was eighteen, sailed, as the wife of a missionary, for China. In reading such a book we feel how the distinctions of *sect* melt away in the fervor of a genuine devotion. — *Ch. Register.*

We commend it to our readers as a precious memorial of a heroic and faithful missionary of the cross, and wish it a wide circulation. — *N. Y. Recorder.*

Its descriptions of Life and Scenes in China are very interesting. — *Zion's Herald.*

MEMOIR OF REV. WILLIAM G. CROCKER, late Missionary in West Africa, among the Bassas. Including a History of the Mission. By R. B. MEDBERRY. With a likeness. 18mo, cloth, 63 cts.

This is a very interesting volume; we have a graphic account of the appalling difficulties attending the missionary work upon the fatal coasts of Africa. — *Puritan Recorder.*

This interesting work will be found to contain much valuable information in relation to the present state and prospects of Africa, and the success of missions in that interesting country. It is commended to the attention of every lover of the liberties of man. — *Watchman and Reflector.*

Lovers of the missionary enterprise will read this book with deep interest; nor they alone, for to the philanthropist and Christian it presents an important field. — *N. Y. Commercial.*

The whole of this memoir is so interesting, that we feel assured it will be read. — *Phil. Ch. Chronicle.*

Every *good* Memoir is a valuable accession to our religious literature. We hail this addition to the number with pleasure. It gives us the experience of a *good man* engaged in a *good cause.* In addition to the religious history of the man, which is a subject of interest to every Christian, we have a brief history of the Baptist Mission in Africa. — *Watchtower.*

MEMOIRS OF DISTINGUISHED MISSIONARIES.

MEMOIR OF ANN H. JUDSON, First Female Missionary to Burmah. By PROF. JAMES D. KNOWLES. A new edition. Fifty-seventh thousand. 18mo, cloth, 58 cts. FINE EDITION, plates, 16mo, cloth, gilt, 85 cts.

The Life of this remarkable woman necessarily includes much of the most interesting and important portion of the History of DR. JUDSON, *and of the Burman Mission. The good accomplished to the cause of Christ, at large, and especially that of Missions, by the wide circulation of this work, can never in this life be fully estimated.*

The sale of nearly *sixty thousand copies* of this work in the United States, besides several editions in England; it having been translated into the French, and also into the German language, by Rev. J. G. Oncken; is gratifying evidence of general approbation. The testimony too of Dr. Judson, the individual whose judgment in the matter is most valuable when he says, "I am extremely gratified, perhaps too much so, with the execution of the work in all its parts," is also strong evidence of its real worth and interest.

If any woman, since the first arrival of the white strangers on the shores of India, has, on that great theatre of war, rightly earned for herself the title of *heroine*, Mrs. Judson has, by her doings and sufferings, fairly earned the distinction. Her sufferings were far more noble than any, which in more recent times have been so much pitied and so much applauded: but she was a simple missionary's wife, an American by birth. She was a real heroine. The annals in the east present us with no parallel. — *Calcutta Review.*

This is the most interesting female biography which has ever come under our notice. It ought to be immediately added to every family library. — *London Miscellany.*

"Mrs. Judson was an honor to our country — one of the most noble-spirited of her sex. It cannot, therefore, be surprising, that so many editions, and so many thousand copies of her life and adventures, have been sold. The name — the long career of suffering — the self-sacrificing spirit of the retired country girl, have spread over the whole world; and the heroism of her apostleship and almost martyrdom, stands out a living and heavenly beacon fire, amid the dark midnight ages, and human history and exploits. She was the first *woman* who resolved to become a missionary to the heathen countries." — *American Traveller.*

THE KAREN APOSTLE; or, Memoir of KO-THAH-BYU, the first Karen Convert. With notices concerning his Nation. By REV. FRANCIS MASON, Missionary. Edited by PROF. H. J. RIPLEY. 18mo, cloth, 25 cts.

*** "This is a work of thrilling interest, containing the history of a remarkable man, and giving much information respecting the Karen Mission. It also gives an account, which must be attractive from its novelty, of a people concerning which little has been known till within a few years."

Few will commence this book without reading it through, and no real Christian will read it through without gratitude to God that he ever stirred up the spirit of a Judson, a Wade, and a Boardman, and thrust them into the strongholds of heathenism, to do battle with the prince of darkness upon his own ground. Get "The Karen Apostle," and read it by all means. — *Methodist Quarterly.*

MEMOIR OF GEORGE DANA BOARDMAN, late Missionary to Burmah, — containing much intelligence relative to the Burman Mission. By REV. A. KING. With an Introductory Essay, by W. R. WILLIAMS, D. D. New edition, with a beautiful Frontispiece. 12mo, cloth, 75 cts.

A distinguished reviewer says, "The introduction *alone* is well worth the price of the book."

One of the brightest luminaries of Burmah is extinguished. He fell gloriously at the head of his troops — in the arms of victory, — thirty-eight wild Karens having been brought into the camp of King Jesus since the beginning of the year, besides the thirty-two that were brought in during the two preceding years. Disabled by wounds, he was obliged, through the whole of the last expedition, to be carried on a litter: but his presence was a host, and the Holy Spirit accompanied his dying whispers with almighty influence. - REV. DR. JUDSON.

No one can read the Memoir of Boardman without feeling that the religion of Christ is suited to purify the affections, exalt the purposes, and give energy to the character. Mr. Boardman was a man of rare excellence, and by a just exhibition of that excellence important service has been rendered to the cause of missions and the interests of personal godliness. — REV. DR. STOW.

A very interesting, instructive, and popular work, which has been highly commended, on both sides of the Atlantic. The perusal of such works is well calculated to awaken our gratitude, enkindle our love, strengthen our faith, confirm our hope, increase our zeal, and urge us to more liberal contributions and to nobler deeds of daring in the cause of Christ. — *Ch. Observer.*

DR. GRANT AND THE MOUNTAIN NESTORIANS.

BY THE REV. THOMAS LAURIE,

Surviving associate of that Mission. With a Portrait, Map of the Country, Illustrations, etc. 12mo, cloth, $1,25.

A most valuable Memoir of a remarkable man; with an account of an interesting country and people, concerning which little has heretofore been known.

The work has all the charm of romance, proving conclusively that facts are not only better, but are sometimes, at least, far more thrilling even than fiction. It cannot fail to interest as well as instruct every class of readers.

Rev. Doctors Anderson and Pomroy, Secretaries of the American Board of Commissioners for Foreign Missions.

We regard the work as among the best of missionary biographies. A remarkable man is there well delineated. Perhaps no other person could have done equal justice to the rare combination or qualities in Dr. Grant's character. We see the boldness of the man unconscious of fear, his enterprise regardless of suffering, his benevolence amount almost to self-crucifixion, yet without rashness, prudent and cautious; and so venturing into regions, and going safely, where few would care to venture. His was an eventful life, and his name will be as imperishable as the history of the present revival of religion in the ancient, degenerated churches of Asia. Dr. Grant will be especially remembered as having opened the way for the gospel into the wild regions of Koordistan. This well-written and interesting volume, while to Mr. Laurie evidently a labor of love, has placed the reading community under obligations to the author, which can hardly fail to be recognized.

RUFUS ANDERSON.
S. L. POMROY.

Missionary House, Boston, June 21, 1853.

Rev. Nathan Dole, Editor of the Journal of Missions.

A book which for interest can hardly be excelled. It is not often that circumstances combine so favorably for an interesting work, as in respect to this biography. In the first place, *the man whose labors for Christ it commemorates*, was a missionary of no ordinary excellence; enterprising; observant; by his inherent traits of character, even more than by his profession as a physician, obtaining great influence over the people with whom he had intercourse; indefatigable in his labors; not knowing what fear was, whether threatening him in the wild mountain-pass from men whose hearts were steeled to pity, or from a deadly pestilence; of rare judgment; glowing with love to Christ, and to the souls of his fellow-men. Then, *the people for whom he spent his life*, aside from his cherished belief that they are the lost ten tribes, are unsurpassed in interest by any other for whom missionary labor has been undertaken. The *period, moreover, in their history* which is covered by this biography, is crowded with exciting events. *Their country* also, so unknown to the civilized world till Dr. Grant explored it, presents scenery of the grandest character; and he had an eye to see, a heart to feel, and a pen to describe. And, FINALLY, the *biographer knew him, knows the people, knows the country*, "was part" of what he tells so well; and though disease drove him home "in person," not a fibre of his heart, by his return, has been unclasped from the work to which in his earliest life he was devoted. The author's part is thoroughly done. His heart was evidently in it. The reader feels that he has a well-informed and trustworthy guide, as he is borne along the current of a narrative, or is carried across the Assyrian plain, or through the rugged and difficult gorges of the mountains. Apart from its value as a record of missionary labors, it possesses high merits as a book of travels.

But, it is as *the life of a devoted missionary* that we here recommend it. Let it be circulated as it deserves, and not a few parents, mothers especially, will be found training their little ones for the service of Christ among the heathen; and not a few young men will be found emulous of a life so full of devotion to the Saviour, and so fruitful of good to others, as was that of Dr. Grant. Above all, let physicians, and those looking forward to the medical profession, read it. Other missionary physicians are needed, several very urgently, in fields scarcely less promising than that occupied by him.

Rev. Selah B. Treat, Editor of the Missionary Herald.

This is the life of a missionary who possessed high qualifications for his chosen work. First of all, he had the genuine spirit of his calling. His piety was deep, constant, unwavering. When he became a soldier of Christ, he enlisted for whatever service should be appointed unto him. He felt that he had only to follow the Captain of his salvation; and this he ever delighted to do. Dr. Grant, moreover, had some elements of character which were seldom combined in the same person, at least to the same degree. He was emphatically a brave man. Few would have ventured to go, where he often went during his eventful history. And yet he was not rash. Few men have exhibited more of the spirit of Paul than our lamented brother. But this brief notice is not the place for a sketch of his character. Mr. Laurie seems to have a just idea of it; and he has been quite successful in his portraiture. And the friends of missions will rejoice that he consented to undertake it.

Pp

GOULD & LINCOLN, PUBLISHERS, BOSTON.

HYMN BOOKS.

THE PSALMIST; a New Collection of HYMNS for the Use of the Baptist Churches. By BARON STOW AND S. F. SMITH:

Assisted by W. R. Williams, N. Y.; Geo. B. Ide, Pa.; R. W. Griswold, N. Y.; S. P. Hill, Md.; J. B. Taylor, Va.; J. L. Dagg, Ala.; W. T. Brantley, S. C.; R. B. C. Howell, Ten.; Samuel W. Lynd, Ky., and John M. Peck, Ill. With SUPPLEMENT, containing a variety of CHANTS, and SELECTIONS OF SCRIPTURE FOR CHANTING.

Pulpit edition, 12mo, (large type,) Turkey morocco, gilt edges, 3,00; morocco gilt, 1,75; plain morocco, 1,50; sheep, 1,25.

Pew edition, 18mo, sheep, 75 cts.; morocco, 1,00; morocco, gilt, 1,25; Turkey morocco, gilt, 2,63.

Pocket edition, 32mo, sheep, 50 cts.; morocco, plain, 75 cts.; morocco, gilt, 83 cts.; embossed morocco, gilt edges, 1,00; tucks, gilt, 1,25; Turkey morocco, 1,50.

THE PSALMIST; WITH SUPPLEMENT. Containing an additional Selection of *more than one hundred* HYMNS, (in place of the Chants and Selections for Chanting.) By RICHARD FULLER and J. B. JETER. *Same sizes, styles of binding, and prices, of the other edition.*

☞ The Psalmist is, unquestionably, the best collection of Hymns in *the English Language*. It has been almost universally introduced into the Baptist churches throughout the United States, and also in the British Provinces, and supplies have been ordered for London.

The united, and unsolicited testimony of pastors of the Baptist churches in Boston and vicinity, New York, and Philadelphia, of the most *decided and flattering character*, has been given in favor of the book. Also, by the Professors in Hamilton Literary and Theological Institution, and the Newton Theological Institution. The same, also, has been done by a great number of clergymen, churches, associations, conventions, etc., in every State of the Union. So that it not only may be said to have been sanctioned *by*, but become *the* HYMN BOOK OF, THE BAPTIST DENOMINATION.

The work contains nearly *thirteen hundred* CHOICE HYMNS, original and selected, by one hundred and seventy-two of the most celebrated writers of the present, as well as past times, (allowing Watts the authorship of about one third of the whole number,) besides pieces credited to forty-five collections of hymns or other works, the authorship of which is unknown. Forty-five are anonymous, being traced neither to authors nor collections.

Two sets of stereotype plates have been worn out in printing the *Pew edition* of the work, and the publishers have just been at great expense in procuring from the Boston Stereotype Foundry a new and elegant Electrotype set of plates, giving an impression equal to copperplate, with an enlargement of the SCRIPTURE INDEX, and the addition (to the Index of First Lines of *Hymns* previously given) of an INDEX OF FIRST LINES OF EACH VERSE IN THE BOOK, the great advantage of which must at once be seen by those who frequently wish to quote, or refer to some particular verse, or find some hymn containing the same, and can remember only a line or two of that one stanza.

THE SUPPLEMENT, occupying the place of the Chants of the other edition, which, in many sections of the country, are seldom if ever used, was undertaken by Rev. Messrs. Fuller and Jeter, at the solicitation of friends at the South.

"The Psalmist, (say they in their preface,) contains a copious supply of excellent hymns for the pulpit. We are acquainted with no collection of hymns, combining in an equal degree poetic merit, evangelical sentiment, and a rich variety of subjects, with a happy adaptation to pulpit services. Old songs, like old friends, are more valuable than new ones. A number of the hymns best known, most valued, and most frequently sung in the South, are not found in the Psalmist. Without them no hymn book, whatever may be its excellences, is likely to become generally or permanently popular in that region. To supply this deficiency is the object of the Supplement.

"The hymns have been mostly selected, not on account of their poetic beauty, but their established popularity. They will, we think, be found not seriously defective as metrical compositions; but their chief excellence consists in their adaptation to interest and affect the heart. If we are not deceived, they will form an acceptable appendix to the Psalmist. Adapted chiefly to *social worship*, they will, we trust, contribute greatly to the interest and profit of our prayer and protracted meetings.

"Though this selection has been made with special reference to the taste and wants of the South, we know no reason why it should not be acceptable to other portions of the country."

WINCHELL'S WATTS, with a Supplement. 12mo, sheep, 50 cts.

WATTS AND RIPPON. 18mo, sheep, 88 cts. 32mo, sheep, 55¼ cts.

HYMN BOOKS FOR THE VESTRY.

THE SOCIAL PSALMIST; a Selection of Hymns for Conference Meetings and Family Devotion. By BARON STOW and S. F. SMITH. 18mo, sheep, 25 cts.

This selection has been in preparation nearly five years, during which time it has been subjected to repeated examinations and careful revision. The object in its preparation has been to furnish a selection of choice hymns for the vestry and the family circle, of moderate size, and at trifling expense, exactly suited to the various stages and conditions of the conference, and other devotional meetings usually held in the conference room, as well as in family worship.

The work forms an admirable companion to the Psalmist, and we hope will be widely used in connection with it. — *N. Y. Recorder.*

A charming collection it is indeed, and many of the hymns are those familiar to the Christian, and peculiarly dear to his heart. It is not only well suited for conference and family worship, but would make an excellent supplement to the Psalmist. — *N. Y. Bap. Reg.*

The Social Psalmist is a good compilation, and we wish it abundant success. — *Religious Herald.*

The preparation of this work was undertaken by the right hands. We doubt not the work will be popular and its use coextensive with that of the Psalmist. — *Mich. Ch. Herald.*

The standard hymns of the Christian church are the most fit to be enshrined in the memory of the devout, as helps of their worship and their piety. Their familiarity, instead of being an objection to them, is their highest praise. We commend the work to the ministry and laity of the denomination. — *Southern Baptist.*

It is printed on good paper, and strongly bound in sheep, and is afforded at the very low price of 25 cents per copy, and 2,50 per dozen.

THE CHRISTIAN MELODIST; a new Collection of Hymns for Social Religious Worship. By REV. JOSEPH BANVARD. With a CHOICE SELECTION OF MUSIC, adapted to the Hymns. 18mo, sheep, 37½ cts.

The work contains 600 hymns, and each hymn has the name of an appropriate tune prefixed. The notes of these tunes, occupying more than sixty pages, are inserted at the *end of the volume.*

There is a copious variety of hymns, adapted to all the regular and the occasional meetings of the church, printed in large, open type, so as to be easily read. Price 37 1-2 cents. 4,00 per dozen.

From the Rev. Daniel Sharp, D. D.: "I take pleasure in saying, that I consider the 'Christian Melodist' a valuable work. It contains original hymns which are beautiful, and well-known hymns that to Christians will never be uninteresting. The collection is a very great improvement on hymn books of the class to which it belongs. I consider the tunes which are added as highly increasing the excellence of the publication."

Similar testimonials have also been received from other pastors in Boston, viz.: Rev. Messrs. R. H. Neale, P. Church, N. Colver, Geo. W. Bosworth, Wm. Howe, P. Stow, and M. Sanford.

From Rev. R. Turnbull, D. D., Pastor 1st Baptist Ch. Hartford, Ct.: "Generally, the hymns are at once poetical and devout and well fitted to express the emotions of a Christian heart. The addition of the tunes at the end of the volume is a great improvement. Indeed it is the best hymn book for the vestry which I have ever seen."

From S. H. Cone, D. D., Pastor of 1st Baptist Ch. New York: "It affords me pleasure to commend it as one of the most copious and judiciously arranged hymn books I have met with. The introduction of appropriate tunes is a valuable addition, and will have a tendency, I trust, to restore to our churches the primitive practice of 'speaking in psalms and hymns and spiritual songs,' in which the congregation may make melody to the Lord."

Like recommendations have also been received from the following clergymen in New York city, viz.: Rev. Messrs. C. G. Somers, E. Lathrop, W. H. Wyckoff, W. W. Everts, S. Remington, Henry Davis, J. T. Seely, D. Dunbar, C. Morton, and J. L. Hodge, Brooklyn.

From G. B. Ide, D. D., Pastor of 1st Baptist Ch. Springfield, Mass.: "An excellent collection of hymns. It has the advantage of being adapted to the sanctuary and to the wants of social worship. While all will find it a profitable help in the prayer meeting and in seasons of revivals, it will be particularly desirable to those churches who do not wish a more expensive book for the Lord's day, or prefer one suited to both public and social worship."

☞ The above works are both admirably adapted to conference and other devotional meetings, and also for the family circle, and at family worship, etc.

Ww

[June 1st, 1856.

SUPPLEMENTARY CATALOGUE

OF

VALUABLE WORKS,

RECENTLY PUBLISHED.

THE CAMEL: His Organization, Habits and Uses, considered with reference to his Introduction into the United States. By George P. Marsh, late U. S. Minister at Constantinople. 16mo, cloth. 75 cents.

This book treats of a subject of great interest, especially at the present time. It furnishes a more complete and reliable account of the Camel than any other in the language; indeed, it is believed that there is no other. It is the result of long study, extensive research, and much personal observation on the part of the author; and it has been prepared with special reference to the experiment of domesticating the Camel in this country, now going on under the auspices of the United States government. It is written in a style worthy of the distinguished author's reputation for great learning and fine scholarship.

DR. GRANT AND THE MOUNTAIN NESTORIANS. By Rev. Thomas Laurie. With a Portrait, Map of the Country, and Illustrations. 12mo, cloth. Price $1.25. Third edition revised.

This edition has been thoroughly revised by the author, with the view of making the work scrupulously accurate. The map is the first correct one of the Nestorian country yet published. The work itself is one of the most permanently valuable of its class, while it presents a full view of the life and labors of the heroic missionary whose name it bears; it also makes the reader familiar with the striking features of a country which, both in ancient and modern times, has been memorable in history. It embraces the scene of Xenophon's immortal Anabasis, the site of Nineveh, that mighty seat of ancient civilization, and the cities of Kars and Erzerum, so recently the scene of deadly strife between the Russians and the Allies.

ANALYTICAL CONCORDANCE TO THE HOLY SCRIPTURES; Or, THE BIBLE PRESENTED UNDER DISTINCT AND CLASSIFIED HEADS OR TOPICS.

BY JOHN EADIE, D.D., LL. D.,

Author of "Biblical Cyclopedia," "Ecclesiastical Cyclopedia," "Early Oriental History," "Dictionary of the Bible," etc. etc. One volume. Octavo. P. 836. (In press.) The subjects are arranged as follows, viz.:

Agriculture,	Family,	Metals and Minerals,	Sabbaths and Holy Days,
Animals,	Genealogy,	Ministers of Religion,	Sacrifice,
Architecture,	God,	Miracles,	Scriptures,
Army, Arms,	Heaven,	Occupations,	Speech,
Body,	Idolatry, Idols,	Ordinances,	Spirits,
Canaan,	Jesus Christ,	Parables and Emblems,	Tabernacle and Temple,
Covenant,	Jews,	Persecution,	Vineyard and Orchard,
Diet and Dress,	Laws,	Praise and Prayer,	Visions and Dreams,
Disease and Death,	Magistrates,	Prophecy,	War,
Earth,	Man,	Providence,	Water.
	Marriage,	Redemption,	

The object of this Concordance is to present the entire Scriptures under certain classified and exhaustive heads. It differs from an ordinary Concordance, in that its arrangement depends not on words, but on subjects, and the verses are printed in full. Its plan does not bring it at all into competition with such limited works as those of Gaston and Warden; for they select doctrinal topics principally, and do not profess to comprehend, as we do, the entire Bible. The work also contains a Synoptical Table of Contents of the whole work, presenting in brief a system of biblical antiquities and theology, with a very copious and accurate index.

The value of this work to ministers and Sabbath school teachers can hardly be over-estimated; and it needs but to be examined to secure the approval and patronage of every Bible student.

VALUABLE WORKS.

THE SUFFERING SAVIOUR; or, Meditations on the Last Days of Christ. By Fred. W. Krummacher, D.D., Chaplain to the King of Prussia, and author of "Elijah the Tishbite," "Last Days of Elisha," "The Martyr Lamb," etc. etc. Translated under the express sanction of the author, by Samuel Jackson. 12mo, cloth. $1.25.

The leading article in a recent number of the New York Independent is wholly devoted to the subject of this work. Respecting the work itself and its author, it speaks as follows:

"It is refreshing at times to meet with one who views the work of Christ from the emotiona stand-point, without immediate reference either to the dialectic or the practical. Such, in an eminent degree, is Krummacher — THE Krummacher of 'Elijah, the Tishbite.' A series of meditations from his pen on the last days of Christ upon earth has just appeared under the title of 'The Suffering Saviour.' The style of the author need not be described to those who have read his 'Elijah;' and whoever has not read an evangelical book of our own time that has passed through many editions in German, English, French, Dutch, Danish, had better order the CHINESE edition, which has recently appeared. * * * We like the book — LOVE it, rather — for the vivid perception and fervid emotion with which it brings us to the Suffering Saviour."

"Krummacher is himself again! Till the present work appeared, he had done nothing equal to his first one, 'Elijah, the Tishbite.' We felt that the productions which he gave to the world during the interval were scarcely up to the mark. In the present he comes upon the literary firmament in his old fire and glory, 'like a re-appearing star.' The translator has done his work admirably. * * Much of the narrative is given with thrilling vividness, and pathos, and beauty. Marking as we proceeded, several passages for quotation, we found them in the end so numerous, that we must refer the reader to the work itself." — News of the Churches (Scottish).

"All those characteristics which made 'Elijah, the Tishbite,' so deservedly popular, — as, due appreciation of the subject; a comprehensive treatment, which, while it embraces a grand whole neglects not even the minutest details; fertility of illustration; and earnest and impressive lessons inculcated by the way, and in affectionate terms, — all re-appear in the present work, which, so far at least, as concerns the dignity of its subject, is of infinitely greater importance to us than its predecessor." — British Critic.

THE PROGRESS OF BAPTIST PRINCIPLES IN THE LAST HUNDRED YEARS. By T. F. Curtis, Professor of Theology in Lewisburg University, Pa., and author of "Communion," etc. 12mo, cloth. $1.25.

This work is divided into three books. The first exhibits the progress of Baptist principles, now conceded in theory by the most enlightened of other denominations. The second presents a view of the progress of principles still controverted. The third sets forth the progress of principles always held by Evangelical Christians, but more consistently by Baptists.

It is a work that invites the candid consideration of all denominations. In his preface the author says: "If, in a single line of the following pages, there should appear to the reader the slightest unkind allusion to any other denomination or individual, the writer would at once say that nothing has been further from his intentions or feelings. * * * His aim has been to draw a wide distinction between parties and opinions. Hence the object of this volume is not to exhibit or defend the Baptists, but their principles."

"The principles referred to are such as these: Freedom of Conscience and Separation of Church and State; a Converted Church Membership; Sacraments inoperative without Choice and Faith; Believers the only Scriptural Subjects of Baptism; Immersion always the Baptism of the New Testament; Infant Baptism Injurious; Open Communion Unwise and Injurious. To show the progress of these principles, statistics are given, from which we learn that in 1792 there was but one Baptist Communicant in the United States to every fifty-six inhabitants, while in 1854 there was one to every thirty inhabitants. The Baptists have more than one quarter of the whole Church accommodation in the United States. * * * The entire work is written with ability and unfailing good temper." — Quarterly Journal of American Unitarian Association.

"We know of no man in our Churches better fitted to prepare a fair exhibition of 'Baptist Principles.' He is no controversialist; and his discussions are in most refreshing contrast with many both of Baptist defenders and their opponents." — Southern Baptist.

"The aim of the work is important, the plan ingenious, yet simple and natural, the author's preparation for it apparently thorough and conscientious, and his spirit excellent." — Watchman and Reflector.

"The good temper of the author of this volume is obvious, the method of arranging his material for effect admirable." — Presbyterian.

"The work exhibits ample learning, vigorous argumentative power, and an excellent spirit toward those whose views it controverts. Apart from its theological bearings, it possesses not a little historical interest." — New York Tribune.

www.ingramcontent.com/pod-product-compliance
Lightning Source LLC
LaVergne TN
LVHW010227110826
845151LV00004B/1210

* 9 7 8 1 4 2 5 5 2 6 0 0 9 *